Political
Empiricism

PRAEGER SERIES IN POLITICAL COMMUNICATION
Robert E. Denton, Jr., *General Editor*

Enacting Political Culture: Rhetorical Transformations of Liberty
Weekend 1986
David E. Procter

Within These Walls: A Study of Communication between Presidents
and Their Senior Staffs
Patricia D. Witherspoon

Continuity and Change in the Rhetoric of the Moral Majority
David Snowball

Mediated Politics in Two Cultures: Presidential Campaigning in the
U.S. and France
Lynda Lee Kaid, Jacques Gerstle, and Keith R. Sanders

Crime and the American Press
Roy Edward Lotz

A Shining City on a Hill: Ronald Reagan's Economic Rhetoric, 1951–
1989
Amos Kiewe and Davis W. Houck

The Cold War as Rhetoric: The Beginnings, 1945–1950
Lynn B. Hinds and Theodore O. Windt, Jr.

Presidential Perspectives on Space Exploration: Guiding Metaphors
from Eisenhower to Bush
Linda T. Krug

Political Campaign Communication, Second Edition
Judith S. Trent and Robert V. Friedenberg

Ethical Dimensions of Political Communication
Edited by Robert E. Denton, Jr.

Cordial Concurrence: Orchestrating National Party Conventions in the
Telepolitical Age
Larry David Smith and Dan Nimmo

Political Empiricism

Communication Strategies in State and Regional Elections

Rita Kirk Whillock

Praeger Series in Political Communication

New York
Westport, Connecticut
London

Library of Congress Cataloging-in-Publication Data

Whillock, Rita Kirk.
    Political empiricism : communication strategies in state and
regional elections / Rita Kirk Whillock.
        p.   cm.—(Praeger series in political communication)
    Includes bibliographical references and index.
    ISBN 0–275–93554–X (alk. paper)
    1. Electioneering—United States—Case studies.   2. Advertising,
Political—United States—Case studies.   3. Communication in
politics—United States—Case studies.   I. Title.   II. Series.
JK1976.W47 1991
324.7'0973—dc20   91–19412

British Library Cataloguing in Publication Data is available.

Library of Congress Catalog Card Number: 91–19412
ISBN: 0–275–93554–X

First published in 1991

Praeger Publishers, One Madison Avenue, New York, NY 10010
An imprint of Greenwood Publishing Group, Inc.

Printed in the United States of America

The paper used in this book complies with the
Permanent Paper Standard issued by the National
Information Standards Organization (Z39.48–1984).

10   9   8   7   6   5   4   3   2   1

Dedicated to my husband, Dr. David E. Whillock,
and to my son, Robert Kirk Whillock

In honor of our parents
John and Thelma Beard Kirk
Everett and Bernelle Wilson Whillock

Contents

About the Series

Those of us from the discipline of communication studies have long believed that communication is prior to all other fields of inquiry. In several other forums I have argued that the essence of politics is "talk" or human interaction.[1] Such interaction may be formal or informal, verbal or nonverbal, public or private, but it is always persuasive, forcing us consciously or subconsciously to interpret, to evaluate, and to act. Communication is the vehicle for human action.

From this perspective, it is not surprising that Aristotle recognized the natural kinship of politics and communication in his writings *Politics* and *Rhetoric*. In the former, he establishes that humans are "political beings [who] alone of the animals [are] furnished with the faculty of language."[2] And in the latter, he begins his systematic analysis of discourse by proclaiming that "rhetorical study, in its strict sense, is concerned with the modes of persuasion."[3] Thus, it was recognized over two thousand years ago that politics and communication go hand in hand because they are essential parts of human nature.

Back in 1981, Dan Nimmo and Keith Sanders proclaimed that political communication was an emerging field.[4] Although its origin, as noted, dates back centuries, a "self-consciously cross-disciplinary" focus began in the late 1950s. Thousands of books and articles later, colleges and universities offer a variety of graduate and undergraduate coursework in the area in such diverse departments as communication, mass communication, journalism, political science, and sociology.[5] In Nimmo and Sanders' early assessment, the "key areas of inquiry" included rhetorical analysis, propaganda analysis, attitude change studies, voting studies, government and the news media, functional and systems analyses, technological changes, media technologies, campaign techniques, and research techniques.[6] In a survey of the state of field in 1983, the same authors and Lynda Kaid found additional, more specific areas of concern such as the presidency, political polls, public opinion, debates, and advertising, to name a few.[7] Since the first study, they also noted a shift away from the rather strict behavioral approach.

Today, Dan Nimmo and David Swanson assert that "political communication has developed some identity as a more or less distinct domain of scholarly work."[8] The scope and concerns of the area have further expanded to include critical theories and cultural studies. While there is no precise definition, method, or disciplinary home for the area of inquiry, its primary domain is the role, processes, and effects of communication within the context of politics broadly defined.

In 1985, the editors of *Political Communication Yearbook: 1984* noted that "more things are happening in the study, teaching, and practice of political communication than can be captured within the space limitations of the relatively few publications available."[9] In addition, they argued, the backgrounds of "those involved in the field [are] so varied and pluralist in outlook and approach, . . . it [is] a mistake to adhere slavishly to any set format in shaping the content."[10] And more recently, Swanson and Nimmo called for "ways of overcoming the unhappy consequences of fragmentation within a framework that respects, encourages, and benefits from diverse scholarly commitments, agendas, and approaches."[11]

In agreement with these assessments of the area, and with gentle encouragement, in 1988 Praeger established the series entitled "Praeger Series in Political Communication." The series is open to all qualitative and quantitative methodologies as well as contemporary and historical studies. The key to characterizing the studies in the series is the focus on communication variables or activities within a political context or dimension. Scholars from the disciplines of communication, history, political science, and sociology have participated in the series.

I am, without shame or modesty, a fan of the series. The joy of serving as its editor is in participating in the dialogue of the field of political communication and in reading the contributors' works. I invite you to join me.

Robert E. Denton, Jr.

NOTES

1. See Robert E. Denton, Jr., *The Symbolic Dimensions of the American Presidency* (Prospect Heights, IL: Waveland Press, 1982); Robert E. Denton, Jr., and Gary Woodward, *Political Communication in America* (New York: Praeger, 1985, Second

Edition, 1990); Robert E. Denton, Jr., and Dan Hahn, *Presidential Communication* (New York: Praeger, 1986); and Robert E. Denton, Jr., *The Primitive Presidency of Ronald Reagan* (New York: Praeger, 1988).

2. Aristotle, *The Politics of Aristotle*, trans. Ernest Barker (New York: Oxford University Press, 1970), p. 5.

3. Aristotle, *Rhetoric*, trans. Rhys Roberts (New York: The Modern Library, 1954), p. 22.

4. Dan Nimmo and Keith Sanders, "Introduction: The Emergence of Political Communication as a Field," in *Handbook of Political Communication*, Dan Nimmo and Keith Sanders, eds. (Beverly Hills, CA: Sage, 1981), pp. 11–36.

5. Ibid., p. 15.

6. Ibid., pp. 17–27.

7. Keith Sanders, Lynda Kaid, and Dan Nimmo, eds. *Political Communication Yearbook: 1984* (Carbondale, IL: Southern Illinois University: 1985), pp. 283–308.

8. Dan Nimmo and David Swanson, "The Field of Political Communication: Beyond the Voter Persuasion Paradigm" in *New Directions in Political Communication*, David Swanson and Dan Nimmo, eds. Beverly Hills, CA: Sage, 1990), p. 8.

9. Sanders, Kaid, and Nimmo, p. xiv.

10. Ibid., p. xiv.

11. Nimmo and Swanson, p. 11.

Series Foreword

If confession is good for the soul, then let me say up front that I have
worked in advertising for several years. I have created persuasive messages and designed strategies and campaigns for consumer and political
"products." The basis for my confession is not shame or doubt, but
pride. As a communication scholar and professional, it is gratifying to
analyze a situation and then create a strategy and message that generate
the desired results. I simply reject the notion that "those who can, do,
and those who can't, teach."

There is a tremendous wealth of research in the area of political communication. Most of the research, however, has been done from a distance with the advantage of 20/20 hindsight. There continues to be, as
Robert Meadow recognized in 1985, "a widening gap between the practice of political communication and political communication research"
(p. 136). Our failure as a field is in not addressing the concerns of political
professionals and practical politics. Many studies are too narrow and
episodic, and they seldom provide conclusions or generalizations beyond the event or situation being analyzed. Too many studies ignore
the vast literature and research of other disciplines. I am amazed at how
many of my colleagues ignore the works of political scientists and how
many political scientists ignore the works of communication scholars.
Both groups fail to utilize insights from the fields of sociology and psychology. Moreover, too many of our studies focus on national politics
and issues, ignoring more local political activities.

Perhaps most important is the fact that many of our studies tend to
forget not only that politics is both an art and a science, but also *that it
is*, above all, a *pragmatic* activity. To ignore the political realities of a

situation is to provide naive analyses of little value. I suggest that this is one reason why politicians seek the assistance and advice of individuals other than scholars of political communication.

Thus, there are several reasons why I echo the call by Robert Meadow (1985) for more applied political communication research. First, we simply need to make our work relevant to the practice of politics. I firmly believe that, as a field of study, we can help improve the quality of electoral politics, and hence democracy, in the United States. Our field of inquiry must extend beyond the simple notion of knowledge for knowledge's sake. We have a responsibility to make our work accessible, informative, and descriptive as well as prescriptive in nature. Our audience must extend beyond fellow colleagues and students to include the general citizenry of the nation.

Second, political campaigning has become a large, complex, and extremely professional business. Today, running for local office requires money, strategy, and media sophistication. Highly trained professionals have invaded politics at all levels, utilizing the latest communication technologies and social science methods. Much of their work is secret and most of their insights are proprietary. We in political communication can ill afford to lag behind in understanding the practices, principles, and techniques of professional politicians if we hope to do our job in preparing students for democratic citizenship.

Finally, scholars of political communication should provide leadership in asking research questions. Politics is too important an endeavor to be left to practitioners alone. By putting theory into practice, scholars can learn firsthand what works and why, thus better informing all of us about the nature of human communication. Political communication scholars can also serve as innovators in, as well as watchdogs of, the political process.

Political Empiricism: Communication Strategies in State and Regional Elections is a valuable and important addition to the field of political communication. The study clearly demonstrates the value of applied communication research, and each chapter presents an appropriate mixture of theory and practice. In discussing various actions and strategies, Rita Kirk Whillock provides linkage between current scholarship and various campaign decisions.

In addition to the informative integration of theory and practice, the case study approach is a useful way to explore key issues, concerns, and topics of political communication such as incumbency, image, gender, fund-raising, advertising, and message strategies, to name only a few.

This study demonstrates that a communication scholar *can* make a difference. Throughout the book one sees the influence of classical concerns on the well-trained student of rhetoric—belief in the character of the speaker, good reasons for arguments, and faith in the democratic political process. Good citizenship demands informed political participation. I am thankful that Dr. Whillock is an active participant in the political process. The practice of U.S. politics benefits from her insight, experience, and dedication.

With my enthusiasm for applied communication research, some critics may argue that the participant/scholar model of inquiry lessens objectivity. It is widely believed that distance is needed for reflection and analysis. I prefer the wisdom of Plato, Aristotle, Cicero, and Quintilian, who all argued for the citizen politician—one who is moral, informed, and committed to the common good of the polis. I also prefer the wisdom of my grandfather, who was fond of saying, "I would rather see a sermon than hear one."

Robert E. Denton, Jr.

REFERENCE

Meadow, Robert G. (1985). Political campaigns, new technology, and political communication research. In K. Sanders, L. Kaid, & D. Nimmo (eds.), *Political communication yearbook: 1984* (pp. 135–152). Carbondale: Southern Illinois University Press.

Acknowledgments

As I reviewed the final manuscript for this book, I became increasingly aware of how much the lectures, readings, and research of my colleagues have influenced my judgments and thinking. Among those scholars is the series editor, Robert E. Denton, Jr. I am indebted to him not only for the opportunity to write this book but also for his cheerful disposition and scholarly encouragement. I would also be remiss if I did not note the influence of Buddy Goodall, who prodded me into writing down my experiences. My life has been enriched by his friendship and his scholarship.

There are a host of people who shared their insights into the political process during the writing of this book. The four profiled candidates—Mayor Steve Hettinger, State Senator Bill Smith, Judge Laura Jo Hamilton, and U. S. Representative Ronnie Flippo—are persons of extraordinary courage. Not only did they grant permission for me to write about their campaigns, they also offered me information and permitted me to write about my experiences without interference. In addition, there are a number of consultants, politicos, and campaign officials who offered their insights, including Dr. Jesse Brown, Roger Schneider, Rick Liles, Bill Jones, Carter Sibley, Dwight Jennings, Richard Gipson, Brenda Martin, Tom Woodall, State School Board Member Taze Shepard, and State Representative Tom Butler.

A number of talented students who have worked with me on various projects also deserve recognition. Their eagerness to learn and their desire to test communication theories in real-time contexts have strengthened my commitment to teaching and research. I would particularly like to acknowledge Matt McGary, Lee Logston, Lori Grimwood, Rita Reynolds Edwards, Daryl Bailey, Tina Hicks, Julie Preston, and Tom Dahm.

I am deeply grateful to my colleagues at the University of Alabama in Huntsville who have offered constructive suggestions, including Elaine Fredericksen, Susan Gill, Julia Langford, Dr. Carol Roach, and Dr. Tom Addington. Bert Yaeger, Anne Kiefer, and the staff at Praeger have made invaluable contributions toward the completion of this manuscript. I am indebted to them for their thoroughness and attention to detail. I am especially thankful for the help of my husband, Dr. David Whillock, who encouraged me, talked with me late into the night as we debated strategies, and still remains my best friend.

PART I

FOUR "GIVEN" CASES

Chapter 1

The Triumph of an Underdog: The Role of a Communication Scholar as a Consultant for One Mayoral Election

My students usually snicker when I first read to them Berelson's (1948) classic analysis of communication effects: "Some kinds of communication on some kinds of issues brought to the attention of some kinds of people under some kinds of conditions have some kinds of effects" (p. 351). They mistakenly assume that Berelson was summarizing what we know rather than setting parameters that influence our conclusions. When examined, the students determine that Berelson simply confirmed Aristotle's stipulation that we study and draw conclusions about persuasion in terms of a "given case." Using this perspective, applied research can perhaps best be viewed as the examination, application, and evaluation of generalized premises in a particular research setting.

However, applied research is more complicated. In the uncontrolled setting of a nonlaboratory environment, the problems to be addressed arise from the situation. We cannot anticipate beforehand what premises of persuasion may apply or what we will see (given our particular biases and information) that others might view differently. As scholars, we can only hope that the tools we have are in good working order and that we can remember how to use them.

This chapter will examine the role of a communication consultant in political campaigns from the perspective of an academic who also manages such campaigns. I first address the unique contributions that communication researchers have to offer as media strategists for political

An earlier version of this chapter appeared as R. K. Whillock (Fall 1989), Political empiricism: The role of a communication scholar as a consultant for one mayoral election, *Southern Communication Journal, 55,* 55–71. Reprinted by permission.

campaigns. Then I examine the persuasive strategies designed for a mayoral race in a Southern city of approximately 163,000 residents. Finally, I assess the value of applied research in light of the limitations and intervening variables that impacted its execution.

THE ROLE OF THE COMMUNICATION CONSULTANT

The general public often regards academics as soothsayers. They feel that we possess greater knowledge and understanding of political events and that such wisdom somehow allows us to foresee the outcomes of those events with greater precision than our nonacademic colleagues. These attitudes are bolstered by the media where every breaking story is analyzed by professors at major universities with the intent of helping the public understand the significance and nuances of events.

These are positive attributes, and there is some validity to these claims. After all, most academics are highly trained specialists; we have read the relevant literature of our particular subfield, seeking to gain a greater understanding of communication processes and relationships in a variety of settings and engaging in academic debate both within our journals and among our colleagues about the validity of our assumptions and the relative worth of our theories and findings. These are the kinds of myths grounded in reality that we hope to promote. They reinforce our belief that the work and costs of our graduate educations were not in vain and that even if we are not financially rewarded for the work we do in our "ivory towers," we are at least respected.

Given the recent exploitation of the communication discipline by "consultants," it is amazing that these public attitudes are still even tacitly maintained. We are all too familiar with those who teach what one of my colleagues describes as "adult show-and-tell" for astonishing prices. Moreover, most of us have probably suffered the whiplash effect of companies who have hired a communication consultant who has failed to "correct" company problems. We are also plagued by the faulty assumption that consultants specialize in (all phases of) communication. Recognizing these constraints, when a client asks me what I can offer a campaign that pollsters, advertising agents, and election specialists cannot, I am not surprised, but neither am I reluctant to respond.

I begin my explanation by talking about Aristotle. Aristotle asserted that "rhetorical study, in its strict sense, is concerned with the modes of persuasion" (Aristotle, 1984, p. 22). That is both what I teach and what I study. What, to use the Aristotelian line again, in a given case are the available means of persuasion? A client hires me to find out what those options are and to receive my recommendations as to which ones are most likely to be appropriate for a given situation.

To accomplish this purpose, I do research. Furthermore, I charge money for the billable hours I spend doing the research and briefing my client. The money is good but it hardly covers the hours I spend reading, researching, and formulating what I judge to be clearly argued positions. I respond to all issues from the relatively trivial (what clothes look best in televised debates?) to the supremely sublime (what can we do to provide "good reasons" for the public to vote for a particular candidate, and what can we do to motivate the public to act on those reasons?).

The information that clients seek is, in many cases, simple to find. Who among us could not list ten or fifteen suggestions for improving a presentation after having spent years critiquing our basic speech students? However, that is the point. We academics can see the impact of those small changes because we have observed their execution over and over again. Further, the information is not any more "trivial" to those who are unfamiliar with the skills of public presentations than a question of legal clarification is for someone who does not understand the law. Those are merely the incidentals that come along with a package of more substantive kinds of information that I am qualified to provide.

From this initial explanation of my perspective, I explain to the client how I fit into the campaign structure. I do not claim to be an expert on which political attitudes are most important to the voters in a given district. Polling data and politicos supply that information. I do not purport to have a mastery of graphic layout and design. Advertising agencies are better positioned for that kind of direction. Furthermore, I do not claim to be a campaign manager. The thousands of organizational details in the day-to-day operations of the campaign are best handled by professionals who are practiced in those areas.

Research, strategy, and analysis are my primary functions. For example, before negotiations begin between campaigns on the ground rules for a public debate, my job is to analyze the situation and prepare the guidelines for our negotiators. This, of course, means that I am best suited to well-defined campaign structures. Less structured campaigns too frequently employ a crisis mentality and rarely know what questions they want answered.

Within the campaign, I explain, there must be someone who remains detached from the emotional strains—someone who can, with some objectivity, judge events as they unfold. That is one reason why I do not hang around the headquarters or become involved in the campaign's day-to-day operations. Instead, I attend only those sessions in which the candidate and campaign managers are briefing me on a particular problem that they need me to research or when I am presenting the arguments for a particular strategy with which to respond to a situation.

Another reason for establishing a detached perspective lies in the benefits gained from formal briefing sessions. During these sessions with the campaign staff, a specific problem or issue must be articulated, complete with the staff's judgments about the relevant information. In campaigns with many specialists, some viewpoints are often not expressed for fear of intruding in someone else's domain even though those perspectives of events might provide critical information. However, when faced with a potential problem on which the consultant will be acting using the information provided, it is not unusual for the staff to be direct and to openly disagree. They disagree on the importance of certain details, they disagree about the severity of the problem or its potential for damaging the campaign, and they disagree about what should be done. When used constructively, this sort of debate frequently leads to a consensus of ideas that unites the participants in eventually executing a strategy to rectify the problem. Even when that kind of unity does not become manifest, I am convinced that people respond more positively to a direct rejection of their position than to the isolation that comes as a result of action taken without their knowledge.

I also talk with the client, if we are still negotiating at this point, about the projects I am currently researching. For example, over the last few years I have examined a number of political advertisements used in regional political races which I have compared with the more visible national strategies. As the client and I watch a few of the ads, I can share some of my insights on the strategies being implemented. In this way, the candidate can learn something about the way in which I approach my research.

In my remarks to the client, my own credo on consulting becomes clear. I am still a believer in the political system. Even though there is a lot of bantering about the "empty rhetoric" of political candidates, I will not work for a candidate who wants me to coach him or her on style without addressing content. I consult because I empathize with the position taken by Corax and Tisias that citizens are not very well educated about how to defend themselves and their ideas. Put simply, some candidates are frequently "out-imaged" by their opponents. I am deeply concerned that (to turn Quintilian's phrase) some "good" people lose because they do not "speak well."

Further, I find myself to be in a unique position. As a consultant who is already gainfully employed, I do not have to have any particular client in order to pay the monthly bills. The honesty that this sort of financial independence provides allows me to do my job regardless of whether a candidate or any member of the campaign staff likes or dislikes my opinions. Professionally, my loyalty resides with academics. Consulting is simply an opportunity to practice theory in "real time."

I will admit that I am an idealist. I am still not a hardened consultant, and maybe, with a little luck, I will never become one. After my spiel, if I am hired, I begin work in earnest.

The following is an excerpt of research/consulting from a 1988 mayoral race in Huntsville, Alabama. Notice that I use the term "excerpt." This is normally the place where academics tell what they have learned (and do so for free). However, I am enough of a sophist to know that some parts of a winning strategy are not disclosed. They are saved for the next election in order to help repeat the victory.

CAMPAIGN STRATEGIES

In order to understand something about the political culture in which this particular election functioned, I begin by introducing the players and the setting, with an emphasis on the candidate for whom I was working. I then explore the decisions made about the type of communication that seemed most appropriate for communicating the candidate's message. The next phase explores the specific strategies of persuasion instituted to accomplish the campaign goals. Finally, I examine the way in which we sought to draw closure to our requests in the election drama.

The Particular Case

By the filing deadline for the mayoral race in this particular election, there were five candidates. One candidate had no previous political experience. At the time, the other four held elected office.

The incumbent had been mayor for twenty years. He had first been elected during the years in which the city was still a relatively small farming community characterized by the antebellum mansions of another era and a military base that grew out of the missile research efforts during the space race. During the 1970s and 1980s, this city experienced a tremendous population growth accompanied by an economic transition from agriculture to a high-technology base supported by space and military research spending. Indeed, by the time of the election, forty Fortune 500 companies had operations here.

The citizen profile also changed in at least two significant ways during the incumbent's terms as mayor. First, the population became more mobile, lessening the sense of history that usually provides an individual with a record of achievement over time. Put simply, candidates could not rely on voters to remember the public services performed before the latter group moved here. This becomes a significant factor when, by conservative estimates, 10 percent of the voting-age population rely on military or government-contract jobs with high transfer potential. A more stable trend in voter change, however, was that of education level. Given the nature of career opportunities in the area, the city attracted a more highly educated population than the national average. Indeed, it now boasts that there are more than 700 residents with doctoral degrees in nonmedical professions and over 6,000 engineers. The profile indicates that these citizens read more, are more aware of current events, and are more self-reliant in opinion formation than less-educated voters.

Every student of politics understands the difficulty involved in unseating an incumbent. However, it is important to note that the rapid expansion of the city as well as the significant revisions in voter profiles contributed to the diminished effects of such variables as name recognition and constancy (aversion to change). These and other indicators (such as the mayor's health problems) contributed to a favorable climate of opinion for a challenger to unseat the incumbent.

Five weeks before the general election, one of the challengers, Steve Hettinger, contracted me to make recommendations on the direction of his campaign. After some initial consultation and a review of available polling data, some fairly obvious facts about his campaign emerged. First, Hettinger had poor name recognition, and even among those who had read his last name on signs around town, few were sure how to pronounce it. Second, Hettinger had frequently been out of town during much of the election period. As a state legislator, he needed, of course, to be at the capital during the legislative sessions. This was a handicap because it took him away from the voters, and his position as legislator did not afford him much media attention. By contrast, two other contenders serving on the city council, as well as the incumbent, were receiving a considerable amount of free publicity due to some volatile issues facing the city. Additionally, the legislature had been made a scapegoat for local problems by the mayor and members of the city council. If the voters found that scenario plausible, Hettinger stood to receive the brunt of the attack during the election. In addition, he was the only candidate in the field who had been elected as a representative of a political party; therefore, his political affiliation was a matter of record. The other candidates had won in nonpartisan elections even though there was strong party support for one of them. Moreover, Hettinger was a Democrat. While that at one time had been a strong advantage in the South, this city (with its dependence on federal money) had voted decisively Republican in the last few major races. Given that 1988 was a presidential election year and that George Bush was leading the race by wide margins in local polls, Hettinger's Democratic party affiliation was a liability.

On the positive side, the mayoral election would not take place on Super Tuesday. As it was a nonpartisan race, a special election date was called. Hettinger had a very strong campaign organization headed by two veteran campaigners, an aggressive finance chairperson, an insightful pollster-analyst and an exuberant, though not politically seasoned, advertising agency. Under the latter's direction, the normal campaign activities, from door-to-door contacts to billboards and palm cards, were already being exercised. The campaign theme—"Bold, New Leadership"—had already been established. Several position papers on key issues had been researched and prepared. Finally, Hettinger was an engineer. In a city of engineers, this potentially gave us a major strategic advantage.

Available Means

The first question I was asked was, "Where do we go from here?" My recommendation was for a full-scale televised media assault coordinated with the accelerated campaign activities that were already being planned. As it turned out, that was good advice because the candidate and campaign staff had already come to this conclusion.

I suppose they wanted confirmation that the cost would be justified and that my services would offer some hope of catching up. That would take some doing. Our polls indicated that Hettinger was running a weak fourth with only four weeks to go in the election. A local Press Club poll released three weeks before the campaign (on the day that our media coverage began) indicated that Hettinger was, in fact, running fourth and would receive only 10 percent of the vote if the election were to be held that day. The mayor and another challenger held 23 percent of the vote each, the third-place candidate held 13 percent of the vote, and the fifth-place candidate held less than 1 percent. Fortunately, some 20 percent of the voters were still undecided. From all indications there would probably be a runoff, because even if one of the leaders were to gain all the undecided voters, there would still not be a clear majority. Our objective, then, was for Hettinger to be one of the two candidates in the runoff.

Mass media is certainly not the cure-all of modern campaigns, but in this case it provided the best channel for communicating our message. Research indicates that mass communication is most likely to be effective when there is the absence of "a nexus of mediating factors" such as previously held attitudes and social influences (Klapper, 1960, p. 8). Our data indicated that these mediating factors were not at play in this race. The citizens wanted a change but showed relatively little commitment to any of the challengers. Those polled indicated that they were planning to vote *for* a candidate rather than against one, meaning that the candidates had few negative images to overcome. Moreover, there were few social pressures to vote for any one particular candidate. Remember, the one social pressure (party influence) that is typically considered to be a major influence on voter choice was nullified (we hoped) by the nonpartisan nature of the mayoral race.

Was the money spent for this kind of media barrage worth the gamble? It was. There was certainly a good reason to believe that we would be more likely to persuade the audience via televised spots than through other channels. When the normal mediating factors are neutralized, "broadcast spending seems to be a significant determinant of outcomes" (Diamond & Bates, 1984, p. 352). By this time in the campaign it had also become painfully obvious that other discursive means were not working well. Put succinctly, televised advertising was our best shot.

Strategies of Persuasion

Perhaps the clearest way of analyzing the media campaign in hindsight is to apply the rhetorical typology identified by Diamond and Bates (1984, pp. 302–345; see also Baukus & Payne, 1984) to the commercial campaign we produced. I hasten to add a note of caution to would-be consultants who are looking for a recipe for success. This is not a cookbook for political advertising. The more successful consultants know and apply a variety of rhetorical approaches depending on the candidate, the specific circumstances, and their own artistic abilities. The Diamond-Bates perspective is effective as an analytical tool to explain something of the general movement of the campaign, and this article provides insight into one successful application of rhetorical principles in a political race. Given this context, the following information can be put into its proper perspective. This is also the appropriate time to notice that I now begin to use the collective term "we" instead of the singular "I." Given that so many people contributed to the final product in terms of ideas for commercials, specific camera angles and shots, talent, and the use of key images and words, to imply ownership would be misleading.

Our first priority was to establish candidate identification. The advertisement we produced focused on Hettinger's name recognition. Achieving this was important if we accept G. C. Jacobson's premise that "candidate recognition should be understood as a minimal threshold voters must necessarily cross before acquiring any more extensive information about a candidate" (1975, p. 773); see also Sabato, 1981, p. 127). Available evidence suggests that the use of polispots (or political commercials) can achieve candidate identification very quickly (see, e.g., Diamond & Bates, 1984, p. 358).

While the primary goal was name recognition, all the ads had to tie into the campaign theme. Using an adaptation of the well-worn question, "How do you spell relief?," the first advertisement keyed in on our campaign theme of leadership. Fortunately, we had the sense to salvage this insult to voter intelligence by subsequently setting up some positive, symbolic issues—issues that we would argue more clearly in the next phase of the advertising schemata. Using one of the community's more senior and well-loved elementary school teachers (by report, she had taught half the city), we keyed in on education as an issue. Of course, we had a classroom full of adorable children and featured a gap-toothed boy named "Bo" (short for Beauregard, perhaps) to spell our candidate's name. I suppose even the kids knew that this was pretty silly. They laughed; the audience laughed; and every parent and grand-parent tuned in to see their kids in their first starring roles (this was a subtle introduction for family issues such as combatting drugs in the public schools). We moved to the next phase quickly.

The next phase of the media campaign was to begin establishing an argument for the public to vote for Hettinger. Numerous studies have indicated the importance of keeping the campaign organized around a well-constructed, simple issue theme (see, e.g., Greenfield, 1980; Leut-hold, 1968; Nimmo, 1970). The campaign theme ("Bold, New Leader-ship") had already been researched, selected, and initiated. Indeed, one of the more stable election issues for challengers running against incum-bents is a crisis in leadership (see Deardourff as cited in Diamond & Bates, 1984, p. 343). The potential use of the word "bold" was intriguing. It permitted us to assert that leadership alone was not the solution. It also gave us the leverage to assert that Hettinger was not just a leader but would, in an aggressive, positive manner, take hold of some prob-lems that had become unmanageable under the current administration.

The problem lay in selling Hettinger as a bold leader. He was not really *bold*. In fact, one newspaper headlined an article, "Serious Steve a 'typical engineer.' " We had to differentiate between bold leadership and a bold person. Hettinger could be viewed as bold based on the type of legislation he had sponsored and the policies he was advocating. Our writer was able to mix the two concepts in an advertisement he titled "Quietly." The spot showed "Serious Steve" working in his office. The voice-over recounted a list of Hettinger's more innovative (read "bold") legislative successes. We continued to respond to the education and family issues that had been symbolically initiated in the first phase. We also recounted Hettinger's record on two emerging issues resulting from city-planning problems. We argued that quiet people could make bold leaders. They would listen; then they would act.

If we were to achieve success, this was also the time to diffuse potential time bombs (see Sabato, 1981, p. 127). Up until this point in the cam-paign, Hettinger had been relatively unattacked by opponent attacks. After all, the polls indicated that he posed no real threat to the other candidates. The major obstacle we identified was that as a state legislator, Hettinger could be made the scapegoat for local problems. By highlight-ing his accomplishments, we hoped to stall any argument that Hettinger was one of the incompetent or ineffective people that the mayor and the council had attacked.

We also wanted to key in on Hettinger's experience as an elected official. This was important since another potential time bomb was the fact that Hettinger had no city government experience. He had done postgraduate work in public administration and city planning, which we wanted to emphasize, but he had not been given the opportunity to prove his leadership skills as a city administrator. This is one of those areas in which image can help. We could show that Hettinger had the qualifications. Now it was necessary to bolster the perception that he was competent to employ those skills.

This approach was designed to establish familiarity and credibility for both our campaign theme and our candidate. We all know the important role of credibility in attitude change. Research indicates quite clearly that short-term attitude change (something that was highly desirable given that the election was only eighteen days away by the time our commercials were aired) is facilitated by sources considered to be "highly credible" (see, e.g., Hovland, Lumsdaine & Sheffield, 1949; Hovland & Weiss, 1951).

To accomplish our objectives, the argument phase was one of the two longer parts of the media campaign. We wanted to take advantage of the repetition that polispots provide. If a voter hears a speech, attends a candidate forum, or watches a debate, the argument that a candidate makes on a specific issue will be heard only once (except for the occasional ten- to twenty-second "news bite" covered by the evening newscast). On the other hand, a commercial has the advantage of exposing the voter to the argument several times. This extensive exposure to and familiarity with the argument, provided it is not used to excess, makes it more likely that the listeners will be persuaded (see Belch, 1982; Cacioppo & Petty, 1979).

Further, before any comparative ads could be effective, there had to be enough goodwill built up that the candidate's motives would appear sincere and his claims would be believed (see Deardourff as cited in Diamond & Bates, 1984, p. 359). Goodwill helps in other ways as well. Being familiar with and liking a candidate have been demonstrated to have a positive effect on voting decisions (see Grush, 1980; Grush, McKeough, & Ahlering, 1978).

The other lengthy phase of the media campaign consisted of drawing comparisons between our candidate and the others. As mentioned earlier, Hettinger and other state legislators were being blamed for the city's problems. We had to attempt to shift the blame back to the mayor and the city council. Given limitations of time both for the production and for the airing of the spots, we needed to find a way in which to lump our opponents together. Given that the three front-runners were all involved with the current city administration, the task was simple.

We had already selected the issues that would provide a strategic position for Hettinger among the field of candidates during the argument phase. We had focused on Hettinger's record in terms of positions that were important to the constituents and consistent with the public's perceptions of issues about which Hettinger might be most concerned.

In the argument phase we demonstrated Hettinger's concerns for these issues and the ways in which he had acted to help find solutions. Thus we sought to bolster Hettinger's issue credibility (see, e.g., Mauser, 1983, pp. 19, 109–141). As we saw it, each viable candidate was required to address the timely problems that emerged during the campaign. Therefore, voters expected responses, or what many call "empty rhetoric," about how each candidate could best solve the problems. What we sought to introduce was the belief that a particular set of issues (which were, of course, important to the voter as well) were personal to the candidate. If we could demonstrate, for example, that drugs in the schools were a problem that affected Hettinger personally, a fact easy to demonstrate given that he had two school-age children, we would have a better chance of convincing the voters that Hettinger was committed to finding solutions rather than merely responding to an abstract issue. By contrast, we hoped the other candidates would not be perceived as favorably.

During the attack phase, we sought to weaken the credibility of our opponents, who claimed that they, too, were concerned about these pressing issues. Our central thesis was that they had been in office for at least four years now, entertaining a host of other, less significant issues, and only now during the election were telling the voters about the solutions they could offer. The spot, entitled, "Where Have They Been All Along?," reinforced the frustration that many citizens felt about city-planning and public safety issues. Hillside blasting had been literally rocking homes off their foundations. Cars were often stalled for miles during rush hour due to the poor planning of major traffic arteries around the city. Drug problems in the public schools were worsening. Furthermore, the crime rate was rising faster than in any other city our size in the state. Playing on the frustrations already felt, and bolstered by the argument that Hettinger had taken positive steps to address these issues, we gave the voters another reason to consider our candidate.

Because research suggests that the public pays "attention principally to messages that reflect their preexisting views" (Diamond & Bates, 1984, p. 351), we sought to demonstrate that the current administration had not been successful in resolving the problems that affected voters the most. If polling merits its costs in no other way, it serves campaigns well by helping identify the issues about which the public is currently most concerned. We sought to hit what Tony Schwartz (1973) called the "Responsive Chord." Schwartz contended that the media is powerful whenever a spot "put[s] them in touch with reality" or when it "strikes a responsive chord with the reality the listener or viewer experience[s]" (see Schwartz as cited in Diamond & Bates, 1984, p. 119). If our campaign had any hope of catching up, we had to attempt to hit that chord.

The choice to run advertisements directly comparing Hettinger to his opponents was risky. S. Merritt (1984) has argued that comparative ads are not effective strategies when there is more than one candidate. She posited that an attack against any one candidate leaves the other opponents as viable voter choices. We hoped to overcome this disadvantage by attacking the other candidates together as part of the current administration. The necessity of lumping the front-runners together cannot be underestimated. Given budgetary constraints, we could not afford to commission polls that would provide us with better insights into which candidate had the "softest" voter support. We also did not want to weaken only one front-runner and leave the voter with two other strong choices. We wanted any voter who might be convinced to make another choice to consider Hettinger.

Timing was critical. We wanted to attack, but we also wanted to limit the time in which our opponents could launch major counterattacks. If they fired the last shot, we were almost certain to lose. I suspect that our opposition never saw the attacks coming. They seemed unprepared to answer. Luckily, our timing was right on target.

Providing Closure to the Election Drama

We still had one more task to perform. In the last two days of the campaign, we wanted to bring the election to a close. Robert Goodman has claimed that "political ads are really classical drama. You try to become the good guy. You dramatize virtue where it exists. You compensate for weakness, real or perceived. You draw a contrast, put the white hat on. You orchestrate it, almost like a production, so that they leave the theater singing your song—or singing your praises" (Goodman as cited in Diamond & Bates, 1984, p. 301).

The resolution phase—what dramatists would call the denouement— is not utilized very much in modern campaigns (see Baukus & Payne, 1984). This is unfortunate. We believed that the one thing most candidates fail to do is to remember to ask the citizen for his or her vote. We sometimes forget that the candidate *needs* the vote more than he or she *deserves* it.

In the last ad we put Hettinger on camera, talking to the voters one-on-one and asking for their votes. It was, in the final analysis, his last opportunity to ask the voters to consider him and to think about his effectiveness to deal with the issues facing the city.

We ran the ad, and then we waited. On election night, Hettinger pulled away from the crowd, garnering 37 percent of the vote and winning 41 of 44 precincts. We had made it to the runoff. Three weeks later, Hettinger went on to win the general election with 65 percent of the vote.

CREDITING SUCCESS

If I were to claim that the media advertisements were the reason why our candidate won, self-respecting academics would not believe it—and they should not. As with any campaign there were a number of factors that influenced the voters' decisions. However, I concur with J. Sabato's (1981) analysis that we should accept the fact "that advertisements make some difference" (p. 134).

I have no hesitation in claiming that in this race the media was critical in getting Hettinger's message out. However, it was Hettinger who won the race. The media only helped the voters learn enough about the issues and the candidates to include Hettinger among the valid choices—to believe that a vote for Hettinger would make a difference.

The campaign had been doing all the normal campaign activities, from bumper stickers to rallies, that would be expected for any race. The door-to-door contacts, the speeches to almost every civic organization, and the nights of shaking hands at the local ballpark should not be overlooked. Nor should the innovative ideas contributed by a host of people on items such as brochure designs and public relations events.

This chapter does not permit the opportunity to explain in detail the intricacies of the campaign nor the frustrations faced in attempting to coordinate the media with the many other campaign activities of the last three weeks of the campaign. It can only attempt to give a flavor of the type of applied research that can be done in the field of political communication.

On election night there were numerous people who shared the excitement of knowing that the work had paid off. Credit had to be given to the candidate and to two campaign managers who had the onerous task of coordinating the campaign and keeping everyone (relatively) pleased with their role within it. However, there certainly exists an unseen audience of researchers who study persuasion and who print their results free of charge. Their work allowed us to make calculated (read educated) decisions about the available options and the potential for success.

CONCLUSIONS

The 1988 elections provided a unique opportunity for campaign and election research at various strata of the political field. While maintaining a critical stance toward the host of presidential candidates—assessing each for the implementation of new strategies, attempting to gauge their effectiveness by analyzing endless reams of polling data, and following news coverage that traced the edges of the flow of political opinion— consultants and professional campaigners in these and other, nonpresidential races kept a watchful eye for some new direction or tactic that might provide their clients with a strategic advantage. However, is that really research? In the sense that these researchers were more interested in success than citations, perhaps it is not. Nonetheless, theirs is the kind of research that has immediate, if not linearly conceived, effects.

Concurrently, academics who consult in political races struggle with another strata of election research. Success is important, but equally driving is the search to discover how the process of communication works in hopes of accounting for the outcomes. In this sense, applied research has the advantage of being inherently heuristic and evaluative. Readings about current events both in academic journals and newspapers like the *New York Times* and the *Washington Post* stimulate questions and generate ideas for adaptations, extensions, and directions of theoretical premises that can be applied to the particular election at hand. Theories no longer stand in isolation; their contradictions suddenly become resolved in the choice of one set of premises over another. Like our nonacademic counterparts, we endeavor to discover what works but we also engage in a form of empiricism that analyzes the variables in an attempt to add power and precision to our theories. These goals may sound lofty given that election research does not take place in a controlled setting.

We cannot deny that research in political communication is far from systematic. In fact, for most consultants the pressure after the election to find and develop new accounts is a greater priority than spending nonbillable hours to assess what worked or why. That sort of research, if it is done at all, is left to academicians who attempt to recreate the events of the campaign.

Perhaps the reason we do not write more about our experiences is that we realize that decisions are not always based on the best available evidence—time does not always permit a full search of the literature. Maybe we are reticent to claim that a particular strategy worked in a particular election knowing that the exigent factors that are relevant in one election will not be reproducible for study in the next. Perhaps we fear being labeled, like the moguls of politics, as practicing what can be best described as media witchcraft. Even noted political consultant Bob Squires has admitted that "the very best people in [politics] probably understand only about five to seven percent of what it is that they do that works. The rest is all out there in the unknown" (Squires as cited in Diamond & Bates, 1984, p. 353). Whatever the reasons, by refusing to acknowledge the role of practical experience in our academic perspectives, we rob ourselves of the opportunity for an experiential critique of the premises we hold true.

The story I have recounted is about the election of a mayor in a thriving Southern city. During the three weeks of the media campaign, something happened. A fourth-place candidate won the top spot for a runoff that he would decisively win three weeks later. I am still struggling with what happened, and I still have questions as to why the voters were persuaded to vote as they did. However, I have also confirmed through experience that some of our scholarship is on target, and that some of our observations appear to be true. Maybe that is why applied scholarship is worthy of our attention and our pursuit.

Chapter 2

Challenge and Recovery: An Incumbent's Battle for Position in a State Senate Race

The Bill Smith–Bob Albright race in Alabama's Seventh Senate District was among the more interesting races in the June 1990 Democratic primary. Smith, a twelve-year veteran of the Senate with an additional four years in the House, had run virtually unopposed since his first election. In the twelve years since, he had been relatively quiet in the performance of his tasks. Nonetheless, he had a visible contingent of supporters. Among them were arts and civic groups for whom he had supplied state funding. Organizations such as the chamber of commerce and the local government administration also endorsed Smith because of his effective work on their behalf.

The down side for Smith was that by fulfilling his obligations quietly, he had ceased to be recognized by many voters for the job he was doing. In addition, most of his campaign support group was twelve years older than when they had first pooled their resources for a Smith victory. They were now to be found in the upper ranks of management and as leaders in civic and social organizations. These supporters offered words of encouragement and financial support, but few had time to devote to the campaign. Look at almost any successful campaign and you will find a cadre of young, eager campaigners: some in college and some newly employed and looking to make their mark in society. This contingent had not been recruited over the years by the Smith campaign.

In other circumstances Smith might have been able to continue along this path of gradual decline. However, this election served as a turning point. Just hours before the filing date had passed, Smith found himself unexpectedly opposed by a well-financed adversary. The result was that the opponent entered the field three weeks before Smith could get organized. The following is an account of Smith's election challenge and his political recovery.

SETTING THE STAGE

The opposition candidate was Bob Albright, a counselor in the city school system. Albright was a colorful local figure who had received mixed reviews from his colleagues and associates. As a former Golden Glove boxer, he maintained a rugged, fighting spirit that had a lot of grass-roots appeal. Albright was elected to the state legislature and served twelve years before being unseated in a hotly contested race.

Albright was not afraid to challenge the system whenever he perceived it to be out of line. He had sued the school system over a pay dispute, the timing of which may have contributed to his defeat in his 1986 reelection bid. Similarly, when Albright lost the 1986 vote, he challenged the party to overturn the election because he alleged that his opponent had not met state financial disclosure requirements.

Albright was also not afraid to be different. Although he conveyed a tough image, he allowed himself to be photographed during one House session knitting a ski cap, a behavior not particularly in line with the macho mentality that sometimes dominates Southern politics.

To say that Smith and Albright were not ideologically compatible is an understatement. At numerous times during their legislative careers they had disagreed on the proper course of action. Philosophically, they were at opposite ends of the political spectrum. Smith believed in the politics of accommodation; Albright was fiercely independent.

Perhaps their greatest distinction was that the two men approached conflict differently. Smith preferred to work quietly to negotiate compromises and build coalitions based on rational paradigms of judgment. Albright, on the other hand, was typically led by his passionate views on a topic, never running from a headline and perfectly willing to engage in battle with little provocation.

There were also issue distinctions between them. One of the major disputes that dominated the local headlines for weeks during one legislative session concerned the dog-track issue. Albright had sponsored a bill that would have permitted legalized track betting in the Huntsville area. He and his supporters argued that the dog track would be a good recreational activity for the area, a boost to local businesses which would serve the clientele during racing season, and a way of enhancing local revenues. Smith and his constituents, on the other hand, viewed the proposal as hastily put together, a condition that they argued made the operation vulnerable to infiltration by organized crime. Smith also received a great deal of support from local churches which expressed concern over the impact of the track on the spiritual health of the community. After numerous weeks of bantering back and forth, Smith and his forces prevailed, killing the bill in the Senate.

The stage for this election was thus set in the headline battle waged on the dog-track issue in 1985. One headline back then had noted that "Albright vs. Smith Could Be Classic Political Battle of 1986." That race never came about. Smith retained his Senate seat; Albright lost his House reelection bid.

Four years later the battle heated up again as Albright entered the race against Smith. Albright had been able to keep the lid on his plan and was therefore successful in throwing the Smith campaign into a state of initial chaos. No Smith fund-raisers had been planned, no field organization had been constructed, and no staff had been assembled. In the meantime, Albright took to the streets and began a direct mail campaign attacking Smith.

THE CREATION OF SMITH'S VULNERABILITIES

Albright cleverly chose the time to launch the attack against Smith. Not only was Smith caught off guard, he was placed in that position by his own neglect.

After twelve years of service with relatively positive community feedback on his performance, Smith may have been overconfident that no serious challenger would emerge. Four years earlier a similar situation had occurred when a relatively unknown opponent entered the race against him. Smith had dismissed the opposition's ability to unseat him and was considerably surprised, by his own accounts, when she came close to winning. However, despite the warning from that race, Smith had done little to shore up his defenses.

This is not a simple issue although it may appear that way at first. Most political figures do not intentionally neglect their constituencies nor their political careers. What many analysts fail to recognize is that in many state and regional offices (particularly state legislative posts), the officeholder also has an outside job. Those interests are in constant competition for the candidate's time. The conflicts can be all-consuming during a legislative session when sensitive public issues emerge. The time constraints are even more ominous when a politician takes the lead in championing a particular issue.

Smith understood the pressures of championing a cause. He led the dog-track fight and was keenly aware of the mental and physical capital that this dispute required. Smith is the president and chief executive officer (CEO) of Smith Advanced Technology, a firm specializing in real-time artificial intelligence and robotics. The necessity for him to stay up to date on technology breakthroughs and current research is evident. However, during the session in which the dog-track issue came up,

Smith had been particularly consumed with matters of state. The result was that his business suffered a significant loss. Smith had vowed to take better care of his own personal matters in the future.

By his own accounts, Smith struggled to achieve a balance in his personal, professional, and political life during the years that followed, although he now admitted that things had gone out of balance in another way: He stopped attending church services regularly because even at church, people would corner him to talk about issues that they wanted him to pursue. On one occasion, a fellow member of the congregation chewed him out just before the services began (and in the presence of a fairly substantial crowd) because he disagreed with a vote Smith had taken. Up to that point Smith had been a Sunday school–teacher and active in church affairs. Rather than face the constant pressure of being "politicked," Smith opted instead to spend Sundays relaxing at his lake house with his family. Similarly, Smith had formerly been a member of the Rotary and other service organizations like the Jaycees. Though he still made it to occasional meetings, he had also divorced himself from these political "shark fests." In essence, Smith had gradually cut himself off from people who might have served as a barometer for his effectiveness.

Smith's isolation was politically significant. He had lost contact with a growing and powerful minority segment of his district. He had avoided social opportunities to meet the young professionals who regularly participated in civic and social organizations. He made the mistake of believing that doing a "good job" was enough. The isolation contributed in no small measure to his constituency's general lack of knowledge about anything—good or bad—that Smith had accomplished in the last few years.

Further, he had not compensated for his absence by an aggressive public relations campaign using mail and news opportunities. In perceptual voids like the one Smith had allowed to emerge, an insightful opponent has the opportunity to put a candidate on the defensive and weaken his or her incumbent status.

Upon joining the Smith election team, our primary fear was that Albright would make Smith's isolation an issue. This perception, we knew, could not be convincingly disputed. It would ring true even to those who knew and respected his work.

Our first task was to attempt to redefine Smith for the voters. We had to make the argument that he had been actively working in their interest. If Albright mounted an attack on Smith's isolation, we could then extend the argument to admit that Smith had a deficiency that could be easily corrected while simultaneously contending that he had successfully accomplished the work he was elected to perform. Defining Smith became our primary task.

OPPOSING DEFINITIONS

Before the Smith campaign team had devised a single strategy, Albright sent out his first direct mail piece. In it, he contended that Smith was the tax collector's best friend, having voted for nearly $410 million in new taxes.

This maneuver was insightful, for it fulfilled two of the objectives of issue selection: It identified an issue that defines the opposition in such a way as to limit its chances to distance itself from the issue, and it selected a topic that constituted a voting concern for the public.

By selecting the tax issue, Albright had found questions to which Smith would have trouble effectively responding. First, there was no source for his claim that Smith had voted for so much money in new taxes. We could show that Smith had voted for less than half that amount during the last legislative session; however, this posed problems. The information would have to be compiled from legislative records since we could find no credible and objective third-party source that could provide the data. Our opponent would then have an opportunity to make an issue out of our calculations. Even that might be acceptable if the majority of the voters were tenacious enough to check on the veracity of the claims one way or the other. However, we did not believe that they were. Then there were also the questions of whether to include measures for which Smith had voted that failed to get Senate approval and of how to include what Albright's letter had defined as taxes (such as user fees, fishing licenses, and driver's learning permits, items that many other people do not). If we chose to wage this battle, we had to recognize that there would be no clear winner.

Second, Smith would have trouble responding to the issue because it is one that few people understand. Suppose we could prove that he had only voted for $205 million instead of the $410 million in new taxes that Albright claimed. Would that seem any less burdensome to the voter making $18,000 a year? We doubted it.

Third, by answering the charge at all, Smith would be placing more attention on the tax issue than it had already received. Simultaneously, such public attention would force him onto the defensive. Given that Albright had defined Smith as the big taxer, we would have to be able to pay a lot of money in advertising time to reach the voter and provide the kind of evidence needed to overturn this image. That kind of big spending would only serve to fuel the perception that we were after the "little guy." Even then, given the nature of a direct mail attack, we could not be certain that we had reached the same people that Albright had in addressing his claim. The result might be to elevate the issue so that it reached an even larger public. We could not take that risk.

We determined that this issue was not worthy of a counterattack. At first glance it seemed as if we had so much ground on which to build an argument that we should not resist. We could point out that Albright gave no source for his claims and argue that he had pulled the figures out of thin air. We could argue that license fees were not typically regarded as taxes and that Albright had padded his figures inappropriately. We could weaken the entire argument by pointing out the fallacies Albright had included in the mail-out. One error in particular served as an excellent bait to get us to respond. Albright had claimed that Smith had been responsible for the recent city sales tax increase in Huntsville, Alabama, a matter that was solely under the jurisdiction of the city and over which Smith had no vote or input.

We even thought that, given the nature of the political process, there might be an argument to support the claim that Albright had voted for more taxes than Smith. Since the House (of which Albright had once been a part) originates all taxation measures and must pass them before they even reach the Senate, we believed that a careful review of the records would show Smith to be the lesser tax advocate. To demonstrate that would have taken an enormous amount of research time, however, by now it was becoming clear that the issue was not winnable and should instead be leveraged against what we perceived to be more positive issues on Smith's behalf.

One advantage of the opposition striking first is that it provides some insight into the type of campaign it is going to wage. You can also measure the strength of the attack strategy in this way. Clearly, Albright had chosen to take his traditional fighter's stance and play hardball from the outset. We had to find issues that would separate us from Albright in the voter's mind and give us an advantage over our opponent before he got us on the defensive again. Fortunately, we had some hunches about the type of issues that might be successful.

RESEARCHING THE PLAYERS

Research in political campaigns typically falls into three areas: voter research, opposition research, and candidate research. Voter information is typically gleaned from survey research and focus group interviews. In more sophisticated campaigns, voter profiles are developed by cross-matching voter registration lists with demographic profile lists purchased from mailing houses. Since voter registration by party affiliation is not required in Alabama, there is no complete state list of registered voters. The available lists have been constructed by certain well-financed campaigns which are generally unwilling to share that information.

Opposition and candidate research can be conducted in-house or purchased through research specialists. For high-visibility campaigns, opposition research can cost a campaign upwards of $10,000. In Georgia, one gubernatorial candidate hired high school and college debaters to construct the research programs. Once the initial research task had been completed, they established networks across the state to compile a daily news clipping and analysis file. Most local races cannot afford such fees. The result is that campaigns often end up with piecemeal research conducted by several volunteers, some of whom are not as thorough as they should be.

The problem with good research is that it takes time. Collecting the material is not easy for local elections. The *Congressional Record* and a number of political action committees (PACs) assist in analyzing federal races. By contrast, states vary in their recording procedures. Many state records and even more local records are neither indexed nor computerized. Local PACs may have information, but a candidate must be endorsed before that information is shared with him or her. Sometimes the demand for information and the schedule for releasing it do not match.

The one type of research that is comparatively simple to perform is candidate research. The candidate's office can usually supply voting records on particular issues. Since Smith shared office space and staff with others in the county delegation, such information had never been compiled. Smith's files were a series of news clips and campaign literature which had been housed in boxes in his garage since the last campaign four years ago. This was another example of the malaise created by neglecting record keeping during nonelection years.

I should note that Smith is not atypical in this regard. Few candidates in down-ballot races have the secretarial support necessary to maintain effective records. Researchers are often thankful for finding a candidate who has kept files of any sort.

The Smith campaign was initially somewhat chaotic. With just six weeks to go before the election, the opponent was already in the field. Luckily, Smith was a veteran campaigner. He was aware of his vulnerability, but he was equally aware of the necessity for a campaign to do its homework and establish a well-thought-out strategy before beginning.

Initial research centered on determining which arguments were perceived as credible associations with Smith prior to their initiation by the campaign. This phase of research was also designed to find voter "hot spots": those issues on the voters' minds that compel a response from some political leader.

Typically, focus group interviews serve as the starting point for this research. In the Smith campaign, however, there was not enough time to be as methodical as we would have liked. After a brainstorming session, Pat Cotter and James Stovall, the pollsters for Southern Opinion Research, constructed a questionnaire designed to assess the market.

Smith's benchmark poll went into the field just before Albright's first mail-out was delivered to the voters. The polling results showed no distinguishing issues between the two candidates. We even attempted to find a coattail effect between Smith, Albright, and the candidates in two more highly visible races: the governor's race and the United States Fifth Congressional District election. The only significant factor that the poll revealed was a slight coattail effect between Albright and one of the five gubernatorial candidates. Given that the governor's race was in a four-way dead heat at the time when the poll was taken, we did not see any particular gain from getting wrapped up in that contest.

At first glance, some people might think that such a poll could tell us very little, but actually it told us a great deal. To begin with, we learned that the issues that we felt truly separated the two candidates were not that distinct in the voters' minds. We knew that we would have to educate the voters and convince them that the differences between the candidate positions were significant. We also confirmed that Smith had not been successful in building up his own public reputation over the years. We had to remind the voter of the causes that Smith had championed and of what he stood for.

Perhaps more important, the polling data indicated that Albright's initial attack on the tax issue was not exploiting an opinion already in the minds of the voters. Although tax issues were certainly a concern, a negative association between the issue and Smith did not exist. Albright was clearly trying to establish a link between Americans' general distaste for taxation and Smith's purported record.

The poll also revealed that the public did not perceive any particular vulnerability on the part of either Smith or Albright. Both candidates appeared to be solidly poised for a good contest. The conclusion of the Southern Opinion Research staff was that the way in which we conducted the campaign would determine the outcome of the election. Everyone fears making *the* mistake that can be exploited by the opposition, but in close elections such as this one promised to be, even a minor exploitable error could work against us.

While waiting for the polling data to be analyzed, candidate research began. We could not afford any surprises once we had laid down the issues for the campaign. The results of these efforts were then matched against polling data to determine the issues that the voters cared about on which Smith had a positive record or agenda. Four significant issues emerged. Smith had an extremely strong voting record on environmental matters. This was by far his strongest press. Smith also had a cluster of concerns that matched the voters' concerns about community standards.

For example, Smith had sponsored the Alabama child abuse law and advocated stronger penalties for driving while under the influence of drugs or alcohol (DUI). He had also assisted in financing an impressive list of community projects in the areas of arts and education. The third area was a fit between Smith and his constituent's profile involving pride in the region's technological sophistication and the primal beauty of the area. Smith personified these concerns in his own business and recreational interests. He was both a businessman in a high-technology industry and an avid participant in outdoor activities. Smith's fourth area of strength consisted of his leadership credentials in the community. His service not only as a legislator but also on boards and civic organizations was still impressive despite the drop-off in these activities over the past few years.

By this time the campaign had hired Doug Bacchus, a college junior majoring in political science at Auburn University. His initial task was to begin compiling opposition research and investigating the charges that Albright was making against Smith in his direct mail pieces.

In the meantime we started making the Smith campaign more visible. As much as we wanted to wait for the research to be completed, we could not afford to delay any longer in getting a positive issue agenda in front of the public. We were now four weeks away from the election.

IMPLEMENTING STRATEGY

While the Smith campaign was buried in research and fund-raising activities, Albright continued his offensive. Another direct mail piece emerged. One thing seemed evident: We could not permit Albright to define Smith to the public before we did, nor could we allow him to dictate the direction of our campaign by positioning ourselves on the defensive. Our first goal was reaffirmed: to redefine Smith for the voters.

The first variable we needed to deal with was the Smith name. "Bill Smith" is, of course, a fairly common name. Ironically, during this same election cycle, the Democratic incumbent for the adjoining Senate district was named Jim Smith. Given that both candidates shared the same media market as well as the same job title and last name, the task was made even more difficult. Fortunately, Jim Smith was not vulnerable in the primary and posed little threat to Bill should people get them confused. Still, we had to deal with the issue of name recognition while we attempted to educate the voter on Smith's record.

The theme that was chosen to capitalize on name recognition was "Re-Elect Bill Smith: A Common Name for an Uncommon Leader." This permitted us to load three important ideas into the campaign. First, we wanted people to know that Smith was the incumbent. Despite the anti-incumbent sentiment that developed nationwide during the general election, people in this district were basically satisfied with the way in which government was functioning for them. Second, we highlighted the problem of name identification. One way to get people to address an issue is to bring it to their attention. Finally, the theme allowed us to bundle the issues around the theme of leadership. That may seem to be a rather generic concept at first, yet leadership is an important quality of an elected official. Based on our preliminary research, we believed Albright could not win in a comparative format.

To begin to explain the sort of leadership roles that Smith had assumed, a palm card was constructed. On one side of the card were Smith's picture, logo, and theme. The other side headlined "Four Reasons to Re-Elect Senator Bill Smith." The reasons given were particularly important for this election. Past history indicated that Albright tended to react out of his strong feelings for a topic; Smith was the more rational decision maker. Although we were not yet prepared to imply anything about the superiority of one decision-making form over another, we wanted to plant the seed. It was also important to give reasons since this was a genuine reflection of the candidate's approach to governance.

Under each of the four reasons given, information was included about the programs Smith supported and what he stood for in Montgomery as state senator. At the end of each of these segments was a summary of the leadership trait involved. For example, after detailing Smith's commitment to the environment, the reader was informed of the fact that his actions were evidence of his commitment. The tag line after the argument read, "That's leadership in action."

The arguments were reinforced perceptually as well. Since the election followed on the heels of Earth Day, the environment was a key concern for us. Using green and white as the colors for the campaign and printing all campaign materials on recycled paper, Smith attempted to claim the environmental issue as his own.

With a central message in place, the contest began to take form. The campaign was organized according to five major functions. The fund-raising segment was the first to take control of the situation and begin working. The fund-raising group functioned as a committee, hosting dinners and personally soliciting contributions. Another segment was headed by a PAC with local affiliations. It provided both phone bank support and the solicitation of other PAC contributions. The door-to-door operation was headed by a man whose analysis, targeting, and organization of neighborhood Get Out the Vote drives are much respected in the area. Headquarters operations became the responsibility of the campaign manager, an efficient support staff, and members of the Smith family. The media and public relations functions were handled by SpeakInc Communication, a local consulting firm.

During the campaign, Smith and his campaign manager served as the central contacts for the various segments of the campaign. No one had time for regularly scheduled meetings to inform one another of the campaign's progress. Occasional phone calls and accidental meetings were more commonplace. The professional orientation of the organization meant that each segment was ultimately responsible for the success of its own operations.

The one common thread of compliance was that all segments of the campaign would focus on Smith's record in a positive campaign. Any attacks or retorts to Albright would be handled through the media/public relations segment of the organization. This was instrumental since the other phases of the campaign were driven by personal contacts, outlets that were essential in establishing the positive rapport necessary before any attack strategy could be implemented. It also permitted the campaign to control the timing of responses better than if the responsibility were diffused.

The initial press for the campaign was to make sure that people knew who Bill Smith was and understood his record on key issues of voter concern. We were searching to build a positive relationship between Smith and his constituents. All other matters were to be subjugated to this need.

The palm card presented a rational, positive message to voters. However, we were looking for a stronger way to kick off the media segment of the campaign. We almost overlooked the obvious in searching for a way to bring Smith and the voters closer together. During this election year, Memorial Day fell eight days before the election. This was particularly important since Huntsville has a sizable number of military and ex-military personnel. Some targeted message for the occasion seemed appropriate, and we needed an angle. We were particularly enthused when we discovered that Smith had served in the military during the Berlin crisis in 1961. Given the fact that the Berlin wall was coming down and that people were acclaiming the victory of democracy over totalitarianism, and recognizing the suitability of the issue for the occasion, we found the right angle.

The radio spots reinforced Smith's commitment to public service. More important, they permitted us to begin the campaign by providing people with the information they needed at a time at which they were prepared to hear it. The positive comments received about the ads helped jump-start the campaign into action.

There were other strategic guidelines for the campaign as well. Given that Albright had chosen a direct mail strategy, personal contact with the voters was valued most highly. We could not risk having an illusive media campaign when the opponent was reaching voters in their homes and calling them by name. The campaign manager coordinated Smith's schedule, making sure that he spoke with a cross-section of the district.

The door-to-door campaign and phone bank combined to reach hundreds of voters with a positive message about Smith's leadership abilities. Although it was not a substantial part of the strategy in the primary, the campaign also utilized person-to-person contacts via direct mail. Through each of these approaches, the first voter impressions were of a highly personalized campaign.

Another guideline formulated for the first phase of the campaign was to maintain a positive message even if Albright continued his assault. Three reasons bolstered this position. First, the voters did not really know either candidate well enough to make judgments about their motives. Once the candidates got into a name-calling battle with each other, voters would not care who started the fight; they would just want it to end. We wanted to make sure that when Smith locked horns with Albright, the voters would know at least one contestant and, preferably, would have already decided to root for a Smith victory. Second, we felt sure that Albright would continue to provoke a confrontation. It was in his nature to fight. If we held off long enough, the public would begin to see Albright as the offender and respect Smith's decision to defend himself when he finally did respond. Third, Albright was on comfortable turf in his fighter's stance. He enjoyed the struggle and the contest. Smith did not, instead preferring a more rational line of discourse. When Smith entered the proverbial ring, he needed to take his best punch and make it count. We were looking for a knockout, but it had to be one that the voters wanted Smith to make.

Yet another guideline reinforced the notion of trust. The campaign must have ready documentation for all the claims that were initiated by Smith. Whether in campaign materials such as palm cards or letters, or in commercials or speeches, we wanted to make sure that there was independent verification of the facts.

Although Smith had high credibility among the people who knew of him, there were many people in the district who were not familiar with him or his record. The people in the latter group were the target of our persuasive efforts. The polling data indicated that each candidate held a sizable following. The battleground was over the undecided voters. The use of evidence in such cases bolsters a speaker's credibility (see Haiman, 1949; McCroskey, 1967; Rybacki & Rybacki, 1991).

The credibility factor would be important to us once we got into a direct confrontation with Albright. People needed to see that Smith was prepared, thorough in his analysis, and willing to substantiate any claim he made against his opponent. The factuality of claims was a potential issue that we also saw developing. In our judgment, Albright had already been altering the facts. The gist of the attacks may have had some truth to them, but the specific attacks often distorted the details.

One guideline was established to assist in setting the stage for an eventual confrontation. Smith needed to make sure that the basis for any disputes was issues, not personality. Albright was a unique, spirited individual. Many people found him a little *too* spirited for their taste. However, we could not allow that to be in any way considered the substance of our disagreements with him. That would be contrary to the rational paradigm that Smith naturally followed. It would also alienate voters who thought we were attacking Albright just because he was different.

Finally, we resolved to end the campaign on a positive note. Despite the fact that we were willing to engage in a fight, we also knew that the way in which a candidate wins or loses can determine how the voters respond. We could win on the issues technically yet still lose the election. The last three days of the campaign were strategically focused to heal the wounds and regain composure after the attack phase had ended.

CONFRONTATION

Billboards erected across the district, along with an active yard-sign campaign, helped voters become aware of Smith's candidacy. The palm card served as the backbone for campaign messages. Once Smith's presence and identity had been reestablished, the campaign began considering how to enter the battle.

Opposition research was now in its final stages of completion. The results were staggering. Everyone knew that the two candidates were far apart on the issues, yet no one within the campaign could believe the number of areas from which we could choose that showed significant differences between the candidates.

We began by attempting to second-guess the opposition. We needed to determine the areas in which Smith was most vulnerable. Based on the campaign literature Albright had already sent as well as numerous statements he had made to public gatherings, we determined that he would establish the race along economic lines. The basic scenario would be to paint Smith as the big spender and big taxer while Albright would be portrayed as the defender of the working-class population. Albright himself expressed this sentiment, saying that the critical issue in this race concerned "the haves against the have-nots."

Albright depicted Smith as one of the "haves." Everyone assumed that Smith would be well financed. He was a proficient fund-raiser. The notion that he would be well financed was fostered by a mock campaign budget constructed to show that we needed over $100,000 to run a decent primary campaign. Although it was intended as an in-house document, word has a way of getting out.

To offset the perception that we were sure Albright would attempt to foster, Smith took defensive action. He was fortunate to have assembled a shrewd finance committee which concurred with the reading of Albright's strategy. They decided to initially limit contributions to $1,000. Although Smith was capable of pulling in substantially more, he knew that voters might read higher contributions as questionable.

Smith also took personal control of campaign spending. He monitored expenses so that workers had all the funds they needed but also so that the campaign got its money's worth out of each dollar spent. This was to be an important variable as we began to consider a media budget.

The advantage of being a late starter in a campaign is that you can concentrate your efforts on the closing weeks of the campaign. Albright had been in the field longer, but he had also been forced to spend more money in order to keep his operations afloat.

Looking at the media buys in the closing two weeks of the campaign, we saw Albright's blueprint for his final media blitz. Whereas Albright was reaching the end of his budget, Smith was just beginning to spend the big media dollars. The campaign was able to buy enough time in the closing ten days to overshadow Albright's final messages. The additional benefit was that Smith could spend that much money and still come in under Albright's total budget.

The strategy paid off handsomely. After the first financial disclosures, the newspaper reported that Albright had spent almost twice as much money as Smith. Further, while Smith had received PAC contributions from a number of small contributors, Albright had relied on one PAC for $24,562, a full *38 percent* of his total budget. Three other PACs had donated over $10,000 each to support his candidacy.

The disclosure took the wind out of Albright's sails. He could no longer make a credible argument that Smith was the big-spending candidate who was reliant on special-interest monies. In effect, he forfeited one of the arguments on which he had rested his campaign.

Opposition research also paid off when we began looking for issues to use in a counterattack. By cross-matching audience interests against Smith's strengths and Albright's weaknesses, three issues emerged. We hoped that these would serve as the knockout punch that we needed in order to win the election.

The first issue to grab everyone's attention was education. Since Albright was a guidance counselor in the city schools, we anticipated that he would naturally win on education issues. He was also heavily financed by the teachers' union. What we found, however, was a law suit in which Albright had sued the school system over a pay dispute. The perception of someone suing the school system over matters of personal interest does not sit well with many voters. Trial records raised additional questions about the legitimacy of his claims. By contrast, Smith had been endorsed by Kid Pac, an action committee whose special interest was child welfare, in order to "signal voters that [Bill Smith] places the needs of Alabama's public school children above all others."

The second area for attack was on the environment. Smith had already carved out a good reputation for his Energy Management Conservation Act. He had also received statewide acclaim for his sponsorship of solar energy legislation. Opposition research dovetailed nicely with the financial disclosures just published. In his last election bid, Albright had accepted money from Chemical Waste Management, Inc., which operates the nation's largest hazardous waste landfill at Emelle, Alabama. Voters did not have to be educated on the issue of hazardous waste. It had been the topic of several attack ads in the gubernatorial race and had been widely covered by the media.

The third area was unexpected as well. As an entrepreneur himself, Smith had always been sensitive to the needs of small businesses. Over the years he had received much support from probusiness groups. Opposition research found a document by the Alabama Alliance of Business and Industry stating that in one session while Albright was in the House of Representatives, he had voted against small business 96 percent of the time.

While we were preparing our attack message, Albright began his television advertisements. True to his nature, this was not an issue-based attack. Instead, Albright attacked Smith on a personal level. He charged that Smith had failed to return phone calls from constituents. The advertisement opened with a shot of a man holding a phone in his hand. He claimed that he had called Smith over fifty-one times and that Smith had never answered his calls. He vowed to hang on to the phone until Smith answered.

That night we put an answering machine in at the headquarters. (Since we were understaffed, there were times when no one would be available to take calls.) Smith's support staff at his business office also instituted strict control over messages to make sure that each phone call was returned promptly. If no one was in, a letter was sent to confirm that Smith had attempted to return the call. None of these defensive measures proved necessary. Few people called the headquarters. Fewer called the business office. No one seemed to care.

Reaction to the Albright ad was not positive. Word around town was that calling someone fifty-one times was harassment. No one blamed Smith for not talking to the guy if he had a chip on his shoulder. There was also no evidence that this was a widespread problem. People who worked with legislators on a frequent basis claimed not to have had any problems reaching Smith when they needed him.

Both men were true to their character in their assaults. Albright focused on a behavior that stirred his emotions. He saw himself standing up for the guy whose voice could not be heard. Smith addressed documented differences between the way in which the two men approached issues. The essential appeals boiled down to a clash between passion and reason. The question was which approach would sway enough voters to create the winning margin.

STRATEGY ASSESSMENT AND REINFORCEMENT

The Smith campaign resolved to end on a positive note. During the entire four-day period during which the attack messages were running, the person-to-person campaign kept advancing a constructive message about the Smith record.

The campaign received positive comments about the palm card, and especially about the fact that it was printed on recycled materials. The card was particularly advantageous to those who already knew and liked Smith. Supporters were given reasons that they could use when asked by their friends why they recommended Smith. Those who had no prior knowledge of Smith also found the information helpful.

The four reasons outlined on the palm card and the accompanying leadership traits were reinforced in a series of newspaper advertisements that highlighted one argument a day from the Wednesday through the Saturday before the Tuesday election.

Although the palm card was the primary tool used in the door-to-door campaign, Smith also capitalized on positive issues through a newspaper-styled advertisement that was thrown to selected homes in the district the last two nights before the election. In this format, the voter could read about Smith and his record in detail.

The paper was designed to reinforce the positive message that was needed to close the Smith campaign. Like the palm card, the front page of the paper was devoted to a picture of Smith, his logo, and his theme. The paper also included a personal note from Smith to the voters asking for their support. The interior pages focused on detailed information about Smith's biography and personal history of service, and his record in the statehouse. The newspaper had a utilitarian function as well as an advertising motive. Included on the back page of the newspaper was a sample ballot and a map of the district.

The inclusion of the sample ballot was a standard political practice for Smith, but it was still effective. Many people like to have a ballot to study before going to the polls. The Sunday paper typically carries one, but newsprint is rather messy. The size of the reprinted ballot on the back of the campaign's recycled stock paper made it convenient to carry and easy to write on.

Timing was critical throughout the campaign, but it was particularly important during the closing days. The last round of attacks was completed Sunday morning when we ran a strong advertisement comparing Smith and Albright on several key areas of voter concern. Once the argument against Albright had been clearly made, the campaign needed to reaffirm Smith as the logical alternative. The newspaper permitted us to provide detailed information of Smith's positions that other formats would not. The information was made readily available to them in an easily digestible format.

CONCLUSIONS

Campaigns openly attempt to depict candidates as symbols for certain issues. Merely telling the public that a candidate has a good voting record on five or six issues is generally not sufficient to sustain a campaign in which the opponent can point out five or six issues on which the candidate has a poor record.

Issues are used to represent habits of mind. The way that candidates approach issues, and even which issues they attend to at all, are indicators of the way in which they view the world. The things they care about—that are of personal concern to them—are bound to be the issues on which they will focus their attention during a legislative session. If these issues match the concerns that are on the minds of the voters, a natural coalition can be forged.

That is why the message of any successful campaign is the candidate. If campaigns are to be effective in establishing perceptual linkages between the candidates and their publics, they must be true to the nature of the candidate.

Both candidates in this District Seven primary amassed sizable followings by staying true to the issues and concerns that drove their personal lives. The battle in the campaign was a battle for self-definition. The candidates told the voter who they were and defined themselves in contrast to the opposition.

In the end, Smith was supported by the majority of voters. The task that lay ahead of him was rebuilding his relationships with those who had felt ostracized by his campaign over the last four years, the same group that had encouraged the candidacy of Bob Albright.

If there is a lesson here it is that the voters will not be ignored. Those who are excluded from representation willingly align themselves with another candidate who better serves their interests. These are words of caution. In Smith's own words on the night on the victory celebration, "Take a few days off, folks. We've got lots of work to do before fall."

Chapter 3

Running on the Family Name: The Impact of Gender and Issue Framing on the Race of a Political Newcomer

In 1988, the First Tennessee Valley Women's Conference was inaugurated. The topic, "Organizing Politically for Your Cause," fit into the overall mission of the organizers. Their intent was to provide a series of workshops focusing on current issues and concerns and directed to an all-female audience.

In the audience that day were a number of women with political aspirations. Many of them were anxious to get an impartial appraisal of their potential to win elective office. Many more openly acknowledged their interest but were reluctant to file because of their belief that others were probably more credentialed or qualified. Still others wanted to explore the idea more thoroughly and find out how to position themselves for a race.

Among those in the audience was Laura Jo Hamilton, an assistant district attorney. Like many of the women there that day, Hamilton had political ambitions. Like many women there and elsewhere, she also wanted to have a family, a decision that in our society often delays a woman's professional goals.

Two years later, Hamilton still had the conference brochure with the names of potential consultants and supporters on it. Two years had made a difference. Her family was now established, she was more confident, and she had spent the time wisely in positioning herself to run. She was now ready to file for the newly created slot of district court judge.

Hamilton initially believed that she was prepared to direct the campaign herself. She had attended seminars, talked to successful judicial candidates, and taken note of her own political experience. By January, with the primary less than six months away, however, she had realized the enormity of the task. She acknowledged the pressures of running a campaign single-handedly and the difficulty in executing strategic considerations while bearing the sole responsibility for campaigning. She also had personal and family obligations that were important for her to maintain. At this juncture Hamilton realized, perhaps for the first time, why campaigns are built around publics and not just around the candidate. In order to run a successful race, she would have to depend on others to bear part of the load. This race was not about Laura Jo Hamilton per se. It was about developing a leader who was capable of inspiring a following. It was about representing the needs of the voters in Madison County, Alabama.

From a research perspective, the Hamilton race provided a number of interesting variables. Gender was one of the more obvious concerns. In addition to the normal implications of a woman running for a traditionally held male role, Alabama still is a chilly climate for women in key governmental positions. Alabama ranks forty-seventh in the nation based on the number of women legislators in the statehouse. Whereas nationally, women comprise approximately 17 percent of the ruling body, Alabama seats just over 5 percent. Even in predominantly appointed positions, there are fewer women in Alabama than in other states. The governor's cabinet, for example, ranks forty-third in the nation on the number of women holding posts. This race was pivotal for the insight it could provide into the problems faced by a candidate in an area that was unaccustomed to successful women politicians.

Another interesting variable was that Hamilton was also a political newcomer. She had never run for office before. Therefore, she did not have an already constructed public image, nor had she developed a publicly viewed style of decision making. Given that a judge's responsibility includes effective deliberation and decision making, the construction of her first public campaign was important. It was true that because of the low visibility of the race, a lot of people would never notice. Nonetheless, the patterns that Hamilton established in her first race would have likely consequences for her political future.

The campaign could not ignore the fundamental strategies that are necessary for any candidate to win. The best predictor of outcome in a lower-level race when there is no incumbent is name identification. Conventional wisdom also notes the importance of money to finance the campaign. Beyond that, there is little research that provides insight into establishing campaign strategy. Little has been written about political elections at this level. As a result, most campaigns tend to apply theories and follow the conventional wisdom constructed for the more visible elections. However, this would certainly not be a high-visibility race. The use of polling data would be negligible except to determine the name recognition levels present at the beginning of the campaign. The intriguing aspect of this campaign was the need for intuitive hunches on which strategies would be built. Indeed, one question that emerged was whether the campaign would continue to follow conventional wisdom and assumptions even when intuitive judgments contradicted the appropriateness of those conclusions.

Given the presence of these determining factors, the following analysis explains how the campaign was conducted and the campaign's approach and interpretation of critical variables.

GENDER

Some research validates the belief that there are differences in the way in which men and women participate in political campaigns (see Almond & Verba, 1963; Anderson, 1975; Campbell, Converse, Miller, & Stokes, 1960; McCain & Koch, 1985; Rappaport, 1981; Shabad & Anderson, 1979; Verba & Nie, 1972; Welch, 1977). However, researchers have a difficult time assessing the impact of gender variables on political outcomes (McCain & Koch, 1985). It is still a relatively new field of exploration by researchers. Although the U.S. public is now familiar with the term, research on the "gender gap" was largely a phenomenon of the 1984 presidential elections. Even less is known about the impact of gender on a person's performance as a candidate (see Trent & Friedenberg, 1983, pp. 113–117). Although some research is surfacing, there is still a lack of generalizable claims as to how female candidates should orchestrate their efforts differently from men. Research into candidate gender in down-ballot races in which name recognition is the primary determinant of electoral outcomes has been negligible.

The fact that gender should even be discussed in a district court judge race is puzzling. One of the symbols of the court is the status of Blind Justice, a woman. According to the ancient mythic roots, the woman rendering justice wears a cloth across her eyes to blind her from those who would try to influence her judgments. The scale in her hands is symbolic of her ability to render a verdict based solely on the weight of the evidence presented. This of all elected positions would seem to symbolically favor women. However, the campaign could not ignore the fact that there are still very few women represented in the judicial branch of government. Despite the fact that the very nature of the position seems to call for unbiased choice, women are seldom elected.

During the early stages of the Hamilton election, two gender-related questions plagued the campaign: "Is gender a determining factor for voters when little other information about the candidates is known? If so, can voter contact with the candidate neutralize the gender issue?" The research in this area is inconclusive. We could find no studies that convinced us that there are predictable patterns in the way in which voters treat men and women. Intuitively, we believed that in the absence of other information, gender could very well be the deciding factor. In the case in which a voter had to choose between a male and a female candidate with equal name recognition, natural prejudices (either in favor or against) would come into play. However, we also believed that familiarity with the candidates would override gender concerns. In that case, we believed that identification with the candidate would overcome other decision considerations.

The question of whether gender would be an influencing factor in this election was a matter of concern. There was some reason to suspect that it would not be critical. Hamilton was well educated and credentialed as an attorney and had been working outside the home for most of her adult life. Her role within the community and her numerous civic services were well noted. On the other hand, Hamilton had two small children, and the younger was only 10 months old. If a person held a bias about the responsibility of women to rear their children, Hamilton could be at risk (see Flora & Lynn, 1974).

One person suggested that Hamilton run under her initials (L. J. Hamilton). That way, the majority of the voting public would not know her gender. This approach is commonly endorsed by some consulting firms with clients in down-ballot races. However, we felt that this would be deceptive. Hamilton had always been known by her first and middle names, Laura Jo. (This practice is not uncustomary in the South.) To change her name at this point would imply that Hamilton herself perceived that there was something wrong with a female running for a judgeship. At the very least, it could be interpreted as an issue that was significant enough to cause her to change her name.

The other two contenders for the position were both male. One candidate was a black attorney in town. The other served as an assistant district attorney in the same office as Hamilton. Both were well-respected attorneys with roots in the city. All things being equal, bets would historically favor the white male over the other two candidates. Hamilton's campaign staff determined that the public should not perceive the race shaping up as either a gender or a racial battle. Hamilton could not afford to split voters along these criteria. The pivotal question, as in other elections, would center around who was able to make the broadest appeal to the largest constituency. However, the perception also needed to be clarified that by virtue of her perspective, Hamilton could offer a more balanced judicial bench. Somehow, Hamilton needed to stress the issue of perspective without inducing the gender claims.

Almost from the outset, it was clear that there would be differences in Hamilton's campaign that distinguished it from other races. The fact that Hamilton was female had a great deal of influence on the campaign

organization. There were more women involved in her volunteer working group than perhaps in any other campaign its size. The finance
committee was gender-balanced, but male workers performing tasks
during the actual campaign were greatly outnumbered by females. There
were times when people within the campaign openly joked about getting
the "sewing circle" or "bridge club" together for another task.

Importantly, the inclusion of more women than men was not a matter
of design. There was no directed effort to this end. Nonetheless, the
fact remained that men tended to support the campaign financially and
through encouragement more than through labor.

There was also another distinguishing factor. Both Hamilton and her
husband were working professionals. George Hamilton, a biomedical
engineer with the National Aeronautics and Space Administration
(NASA), could not bear the sole responsibility for the children during
the long election season. Although he carried a substantially heavier
share of the child-care load during that period, Laura Jo remained an
active family member. During the campaign it was not unusual for Laura
Jo to take her children with her or to find George nailing yard signs
together with his two "apprentice carpenters" at his side.

Differences between this and other campaigns were apparent, yet we
did not want to set up a gender mandate or provoke gender concerns
as points of contention between rivaling candidates. Although the Hamilton campaign saw no percentage in spotlighting her gender, neither
did it perceive a reason to act as if it were hiding something from the
public. In order for gender to become an issue, someone had to make
it one. The campaign resolved to neutralize the negative impacts of the
issue insofar as possible.

All family pictures were shot in order to downplay the youth of Hamilton's children. The picture chosen for her brochure, for example, featured the children sitting on a playground slide with both parents
sharing in the activity. The picture did not hide the fact that Hamilton
had young children, but neither did it draw the contrast as sharply as
might have been done by a traditional family portrait.

If the family shot had been omitted, Hamilton would have been asking
for an attack. Politicians routinely show their families with them. It gives
the reader insight into the personal lives of the candidates. Hamilton's
family deserved no less emphasis in her life and career than a male
candidate's family would.

Further, by openly acknowledging the family linkage, people would
have to either already possess a bias against working women or the
opposition would have to make Hamilton's family an issue by articu-
lating it as one. Hamilton could do little to change the minds of those
who already had those dispositions against women working outside the
home. Given the number of working women who worked or had profes-

sional responsibilities outside the home, the campaign determined that an opponent would dig his own grave by hoping to fan prejudicial sentiments. By placing the photo prominently in the brochure and acknowledging Hamilton's family ties, the opponents were prevented from bringing up gender issues through the claim that Hamilton had omitted an important part of her life.

More important, Hamilton's family was vital to conveying a sense of who she is. She needed to be comfortable continuing to maintain the same kinds of roles and activities she had engaged in before entering a political career.

Although some people were openly concerned about the gender issue, the campaign resolved to define the issue positively before the opposition could define it as a negative attribute. As Christopher Matthews (1988) noted in his book *Hardball*, campaigns should "hang a lantern" on their problems (p. 155). There is little to be gained by allowing someone else to describe a natural trait as a problem.

The campaign had much to gain by redirecting the gender question to make it a family issue. Family concerns are not far from the surface in the South. Extended families are a natural part of the Southern heritage. The Wilbourns and the Herefords, Hamilton's maternal and paternal lines, were reputed by one observer to populate half the county. The rest of the inhabitants, the observer noted, were probably Hamiltons. In truth, the families were well known and much respected in the county. It was one of Hamilton's strongest assets. If the campaign was successful, it would be in no small measure because it was a family campaign.

The first manifestation of the family influence was a playroom constructed in a room of the headquarters for the many children of relatives and volunteers who would come to work. At major campaign events there were numerous kids under foot. The kickoff rally even featured campaign-decorated "Tiny Tyke" car races and a family picnic–style atmosphere.

Another opportunity to highlight the family issues in a positive way was in Hamilton's brochure. Underneath the family photograph Hamilton included a brief statement about her candidacy. In it she advanced an argument that emphasized the impact of her family relationships on her ability to perform the job:

My fourteen years of trial experience have given me the legal insights necessary to be an effective judge. But what qualifies me is not just legal experience. Our laws are designed to uphold and reinforce our community's values. It is the responsibility of the court system to protect those values. *My roots in this community*—as well as my ties to the many civic and service organizations which contribute to its progress—have provided me with an understanding of our community's standards. Knowing what is involved in being a District Court Judge, I understand the impact legal proceedings have upon our communities *and our families*. I know I can make tough, fair decisions *with those interests in mind*. I can do what is required and more—I can make a difference in people's lives for the better. That's why I am running for office and why I need your vote. [emphasis added]

The intent of the statement was to entrench the family perspective while at the same time preempting arguments relating to the gender issue.

The latter began by mentioning Hamilton's experience. A full two-thirds of the brochure dealt with the specifics in detail. She was not asking that people vote for her just because she was a relative or a female. She was a viable, qualified candidate. She deserved the voters' consideration, and the brochure explained why.

At the same time the letter redirected the family issue. "Family" became a code word for roots in the community. Hamilton argued that the stronger a judge's ties to the community, whether through service or lineage, the more capable he or she would be to understand the standards that were to be upheld in the court system.

"Family" was also representative of an approach to decision making. As Hamilton would argue in almost every public appearance, the majority of cases before a district court judge are juvenile cases. These juveniles are not, for the most part, hardened recidivists. They are the children of some family living in the community. The effect of juxtaposing family and legal issues was to project a certain caring and sensitivity about a judge's job. In one radio advertisement this argument was strengthened by a reminder that the district court was usually the court of first appearance for juveniles. The way in which they are treated can have a significant impact on their future as well as that of the community.

At the same time, Hamilton acknowledged a need for voters to understand that she was not going to be a "soft" judge, a trait that might be gender-related in some voters' minds. For this reason, Hamilton's experience as an assistant district attorney was emphasized. She had personally prosecuted approximately 4,000 juvenile cases, 20,000 misdemeanors, 35,000 traffic cases, and 1,000 criminal cases. That was not the record of someone who was soft on criminal conduct.

By taking this approach, the campaign redirected the gender and service issues as necessary requirements for any candidate for a judicial post. The campaign offered voters a standard of judgment for use in comparing the contenders for this office. It seemed an appropriate criterion. If voters accepted the standard as valid, we felt sure that they would vote in favor of Hamilton.

Gradually, as the campaign began to take shape, the fit between the family theme and Hamilton's campaign became apparent. Her family was literally the hallmark of the campaign. Mrs. Wilbourn, Hamilton's mother, canvassed as many neighborhoods as any other worker in the campaign. After suffering heart trouble early in the season, she redirected her efforts to making the campaign environment a pleasant one for volunteers. She would often bring homemade goodies to headquarters to keep up the spirits of the workers there. Others, picking up on Mrs. Wilbourn's lead, quickly followed suit. Workers soon learned that there was always work they could do and usually good food as a reward for service. Mrs. Wilbourn was also instrumental in keeping everyone's spirits up. Though she stayed in the background of the campaign, she provided invaluable assistance in rallying the families and instituting a family atmosphere at the headquarters.

Similarly, the Hamiltons, Laura Jo's in-laws, were active in the campaign. They joined their son in taking responsibility for the silk-screening effort to produce yard signs. They also assisted in placing a good number of the signs around the county. Distant cousins soon became major players in the election process as well. Those who could not devote time, sent money. Those who were well connected kept the campaign aware of activities in the opponents' camps. A solid family front soon became evident.

One other gender-related concern created much campaign debate. Hamilton was a woman with very distinguishing facial features. These were made more prominent by the way in which she wore her hair. She had very long hair but always wore it braided into a bun at the nape of her neck. The look was especially dramatic in black-and-white photographs. (The campaign could not afford to run color photographs in brochures and billboards.) Almost from the first day on which Hamilton began talking about running for office, people tried to convince her to cut her hair to make a softer and more professional appearance. Hamilton did not want to change. That should have been the end of the discussion, but it was not.

The campaign strategists believed that Hamilton's "harsh" look might actually be a benefit to a person running for a judicial post. (The stereotype image of a judge as a white-haired elderly man conveys the same "tough" image.) This was not, after all, a public relations position. Further, Hamilton made a very striking impression. People who saw her photograph were not likely to forget it. Given that one of the goals in this race was to help establish name recognition, the strategists reasoned that the photograph would be an effective memory aid.

Numerous friends, relatives, and professional advertising executives in the area advised against the use of Hamilton's photograph on her billboards. One executive emphatically declared that the photograph would cost her the election. However, the campaign insisted, and remarkably, people on the street began to recognize Hamilton and call her by name. Several of them specifically mentioned seeing her picture.

Hamilton's decision to keep her hairstyle and the campaign's use of her photograph on all campaign materials made another statement about gender concerns. Hamilton was comfortable with who she is and how she looks. Her decision not to conform to public stereotypes reflected a certain confidence and independence in her judgments. This would not be a campaign concerned with image over substance. Hamilton believed that she was the best-qualified person for the job. The campaign's job was to make that argument to the public. Hamilton was content to let the public arbitrate the final decision once her claims had been established.

LESSONS OF A POLITICAL NEWCOMER

Before making a decision to enter political life, a candidate must consider three issues. The first concern is what qualifies him or her to serve. Assuming that the person meets all the legal requirements for holding a particular elective position, he or she must examine personal experiences, memberships, service records, and public leadership positions. These resume items are often used by political insiders to determine candidate competency. They will also eventually be packaged to serve as a candidate's public credentials. Voters generally want proof of public service. They do not accept a person's desire to lead as meaningful when when that person has shown no previous compulsion to serve public needs.

A second concern is the ability of the candidates to raise money. Campaigns cannot function without it. Even if a candidate is the best-qualified person to serve, without financial resources to get the candidacy before the public there is little hope of being elected. This does not mean that a candidate must have personal wealth, although that helps. However, the necessity to accumulate funds does require a commitment on the candidate's part to raise the necessary capital to wage a campaign.

The third consideration involves determining how to go about building a supportive public. This consists of courting both experienced politicians and political hacks as well as the voting public. The politicos are of great assistance to beginning campaigners in offering advice and warning against potential errors. The public is, of course, the ultimate target of the campaign's persuasion.

In each of these categories, Hamilton was a strong contender. She had served in major leadership positions in over fifteen community service organizations. No other candidate could boast as strong a record of public service. Importantly, these were not just resume-building positions. Hamilton had assumed an active leadership role in each of them, as members of these organizations could attest.

Because of her public service commitments, many opinion leaders in the community already knew something of the values Hamilton would represent. She had made a genuine attempt to make the community a better reflection of traditional Southern values. For example, as a founding member of Hospital Hospitality House, she had helped establish a means of keeping the relatives of terminally ill patients close to the hospital while relieving them of some of the financial burden of doing so. She had also been active in education projects and was consequently honored for distinguished service to the Huntsville Community by the United Negro College Fund. Her work cut across social and economic stratifications within the community, providing her contact with a broad constituency.

Another key ingredient of Hamilton's association with so many civic and service groups was her friendship with a large group of people who routinely volunteer and work for worthy projects. Access to these people is critical to a candidate. These are the people who devote time to helping others. They are also the people who are not afraid to put in long hours and hard work.

Each of the candidates contending for office was legally qualified to serve as a district court judge. Each had his or her own set of strengths. The decision of who would eventually win would hinge on the criteria voters used to discriminate among them. On the subject of personal service to the community, Hamilton made a strong case for her candidacy.

As a result of her decision to run for office, Hamilton discovered that she also had strength as a fund-raiser. When the campaign began in January, she had collected no money. She was worried about accumulating campaign debts and about her ability to personally sustain a campaign in the event that she had to rely on her own financial reserves. Once she became aware of the cost of waging an effective campaign, Hamilton committed herself to raising the necessary capital. Her first and only priority in the opening months of the campaign was to raise money.

That decision was difficult for Hamilton to carry through. One opponent circulated an impressive brochure weeks before Hamilton circulated anything. She was worried about that candidate's ability to commit people to his candidacy before they even knew that she was running. However, she finally became convinced that there are other ways of securing commitments from people. Merely handing people a brochure does not secure their vote. Further, the campaign was a long way from worrying about public persuasion. The first target was to secure financial commitments in order to ensure that a well-targeted public campaign could be waged.

The fund-raising effort was directed along three fronts. The first target was Hamilton's family. There were over 200 people on the family mailing list alone. The help of such a large, close-knit family cannot be undervalued. Hamilton could not afford to delay asking for her family's commitments in the race. Nailing down natural constituencies is critical. She also did not want to offend her family by having them learn from someone else that she was running. Protocol required that she notify family members first.

Hamilton received an extremely favorable response. She confirmed one of the old adages of politics: Never take anyone's vote for granted. Hamilton's decision to make sure that her family members were the first to know of her candidacy was not only a courtesy, it was instrumental in securing their later commitments to vote.

The second fund-raising effort was made through personal solicitations. A daily call list was constructed of people with whom Hamilton needed to speak personally. One way in which Hamilton's affiliations paid off for the campaign was in her name recognition among a monied segment of the community. Many of the organizations for whom Hamilton worked brought together the community's financial elite. Name recognition among the philanthropic segment of the community is a major asset to a first-time candidate. These are the people who are accustomed to supporting worthy causes. They are also in a financial position to back their personal commitments with the kind of hard dollars needed to support a campaign.

Similarly, another target for personal fund-raising efforts was within the legal community itself. Every lawyer in town had an interest in the candidate who would be elected to the newly created judgeship. Many of them who were unwilling to take sides contributed to each campaign. Additionally, the legal community is often targeted for various fund-raising projects. The fact that Hamilton had given money to support so many of her colleagues projects over the years led to an easy reciprocal response to her request for support.

When Hamilton reached her tolerance level for personal rejection that accompanies such solicitations, she coordinated the details of two fund-raising events along the third fund-raising front. Candidates in down-ballot races such as this one cannot usually afford paid staff to handle such details. Much of the responsibility rests with the candidates to oversee the development of fund-raisers.

In the opening weeks, contributions obtained through personal solicitations were sufficient to pay for the invitations and mailings to one fund-raiser. Estimating that the response rate would be approximately

one in ten, over 1,000 invitations were sent for the first event. Fortunately, the hosts of the second, more expensive, event agreed to pay
for the invitations and mailings as part of their contribution to the
campaign.

The two public fund-raising events were tailored to specific groups.
The first one was scheduled for St. Patrick's Day. The theme, "Get Out
the Green," served not only as a festive reminder of the holiday but also
clarified the purpose of the event. Appropriately, the event was billed
as an "Irish" coffee and scheduled in the morning to avoid conflicts
with other community events. Fortunately, St. Patrick's Day fell on a
Saturday so the campaign did not have work conflicts to consider. Invitations to the event were sent to the memberships of most of the
organizations with whom Hamilton was affiliated.

This would be the major fund-raising attempt for that audience. Consequently, the campaign needed to make sure that it raised as much
money as it could in one shot. Several factors were addressed. The
campaign wanted to make sure that people understood that the purpose
of the event was to raise money for a campaign. A lot of time was spent
debating whether the amount of the donation should be specified in the
invitation. The fear was that without a specific amount, people might
be uncomfortable. Uncertainty breeds this sort of discomfort. If someone
was not sure of what was appropriate, we feared they would stay at
home rather than risk potential embarrassment. Further, we were targeting many people who had money as well as others whose contributions were usually through service. We wanted to make the event
affordable (with a slight "stretch") for those who wanted to show their
support of Hamilton's candidacy. We also needed to make sure that
there was a profit for the event. For these reasons, the invitation specified
a donation of twenty-five dollars.

Another factor that helped increase the response was the personal
nature of the event. All invitations were hand-addressed—no mailing
labels were used. In this way the campaign made sure that every person
knew that he or she had been specifically invited. This not only happened to be true, it was another reflection of the family environment
created during the campaign.

Attendance was also reinforced through the use of an RSVP card,
which was stamped and enclosed with the invitation. Those who could
not come often sent in a donation with their regrets. Others sent the
money in with their affirmative response. The result was that the event
was in the profit column before the first person walked through the
door.

Another drawing card for the event was its location. The house was
in the Old Town section of the city, in a home that had recently been
remodeled and that held great interest for a number of people. Placing

the event in someone's home is much more personal than having it in a sterile hotel dining room. The fact that it happened to be one of Hamilton's cousins who hosted the event augmented the family front.

Finally, the event took on a personal note by virtue of the reinforcement built into the invitation of homogeneous groups. Reminders of the event were placed in the newsletters of several organizations. Since many of these people saw each other at various events, there were also friendly reminders among themselves of the upcoming fund-raiser. The results were gratifying. Hamilton raised as much money in this one morning event as she did in the second, more expensive and select, fund-raiser.

The second fund-raiser was designed as a special event catering to the upwardly mobile couples in the community. This target group is often ignored by fund-raisers. Professionals argue that while these people have nice cars and homes, they also have very little disposable income. Most of it is tied up in the house, the cars, and the children. Professionals steer away from them as primary backers of a political campaign. That made them a particular asset to this campaign. The governor's race was locked in a five-way tug-of-war for public funds. Several other candidates who had filed for the U.S. House seat were also grappling for money. The pool of community resources was quickly being tapped out. The fact that this was not a lucrative enough crowd to attract the attention of the major fund-raising professionals for the high-visibility races did not mean that their contributions were small fry to a judge's race.

These people were targeted for yet another reason. They did not support the Hamilton candidacy because she was someone to be reckoned with in the future, but because she herself was one of them. While this group likes to meet the up-and-coming leadership, it is not particularly impressed by titles. One function with the gubernatorial candidates usually satiates its curiosity. Hamilton, like other members of this group, would soon be making her mark on the community, and they seemed to like the idea of being a part.

Impression is an important variable for wooing this crowd of supporters. They like to be impressed. They enjoy living in fine homes and tastefully displaying the fruits of their success. Those needs are rarely fulfilled by attending a supper at even one of the more expensive local restaurants. For that reason, Hamilton was able to secure the support of several couples who agreed to host the event themselves at one of their homes. The location was ideal. An antebellum mansion in the historic district of the city provided an appropriate climate for the gathering. This event was clearly a social event with the Hamilton campaign serving as the reason for the party. A festive spirit and an elegant display of finger foods and fine spirits added to the occasion.

During the hectic spring social season and the conflicts with other campaign's events, there was some concern about the turnout. The instinct to target this crowd, however, was a good one. The event was well received and set the tone for the good-natured, personal campaign style that Hamilton would carry through to her final victory in the fall campaign.

Through the combination of these strategies, Hamilton was able to amass a sizable war chest for a judicial campaign. Little money was spent in the early stages of the campaign except as seed money to raise more money. Moreover, the strategy served another function as well. Before Hamilton began reaching out to voters whom she did not know, she solidified her base of support among those she knew. Her financial strategy was designed to target certain groups yet also to include people from across the financial spectrum. Few people who wanted to donate to the campaign were kept from a specific opportunity to do so.

Hamilton proved to be not only a strong-fund raiser but an effective campaigner as well. Her follow-up to each of the fund-raising events demonstrated her organizational abilities and her attention to detail. It also aided in solidifying her base. Thank-you letters were promptly sent to those who contributed. These people were also included on the priority mailing list to receive campaign information as soon as it became available.

Hamilton was also aware that supporters can contribute to a campaign in more ways than one. Just because people give campaign money does not mean that they should not be asked for other types of support as well. Each person who donated money to the Hamilton campaign was also asked to assist in other ways. The minimal request was that the person allow the campaign to put up a yard sign. Other individuals were asked to write letters of support on Hamilton's behalf to their friends and colleagues. Some were asked to help at campaign headquarters. Hamilton was particularly effective at identifying a person's strength and then attempting to get him or her to utilize that talent on her behalf.

Much of Hamilton's support was from the rank and file. She did not have as much assistance from veteran political campaigners as she would have liked. Hamilton was fortunate to have some understanding of election processes. She had worked on several political campaigns before. She had even served as campaign manager for the district attorney, who was also running during this election for a seat in the U.S. Congress. However, she had not been entrenched in party politics. As a result, little help was offered to her by other successful campaigners. The county chair, like other party officials, maintained an appropriate hands-off policy during the primaries and then endorsed and supported the selected candidate for the general election. A few successful politicians were willing to advise her privately, but most were unwilling to be publicly aligned with her during the primaries.

Hamilton's success in building a coalition was influenced by two specific factors. First, she worked to get other people committed to making her campaign a success. Second, she engaged in highly reciprocal relationships with the voters.

From the very beginning, Hamilton's campaign worked to be inclusive. Hamilton asked for and recorded the advice that backers had to offer. In strategy sessions we would debate the merits of each proposal. In many cases we received excellent ideas that might have been rejected since they were not included in the budget priorities or would consume too much time for the limited campaign staff. Hamilton made no apologies for the campaign's priorities, yet no good idea was discarded without asking for further advice on how to fund it or find the people to implement it. The campaign did an excellent job of establishing and following its priority assignments. However, anyone who observed the campaign knows that many of these workable suggestions had as much positive impact on the campaign as did the targeted strategies. By being open and inclusive, Hamilton's campaign became quite innovative.

Supporters also seemed to enjoy implementing their own ideas. Unlike the tasks set by a strategist, these ideas were of their own creation. They zealously protected the quality of the work because of the personal investment it required. They also got a thrill out of seeing its effect.

The inclusive nature of the campaign had another advantage as well. These volunteers took ownership of the campaign. It was as much theirs as it was Hamilton's. By the end of the primary, Hamilton had a sizable support group that would feel personally responsible for the outcome. That kind of commitment was critical in the primary, and it proved to be of even more value in gearing up for the fall race against an opponent who had not faced a primary challenger. Hamilton was amassing a coalition that was committed to her success.

The Hamilton campaign also based many of its specific strategies on personal relationships. The family concept has been amply explained. Another facet of this approach is the way in which Hamilton established a rapport with the voters at large.

The campaign was, of course, concerned about name recognition. In both radio and billboard advertisements, the campaign attempted to lay a solid foundation for the Hamilton candidacy. Heavy concentrations in both mediums proved useful in this regard. The campaign soon became concerned about factors that would determine the vote in cases in which two or more of the candidates had equal name recognition. The campaign strategy was based on the fact that the overriding factor would be personal knowledge of the candidate. Credibility studies suggest that face-to-face appeals are more effective than appeals made through the mass media (for the landmark studies on this phenomenon, see Berelson, Lazarsfeld, & McPhee, 1954; Katz & Lazarsfeld, 1955).

Hamilton took a leave from her job in order to campaign full time once the election season began in earnest. Whereas the other candidates both had office responsibilities, Hamilton devoted herself to the business of campaigning all day, every day. She was not distracted by other work responsibilities. This decision freed her to attend meetings and roam the back roads of the county. Almost every day during the campaign, a portion of Hamilton's time was spent in direct contact with voters whom she had not previously known.

Hamilton also learned the value of campaign specialty items. People often avoid meeting politicians when they can identify them in a crowd. Perhaps they do not wish to be bothered by what they perceive to be a self-serving request for their vote. Give those same people something free, however, whether a yardstick, a comb, or a candy mint, and they will flock to the candidate. Hamilton had one of the better specialty advertising ideas of the election season. Pencils were made up with her logo on them. What made them unique was that they were topped with two erasers, giving them the form of a gavel. The gavel was also a symbol used on her billboards and brochures as a reminder of the judicial post. Kids loved them, and adults admired them because of their uniqueness.

The use of this and other specialty advertising items served as a gesture of goodwill. The implication was that the pencil should be taken in exchange for the favor of reviewing Hamilton's campaign brochure. The tactic worked. At ball games and major public functions at which these items were distributed with brochures, few of Hamilton's campaign materials ended up on the ground. Without these items, we often noticed her brochures littering the ground like everyone else's.

In addition to advertising specialty items, the Hamilton campaign pressed its personal contact with the voter through an extensive direct mail campaign. Almost 20,000 households were targeted with her brochure. Hundreds of personal letters of endorsement from supporters to their friends were written on Hamilton's behalf. Every effort was made to ensure that voters knew that Hamilton needed their vote and intended to ask for it.

The implementation of a personalized strategy is expensive. By using these approaches, the campaign made a decision not to spend money on other advertising devices. Sometimes the campaign questioned this judgment. One opponent brought terror to the campaign by using television advertisements. However, television seemed too impersonal for the type of campaign that Hamilton had committed herself to run. Moreover, the cost for an effective media saturation campaign is prohibitive. As it turned out, for all the good intentions of the opponent, the television saturation he was able to purchase was not sufficient to affect the outcome.

The Hamilton campaign was not without its flaws, but the one thing that dominated it throughout the election season was its steadfast commitment to predetermined goals. Once the issues had been debated and the strategies set, the campaign followed through. The consistency of purpose and dedication to specific goals were instrumental in driving the campaign and keeping it on track.

CONCLUSIONS

There is no magic formula that provides a guide on how Hamilton constructed a winning campaign, but two conclusions seem useful. Hamilton was successful in overriding any preconceived stereotypes about the ability of a woman to fulfill the responsibilities of a judge. In part, she was able to accomplish this by demonstrating her strength as a campaigner. Although there are no empirical findings to support this conclusion, we believe the Hamilton's efforts to establish personal contact with the voters helped override the prejudice that comes from ignorance. Once people knew and liked her, the gender factor did not seem to be important.

Hamilton was also successful because she took the time to build a public. She did not glad-hand voters from the first day on which she made a decision to run. Hamilton's consistent requests for help, her persistent efforts to raise funds, and her dedication to the implementation of coalition-building strategies served her well. The primary did not go into a runoff as many had predicted. Instead, Hamilton was able to win on the first ballot in the face of tough opposition.

Almost exactly one year after Hamilton first put her campaign into motion, the investiture ceremony was held to swear her in as the new district court judge. One person remarked that the event reminded him of a wedding as there were so many relatives and well-wishers standing shoulder to shoulder. The turnout for the investiture of a relatively minor down-ballot race was evidence of the campaign's effectiveness in building a coalition. In addition to the over 500 families that contributed to the campaign financially, others who had worked in the campaign attended the ceremony and joined the festivities at the reception. It was only fitting that Hamilton's campaign family celebrated together.

Chapter 4

Death at the Hands of Consultants: An Analysis of Defeat in the 1990 Alabama Gubernatorial Primary

The first reaction after a devastating personal loss is to question what went wrong and to wonder if the outcome would have been different had other tactics been utilized. These questions are truly "academic": The only people who care are the candidate who lost, the candidate's close friends and relatives, and the academics who try to reconstruct a campaign by evaluating it in hindsight. Moreover, the events cannot be relived. No one can ever know if a different strategy would have produced more favorable results.

The study of losing campaigns is significant for purposes of correcting future problems, yet losing campaigns are seldom analyzed with any care. Campaigns are expensive operations. Immediately after the loss, the motivation is to shut down the operation. The staff gets rid of the phones, the computers, the office space, and the fax machines, and boxes up all the paperwork either throwing it away or storing it in the candidate's garage. In the better-financed campaigns, some paid staff remain to shut down the operations and pay the outstanding bills. In an attempt to distance themselves from the pain created by the loss, no one remains to help sort out what might have happened.

Even the paid consultants who might be expected to have an interest in why the campaign failed will have already turned their attention to the next race from which their future paychecks will come. The pressure of every election for consultants who depend on politics for employment is to find another campaign in need of their particular skills.

This description attempts to fill the gap and account for what happened—or did not happen—in the failed 1990 Alabama Democratic gubernatorial bid of Congressman Ronnie Flippo. "Death at the hands of consultants" is not just a phrase. It is an explanation that clarifies the campaign's major impediment to getting an effective message across to the voters. It is not intended to defer partial responsibility for the defeat away from Congressman Flippo. After all, he was the one who hired the specialists and had the power to control his campaign. Nonetheless, central to an understanding of the race is an appreciation of the strength of the egos that clashed in this campaign, a factor that was beyond Flippo's control. The fact that almost every high-ranking participant professed the superiority of his or her skills is a sign of their individual successes. When they came together in the Alabama electoral climate during this particular election, however, the collective impact was disastrous. It is important to note that the deficiencies identified are not intended as evaluations of the overall capabilities of the individuals involved. Rather, this is an account of their deficiencies in one specific case.

BUILDING A CAMPAIGN TEAM: SOME INITIAL SUCCESSES

Political campaigns in many ways remind me of a learning toy that I once saw. It was a weighted top. The object was to first set the top spinning all by itself. Then, to demonstrate the principles of weight and counterbalance, a series of hooks, magnets, and other ornaments could be added. When some of these additional parts were added, the top became more colorful and dramatic. However, when other parts were added, the top became lopsided and spun out of control.

Political campaigns routinely conduct similar experiments in weight and counterbalance. Developing an effective election team is often equivalent to playing with all the parts of the top in an attempt to give certain aspects of the campaign the proper weighting. As with the top experiment, any number of combinations may conceivably work; the trick lies in balance and counterbalance.

The first contact I had with Congressman Flippo was through a staff member who was newly assigned to the district. Roger Schneider, a native of the Huntsville community, had previously co-owned a computer company in Atlanta. Given his knowledge of computer systems and his location, Schneider was contracted to computerize the operations of the 1988 Democratic National Convention. There Flippo contacted him to work in his congressional office to set up better communications with his constituents. Now the congressman had decided to run for the governor's seat and Schneider was helping to assemble the campaign team.

During our discussions, we batted around a few ideas about the campaign, including what sort of news bites Flippo might include in his speeches. During this time the present governor had inaugurated a new public relations campaign to support Alabama tourism. The theme, "Welcome Home to Alabama," headlined a number of events which included personal invitations to former residents who had moved out of state. Given the wide media coverage of the campaign, I suggested that Flippo might want to argue that since Governor Guy Hunt was welcoming people home, he thought he would just take him up on his offer to come home from Washington. Schneider seemed pleased with this and other ideas and promised to keep in touch as events developed.

Apparently, the congressman liked the ideas. There were more conversations designed to apprise me of the congressman's visits and to discuss other issues. On each occasion we spent a few minutes talking about the possibilities of Flippo's success. Like any campaign in the early, enthusiastic stages, we were excited by the prospects. In late summer I met with the congressman and his wife to discuss working for the campaign and to secure permission to write about the events for this book.

During the first meeting with the staff, potential problems were already surfacing. The struggle for Flippo's attention and favor had begun.

THE WAR OF THE DECISION LOOP

Congressman Flippo had just emerged from his last election in the fall of 1988. Now, only nine months later, he was contemplating a bid for the governor's mansion. Flippo had a keen understanding of some basic considerations of timing. He knew that he had to secure his media advisors, polling firm, and fund-raising advisors before the better firms were committed elsewhere.

Flippo struggled with the decision of whether to hire some of the Washington firms that had amassed impressive win–loss records and prestigious lists of exclusive clients or to choose a local firm. He did not want to be accused of undervaluing local talent but he clearly wanted every advantage that his position in Washington could afford him.

After much internal struggle, Flippo decided to use the Washington crew. However, Flippo never seemed to trust its judgments completely. As he brought the "big guns" on board, he simultaneously established an Alabama oversight and review group to make sure that they ran a "Southern" campaign. The idea sounded reasonable but in actuality it was problematic.

Flippo wanted the Alabama crew to report its judgments to him. In turn, he, as the employer, would express his wishes to the Washington staff. Evidently, the only ones who knew that there was an oversight function was the Alabama crew. The Washington group never acknowledged or accepted the input of the locals. In fact, on several occasions it treated them with disdain. Perhaps as a carryover of the Washington group's attitudes toward Alabamians, as the campaign progressed it even treated Flippo's own direct requests as the ravings of an uninformed candidate. He was listened to but ultimately ignored on numerous issues of major and minor consequence.

The reason for this may be simple. Major consulting firms have their reputations on the line in each election. It would not be in their best interest to take responsibility for a campaign over which they have no control. The better consultants have a basic desire for quality control over all aspects of the campaign for which they may be accountable, and Flippo's firms were certainly no exception.

Flippo may have underestimated another problem in the interrelationship of the Washington and Alabama contingencies. Many people on the local advisory group had never worked side-by-side with firms as prestigious as those Flippo hired. Though they did not discount the worth of their own ideas, they were smart enough to know that the Washington gang presumably had experience on its side. After all, when one of the top fund-raising consultants in the Democratic party tells you to organize in a particular way, what credibility does a veteran campaigner from another generation of politics have with which to refine that strategy? Further, the Washington firms had worked together before. They knew each other and the likely approaches that each would take. They also knew and respected each other's work. They formed, in essence, their own clique. The pressure to conform to Washington peer pressure became enormous. Those who were not ostracized as "hicks from Alabama" spent more and more time as the campaign developed trying to get the praise and approval of Washington rather than challenging any of that groups assumptions.

Washington firms gain their reputation through their ability to produce results. Often they are formula-driven. These formulas are developed at various levels of complexity and sophistication. As with any model, the object is to be able to predict outcomes. What they offer a campaign is the hope of increasing the odds of winning. Failure to heed their advice, they subtly remind the candidate, reduces the likelihood of a win, and winning *is* the object of campaigns. The pressure to win is the ultimate threat used on a candidate. Almost any decision can be countermanded if the threat is exercised appropriately—this is raw persuasion at work.

In this campaign the Washington crew had yet another advantage. They were geographically closer to the candidate than were his Alabama campaign staff. As he was a working congressman, they could easily gain access to Flippo. Though occasionally they traveled to Alabama for a meeting, their overall time in the region was not "required" since they were able to conveniently meet with the candidate elsewhere.

The tension that permeated the campaign as a result of these divided camps syphoned off the energies of the staff. Over the months, the battle for Flippo's attention settled into at least four camps: the Washington campaign staff, the Alabama contingency, the congressional staff, and the major financial contributors and politicos around the state. Reading the signs of who was aligned with whom on what issues on a given day was a never-ending source of puzzlement. Everyone played the game. Who could be shut out of the decision loop today? How could Flippo be positioned to take certain advice? Sadly, Flippo's marathon schedule did not permit him to be a player; instead, he was skillfully manipulated by each of the four camps for their own purposes.

In hindsight, Flippo's major fault may have been his too-trusting nature. He could never seem to realize that people on his own team were conniving and sometimes deceitful. He was a true believer on a righteous mission while he was viewed as tonight's supper by the cannibals who had willingly agreed to assist him through the jungle. That is a trait that I have to admire, but it is also a fatal flaw.

Even at the end of the campaign, the problems that perplexed Flippo at the beginning had never been resolved. This never-ending repositioning of in-groups and out-groups is critical to an understanding of the communication undercurrent that contributed to Flippo's defeat.

THE PLAYERS AND LAYERS OF ORGANIZATION

By mid-fall, the congressman had hired the firm Fraioli and Jost as his fund-raisers, and slowly the campaign began to take form. Steve Jost was the primary campaign contact. At his urging, the campaign developed one goal to extend through the end of the year: to raise money. The congressman already had over $1 million in his campaign coffers. The hope was that the money would be held in reserve in the unlikely event that Flippo should lose. Current laws allow such money to be transferred to state races but do not allow money raised for state races to be applied back to federal elections. By holding the money in reserve, should he lose, Flippo could still conceivably run for another federal job with a cash reserve in place. The goal was to raise 2 million new dollars by the end of the year. That was an unusually high goal but one that everyone seemed to accept as valid, at least for a while.

Fraioli and Jost are among the star consultants of the Democratic party. Their track record of fund-raising is exceptional. Though I never met Fraioli, Jost was exactly what you might expect a fund-raiser to be. He was energetic and professional, always pushing the campaign to set up more events and increase the effectiveness of each fund-raising effort. He was systematic in his approach, often voicing his frustration when someone failed to recognize the method behind the fund-raising plan.

He also appeared competent and confident, and was not easily intimidated by the perceived power of those for whom he worked.

Fund-raising firms do not function as some people might think. They do not raise money for the campaign. Rather, they are composed of practicing organizational scholars who set up a systematic method for achieving financial goals and teach workers how to increase their overall success rate.

Some of Jost's organizational goals were immediately apparent. Jost contended that campaigns routinely allow money to escape from their grasp. Potential donors will verbally commit to making a contribution but fail to send the promised check. In the meantime, the campaign mentally credits the donation to its account before the money is in hand. In order to be successful, campaigns have to establish a method of collecting on these promises. Working with Schneider, Jost established a method for donor tracking that was tailored for the Flippo campaign. In this way, the campaign could keep up with the large number of contributors who were participating. Similarly, Jost provided a systematic way of following up on leads so that field personnel had an adequate resource base to keep them busy with productive leads.

In this campaign, Jost laid the initial organizational framework and literally kicked it into place. There were obstacles to the fund-raising effort. Flippo was surrounded by a cadre of "idea men" who had evolved self-perceived roles as campaign executives. They were not interested in doing the necessary work to make this phase of the campaign a success. As a result, the first paid additions to the campaign were fund-raising field personnel. Once they had been hired, Jost became a tyrant. Unlike the volunteers and insiders who had become comfortable with Flippo over their years of acquaintance, the fieldworkers were hired guns like himself. The campaign hierarchy could be pushed only so far; the field personnel were clearly participating in a shoving match for funds against other campaigns and their fund-raisers.

Like most organizations, campaigns are slow to adapt to change. One contributing factor to the oppressively slow pace in those early months was the perception that the primary was still some eight months away. The window for fund-raising was much shorter, however, and Jost attempted to instill an immediacy to the effort.

Almost everyone in the Flippo organization was anxious to get the public campaign started. Jost had to assume the responsibility of focusing the campaign's efforts. Tension was high among the staff as Jost monitored the profit margin and issued campaign edicts. Flippo was too busy to referee the struggles.

Flippo was already performing two stressful and demanding tasks. He was both a working congressman and, by necessity, an active fund-raiser. Perhaps he had envisioned that Fraioli and Jost would relieve him of the fund-raising responsibility. However, what he no doubt discovered was that he now shouldered the ultimate burden for raising capital.

Fraioli and Jost not only made strong edicts about how Flippo's time should be used but were also specific as to who took priority in scheduling that time. This created another point of contention between the campaign and the congressional staff. The locus of power was beginning to shift and no one seemed pleased with their new responsibilities. Those included in the inner circle now had fund-raising–related tasks. Jost's plan permitted the organization to begin functioning. It also created the first caveat.

Since no campaign manager or similarly powerful figure was yet involved in the campaign, those without fund-raising responsibilities were left out of the initial organization. They were now vying for placement and direction. Unofficially (for there was no official direction), they each began planning for what they perceived would be "their time" during the campaign: A time when they would become the insiders with the candidate's ear and would have the full use of the campaign resources. Although they attended most of the fund-raising meetings, this group of outsiders was never a fully integrated part of the organization. The result was that in mid-November an accounting of campaign resources showed that money was being spent at an alarmingly high rate. Those with fund-raising responsibilities were furious. Campaign expenses had to be brought down, and therefore a virtual spending freeze went into effect.

This chilling effect meant that no one was allowed to spend any money unless it specifically related to fund-raising. Money was to be saved for the election campaign itself. This shut down most of the planning and preparatory operations by the Alabama staff while at the same time allowed the Washington planners free rein. The real issue should have been whether the money was being squandered or if it was being used to judiciously set up operations that would save the campaign money later. However, with no campaign manager in place, and with Flippo's time severely limited, no one was in a position to make those decisions.

Some decisions relative to the public campaign should have been implemented. For example, one proposal focused on preparations for the opening of the public segment of the campaign. In addition to locating regional facilities that might be obtained at exceptionally good rates (if not donated), the plan detailed the formation of regional steering committees. These units would begin to brainstorm for events that could be held during the formal campaign and that might be of particular interest to the local residents. Anything from Earth Day rallies to Memorial Day celebrations were to be evaluated for their potential to draw a crowd. Further, these campaign committees were to establish a feedback loop on the local events and issues. This would permit the campaign to tap into the issues that were on the minds of the voters. In true entrepreneurial spirit, the thinking was that once these committees came up with worthwhile ideas, they would be asked to help the campaign carry off the projects (including donating the time, money, and resources necessary to produce a successful event).

The idea had merit. However, setting up these meetings and developing these contacts was considered too expensive and too risky. After all, people might consider their time to be their donation to the campaign. Since money was the first priority, nothing was approved that might jeopardize the kitty. Further, there was an implied concern that without someone with oversight authority, some people who became involved might prove to be liabilities for the campaign later on. No one asked these exact questions, but they were clearly implied: What if the "wrong" people were invited? What if some important person was left out?

This is national political thinking at work. While it may be prudent on the national level, it is devastating for state and regional elections. In the major political races the attitude often develops that campaigns are run with money, not people. If a campaign has a person's money, they reason, the campaign can print slick bumper stickers and yard signs, it can produce award-winning commercials, and it can control what the public sees in an orchestrated media event. These campaigns prefer not to have high school students painting signs after school (the signs might look tacky and homemade). They prefer not to have some local individual (who might, per chance, be a less than perfect spokesperson for the candidate) taint the campaign's image. Control is the lightening rod.

Some election campaigns cannot afford to be that sanctimonious. A preacher once reminded his congregation that the church is a hospital for sinners and not a hotel for saints. The Flippo campaign needed to heed the same advice. It was beginning to adopt a dangerously pious attitude. The politics of inclusion demand that the voters be allowed to get involved. That involvement breeds loyalty and generates enthusiasm in participants. Further, foes of the plan seemed to overlook the fact that these committees could be expanded as more and more people got on the campaign bandwagon. True to their task, the fund-raisers were able to dramatically focus the campaign to the one goal that they had been hired to reach: raising money. Unfortunately, a number of potentially effective projects were squelched because of their financial implications.

The fund-raisers did their job, but the money-first philosophy became counterproductive for the effort. Quite apart from the Flippo campaign, a fund-raiser for a candidate running for another political office provided some interesting feedback. The clientele consisted mostly of doctors, lawyers, young professionals, and the members of the Junior League. During the evening the conversation occasionally turned to the governor's race. Almost without fail jokes would arise about an invitation to "yet another" Flippo fund-raiser. A woman intervened in one conversation to assert, "Pay $250 for breakfast? When he's already got a million and a half in the bank? I'd rather give money to someone who needs it." Another added, "They don't want you anyway. They just want your money." The campaign was already beginning to set itself up for failure.

GETTING THE CAMPAIGN IN GEAR

By the first months of the election year, the campaign still had no manager. No one within the campaign was given planning authority. Given that initial plans were for Flippo to announce his candidacy January 17, this obvious omission was perplexing. Some insiders reasoned that the decision was delayed because managers cost a good sum of money. Therefore, to delay the hiring would save the campaign money. Others argued that no one was selected because there was a struggle among the Alabama contingency for the post. After a while, rumors developed among politicos that Flippo was being blackballed by the party, who withheld the list of proven, available managers from him. Whatever the reason, the campaign was clearly crippled, and the longer the situation continued, the more suspect was the reason.

The continued struggle to establish favor with the candidate was a daily concern. Given that no one knew where he or she stood with Flippo, the selection of a campaign manager was hotly contested. The way in which each person was regarded by the manager would determine who would be allowed to participate in a meaningful way in the campaign and who would be excluded. Campaign plans to persuade voters were subverted because everyone's attention was riveted on the internal power struggle.

Flippo finally took the initiative to begin finding suitable candidates. However, the process created even more paranoia. Even some of the "loyal insiders" were not sure who was being considered or who might actually be interviewed for the post. Finally, the manager was announced. He was Joe McLean, the former campaign manager for Governor Douglas Wilder's successful campaign in Virginia.

McLean was a likable enough person. He was young, dedicated, and expert in responding to media questions with interesting tidbits of printable analysis. From a perceptual vantage, he was also an interesting "local" choice since he was from neighboring Tennessee. Hiring McLean gave the campaign two advantages: It was able to foster the impression (at least for a while) that locals were running the campaign (and not the big Washington firms), and it was able to perceptually demonstrate that Flippo was concerned about including those sympathetic to the needs of ethnic groups. The natural association of anyone connected with the Wilder campaign was favorably received by the black community. With this announcement, the campaign suddenly sparked a flame of public enthusiasm that had not been previously ignited.

These issues aside, McLean was immediately suspect. The *New York Times* had written extensively about the Wilder campaign. As the first black governor in the cradle of the Confederacy, the strategies and strategists who had contributed had been given wide coverage. However, the *Times* had singled out media consultant Frank Greer as the backbone of the Wilder operation. McLean professed his instrumental role in the effort but fueled suspicions by being vague about his responsibilities in the Wilder campaign. A book on the Wilder campaign later explained that McLean had not been suited to the task. He had been selected for the Virginia state party chair position just prior to being asked to head the Wilder campaign. He was not seasoned and had clearly been pushed ahead of his experience base to run a statewide campaign. McLean was not experienced enough, by their accounts, to reason through the various conflicting positions. Moreover, he was not an organizer: a task that falls squarely on the shoulders of the campaign manager. Accordingly, by the end of the Wilder campaign, McLean had been sent to Virginia Beach to head up the Get Out the Vote (GOTV) phone bank. He was not even to be found in the headquarters during the final days of the campaign. This was not good news. However, the Flippo campaign was enjoying positive press reports at the moment, and it was not receptive to cautionary advice.

In the early days of McLean's leadership, many of these concerns were manifested. He had little time for the area's politicos. He had even less time for local supporters except those who were viewed as having the ear of the candidate. His primary loyalty from the beginning was to the Washington consultants. After all, they were the ones who would be his contacts for finding future jobs. If they liked a campaign manager and could work with him, they might recommend him to some future client.

McLean's first challenge was to resolve the dispute over the location of the state headquarters. The topic had been hotly debated before McLean's arrival. Some wanted it in Huntsville, and others in Flippo's hometown, Florence. Still others suggested Birmingham because of its central location within the state.

Flippo preferred the Florence location. Since it was his home, he hoped that he would be able to maintain some contact with his family and friends, people he believed would help him keep on track during the campaign. The Shoals area also comprised the financial backbone for his election bid. Since that was where most of the money originated, Flippo reasoned, it only made sense to keep the investment in the local economy.

On the other hand, both Huntsville and Birmingham were major media markets within the state. Huntsville had the additional benefit of being in Flippo's congressional district. As a popular fourteen-year veteran of Congress, Flippo had many friends and supporters who would provide a steady pool of workers. Birmingham, while outside the district, had the advantage of being centrally located in the state. Choosing Birmingham, it was argued, would force Flippo into a statewide race and increase his chances of appealing to those voters. Flippo had to be perceived as a statewide candidate, and not a regional one, if he hoped to succeed.

The decision was made to head the campaign in Florence. McLean explained that he made the decision out of necessity. Flippo's advisors in Florence had too much influence on him when he was in the state, and his Washington advisors had too much influence to ignore. If McLean hoped to work as an effective campaign manager, he had to be "in Flippo's back pocket." From his perspective, the decision seemed justified. However, this served as one additional bit of evidence that the insider/outsider mentality was still an issue for the campaign. In fact, McLean was fostering a war of the insiders.

After this decision, the campaign became wrapped up in a struggle for viability. Schneider, who had been hired by the campaign to establish its computer operations, was named deputy campaign manager. As he had served as the main link between the congressman, key constituents, and media operatives, moving Schneider some seventy miles away from the Huntsville media market area left no one of significant rank to oversee a market of over a quarter of a million people. Even the press spokesperson was to be stationed in Florence, a city with no major media linkages.

Four factors began to identify the Flippo campaign. First, the campaign was clearly regional. With so many people worried about "being in the [decision] loop," few people were willing to be away from Florence when Flippo was in town or when they believed key decisions were being made. Additionally, Florence was in the upper northeastern corner of the state. Sending crews into south Alabama was a time-consuming and costly ordeal. Slowly, people found things to do closer to Florence rather than tilling the field in southern Alabama.

The second definitional factor was that the campaign had taken itself out of the media marketplace. The Shoals area has regional reporters who send in transmissions to the Huntsville stations, but it does not have a broadcast station that reaches the Huntsville media market. As part of the Huntsville media link, the reporters sent to the Shoals are not star reporters. At times, the Huntsville stations had to decide whether to send a first-string reporter to the Shoals (a ninety-minute drive each way) to cover a story or let the Shoals reporter cover it. For numerous reasons they generally chose the latter option. As a result, unless Flippo appeared in Huntsville, the seasoned political reporters stayed home. This severely limited news coverage of the Flippo campaign in his own backyard.

That may not sound like a significant issue, but it is. Star reporters get the lead positions in news stories. They also have license to give occasional commentaries. Moreover, they are usually privileged with inside information about evolving stories. Take those assets away from a campaign and it becomes isolated. Reporters are no different than voters in that they like to be courted.

Unlike the setting in national political races, there are no bus loads of field reporters assigned to each candidate to dog them wherever they roam. There is no daily copy about the breaking campaign stories sent in by the field reporters. Neither do they have large travel budgets to sustain the kind of travel necessary to keep up with a busy candidate. Consequently, races receive coverage when candidates appeal to local interests. When the candidate comes to town, the event is covered. Occasionally the candidate will make some newsworthy statement that will be carried statewide, but this typically occurs only during the final weeks of the campaign.

The Flippo campaign forgot the news standards that the local media attempt to maintain. They do not like to be perceived as the public relations arm of campaigns whose job it is to print the daily fluff sent from the press secretary. What news reporters need is help in developing stories. They also need contacts. Those needs cannot be met when senior-level contacts are halfway across the state.

With Schneider gone, the Flippo campaign took all senior contacts out of the area. There was no one to whom a reporter could go to harden up a story when there was nothing much happening in the news that day. Since good campaigns typically pocket three to four good news stories as favors for key reporters to use on slow news days, the campaign lost innumerable free media "licks" through its own isolation. Moreover, it lost the contacts that breed trust, a factor that was to have a considerable impact in the final weeks of the campaign.

The third definitional factor for the campaign was the absence of Flippo's mark. Over his fourteen years of service in Congress, Flippo and his staff had established an efficient, thoughtful response process to maintain contact with the voters. It was a well-oiled machine. Members of the Flippo congressional staff were personally committed to responding to all constituent requests in a timely manner. Each phone call was followed up with a letter telling what Flippo thought about the issue and what he was prepared to do about the request. The perception in the Fifth Congressional District was that Flippo cared about constituent needs. The district claimed ownership of his office and lauded him as a respected representative.

The campaign did not have this image, however. The same people who were accustomed to timely responses and the feeling of inclusion were now clearly being excluded. Several key contributors made it known that they were never sure if their suggestions and advice even got through the channels to reach Flippo. If they did reach him, the proposals must have been rejected because they were never acted upon.

I found myself in the same position at one juncture. Following my normal routing pattern to get information to the candidate, I was told that the "key advisors" (I had no idea who was in the loop that day) had pointed out that the voters were not ready for Flippo to take action. The only ones who cared were "the lieutenants" (like me, I suppose) who wanted to get into the game (meaning, presumably, that we "outsiders" could not yet play). Basically, I was told (as were others) that when our advice was needed, it would be sought.

Ironically, the one thing that the campaign excelled at created another public image problem. The only thing that merited a timely response was a financial contribution. Slowly, the public perception began to build that voters were not as important as their money, and some supporters quietly began contributing to other candidates.

The campaign reflected such an atypical approach from what people had encountered over years of dealing with Flippo's administration that initial speculation placed the blame on the staff. Over the weeks, however, Flippo himself was blamed. If he could not control his staff, some voters reasoned, how could he control a whole statewide administration? Slowly Flippo's base of trust with political insiders was eroding. No one could determine who was in charge of or controlling the campaign.

This leads to the fourth definitional factor: the presence of what Irving Janis (1972) called "groupthink." Those who managed to become part of the inside team "unwittingly developed shared illusions and operating norms that interfered with their ability to think critically and to engage in the required reality testing" (Morgan, 1986, p. 202). When criticisms emerged, supporters were assured that the matter was already being addressed or was insignificant compared to other issues on the agenda. When supporters warned of severe public relations problems, they were ignored and then ostracized from further contact with the candidate.

The most dramatic display of this groupthink mentality was the campaign's overconfidence. Insiders constantly stroked Flippo's ego and assured him that the campaign was right on target. Contradictory information, they asserted, was coming from sources that were ill-informed or politically naive. Flippo soon became surrounded by ego-inflaters. Privately he seemed to be distrustful of their pronouncements, yet he was blinded by a desire to win. He wanted to believe in the truth of their claims. This lack of ability to realistically appraise campaign events and message strategy effectiveness became manifested in the media phase of the campaign.

THE MEDIA GURUS

As the final weeks of the campaign approached, the media moguls went to work. Struble and Totten Communications, which had performed the media responsibilities for Flippo's successful congressional race just two years earlier, was now managing his gubernatorial media campaign.

Struble and Totten's impressive win–loss record is proof of the firm's overall effectiveness at media consulting. However, it was philosophically at odds with local Alabama politics. In the 1988 election, it advised Flippo to run a pure media campaign. There were no bumper stickers, no major campaign events, and no headquarters opened. The firm advocated this type of strategy, arguing that the media is the only thing that matters to voters anyway. The philosophy of Struble and Totten, as Flippo described it, was to spend no more money and time than was necessary in order to get the job done. I can imagine that he had also been advised to save all the money he could for his upcoming gubernatorial bid. In any case, Flippo took their advice.

The by-product of this strategy was that there was also no seasoned campaign organization in place for this election. Flippo must have contemplated running for the governor's seat at the time of his 1988 campaign, yet instead of working to develop an election team that could translate that campaign's efforts into a statewide race, Flippo had no organization. Moreover, the few loyalists who had been with Flippo all along had not had an opportunity to test themselves as campaigners for some time. Even though each had good political insights, skills deteriorate when they are not used. Further, Flippo was not a seasoned campaigner himself despite his fourteen years in Congress. His only highly contested race had been his first one. He also had the disadvantage of being a PAC candidate, and consequently, his fund-raising abilities in the field were not finely honed. By necessity, the Flippo organization was dependent on the media campaign to work the way it had been planned. There was no room for miscalculation.

In the current election, Struble and Totten's strategy was to pull a large percentage of the voters out of Flippo's Fifth Congressional District and for Flippo to hold "his share" of the voters in other areas of the state. Such a formula, they argued, would guarantee him a place in the runoff. With five candidates, four of whom were solidly positioned for race, it was critical for Flippo to carry his own district. Therefore, Struble and Totten recommended a media-intensive campaign outside the district and a media/organization race within the district.

The failure of the plan was that it underestimated the strength of the other contenders. It also may have overestimated Flippo's ability to wage a statewide campaign, raise money, and still perform his congressional duties in Washington. Everyone seemed to agree that the strategy would work, and for a while it was successful.

The first series of advertisements pushed the "American dream" aspects of Flippo's life as a warrant for voters to consider him. Flippo had a life story that seemed to be a perfect rendition of the myth. The ads were successful in portraying him as someone who had a lot in common with other Alabamians and who would serve as a positive role model for others to emulate. In addition to a good story, they had the advantage of strategic timing. Struble and Totten had decided that Flippo should surface early in the media race in an attempt to bring undecided voters into his camp before other candidates entered the field. The result in these initial efforts was a 6 percent increase in the polls. In the week just prior to the surfacing of the other candidate's media campaigns, Flippo enjoyed his highest polling results.

However, the advertisements were also problematic. The biographical advertisement was almost identical to the one used in the 1988 race. Given that the voters could remember having seen the ad only months before, the only thing that seemed new was the tag line. This provided some assurance for the public that Flippo was consistent in his approach, but the down side was that the other candidate's messages seemed fresher to the voters. Novelty has its appeal.

In addition, no one seemed to recognize that each of the other candidates had his own "American dream" story. Flippo's ratings were initially high but the other candidates soon caught up. Once all the candidates had surfaced, the polls reflected a virtual dead heat among the top four.

The strategy clearly overestimated the ability of a media-intensive campaign to deliver votes in a field dominated by viable contenders. The results of this first round of media advertisements sparked controversy once again within the campaign. Tempers flared at times. The focus of the message strategy became distorted as each group of advisors argued for a different remedy for capturing momentum.

Instead of building on a consistent theme, the advertisements changed direction. First there was a barrage of good-guy character advertisements. Supposedly, the strategy was to show the good things that Flippo had accomplished as a congressman. No one seemed to recognize that the argument was not unique to the Flippo candidacy. Each of the contenders had similar histories. The result was a no-win argument: The polls remained constant.

During this phase, the first public stirring of discontent affected the campaign. One person who was asked to voice a testimonial for Flippo had no idea that the piece would be scripted. He had apparently prepared his own remarks and was somewhat disconcerted to find that the version he was asked to read did not reflect his exact sentiments. He agreed to read the scripted version, but word on the street was that he was not satisfied. The blame, fortunately, fell on the media crew and not on Flippo himself.

Another ad featured the mayor of Decatur in a shot with Flippo. The ad implied that the mayor endorsed the Flippo candidacy. The local media and competing candidates went wild. The mayor was forced to virtually recant any implied endorsement of Flippo. This was another major gaffe for the campaign. This time, the blame began to fall on Flippo.

Flippo was advised that the next series of advertisements had been designed to help him break away from the pack. However, the messages were not well designed. One ad claimed that a vote for Flippo would be a vote for change. The ad argued that the voters of Alabama did not need the "same old crowd in Montgomery." Despite polling results that indicated that voters did not accept the argument as valid, the campaign used the theme anyway. Again, nothing was gained.

None of these efforts seemed to produce the desired effect. No clear leader emerged. The attack phase of campaigns usually results in a making or breaking of candidates. Some shift of ground typically occurs at this point. However, this shift did not materialize in the gubernatorial race for some time.

Struble and Totten strongly urged a positive campaign throughout the primary. This advice was well founded in the early stages of the election. The 1986 Democratic primary had proven disastrous for the party. In that heated battle, the two candidates had gotten "down and dirty." After the election, the winner was stripped of his nomination by the party over a rules dispute. The voters were so disgruntled with the way in which the candidates had conducted party business that they voted for a relatively unknown Republican who now serves as governor.

Given that background, the candidates seemed to redirect their strategies away from gaining converts from other contenders' camps and began to focus on how to rally their own supporters in a race for the runoff. This was the apparent strategy of each campaign. Although that was clearly the intent discussed in the staff meetings, in the final weeks before the election, more money was being pumped into south Alabama, where Flippo was sure to be a low scorer, rather than strengthening his north Alabama base. When the error was pointed out to Flippo, tempers flared. Flippo was forced to transfer funds from his congressional account to purchase more media time in the market of the Fifth Congressional District. At this point, the campaign was out of control. No one seemed to know who was responsible for the errors, more money was being spent than was budgeted, and everyone was looking for a scapegoat.

Regardless of who was to blame, the media campaign did not achieve its desired effect. The Flippo campaign produced more advertisements than the campaign of any other candidate in the field. Nonetheless, Flippo did not get his "fair share" of voters in southern Alabama and did not move significantly in the polls from the time he entered the race. In the benchmark poll conducted in November 1989, Flippo held about 15 percent of the voters who were expected to participate in the primary. On election day he drew 18 percent.

Importantly, the failure of the Flippo candidacy was not confined to the media campaign. Old problems began to take on new significance as the campaign faced its ultimate challenge: the handling of a smear campaign. This was the final undoing of the Flippo candidacy.

THE FINAL BLOW

Just three weeks before the election, a fallacious letter was circulated to select Flippo supporters. Printed on Flippo letterhead, the letter announced the establishment of FACT (the Flippo Auxiliary Communication Team). Its stated purpose was to distribute word-of-mouth information about the opposition for which the campaign could not take responsibility in the media.

The gossip sheet was cleverly devised. It even noted that Flippo, campaign manager McLean, and press secretary Steve Cohen would treat FACT as "unofficial and unauthorized," which, of course, they did.

In the letter there were several "talking points" listed as items for discussion about each of the opposing candidates. Some of the charges had a scintilla of truth in them, but the overall theme was racist and bigoted. Charges against the candidates on the basis of religion, race, and personal morals were leveled.

The letter sparked immediate outcries from the supporters who received them. The news media picked up on the story. Most reporters handled the story responsibly, discussing the intent of the letter but not recounting any of the smearing comments. Unfortunately, there were also less scrupulous reporters who wanted to share some of the dirt over the public airways. As predicted in the letter, Flippo and the campaign denied their involvement, but the story persisted.

The letter caused concern for a number of Flippo constituents. The letters were targeted to Flippo supporters, leading to the speculation that the people behind the letter had access to the campaign's data bank. In addition, the letter was on Flippo stationery. It smacked of an inside job. Though no one wanted to believe that the campaign had any connection to the deed, the suspicious evidence called it into question.

The Flippo campaign made a vigorous denial. Flippo claimed to be outraged. Given that the letter had been distributed via federal mail, the postal authorities were notified. The campaign claimed that it would press mail fraud charges against the perpetrator.

The campaign purported to have things under control during the initial hours of the episode. Three critical decisions demonstrated otherwise, however. First, the campaign decided to offer a reward for information leading to the arrest and conviction of the offender. The down side was the amount offered: only $2,500. The person who had gone to the considerable trouble of setting up the letter and who now faced federal charges if caught surely felt reassured by the insignificant award. The supporters were stunned. The action did not portray a campaign bent on catching the violators. This was particularly true since Flippo had such an enormous war chest and seemed so intent on proving his innocence. A reward of $25,000 might have captured someone's attention, but $2,500 was hardly worth the effort.

The second error was in making a negative advertisement implying that one opponent's campaign was responsible for the letter. It is hard to believe that a campaign that had refused to make legitimate arguments differentiating Flippo from the opposition would now be willing to run an ad with charges based solely on innuendo. Campaign insiders spoke of things that they "knew" about the event but that could not be publicly verified. The effect was to hurt Flippo's credibility as a man who acted with reason.

The third error was that the Flippo campaign seemed to want to keep the letter as an issue before the voters. More than anything else, the letter kept Flippo from addressing the more serious issues of the election. He spent so much time crying foul that he neglected to focus his efforts on persuading voters to support him. Had the Flippo campaign nurtured the press contacts throughout the campaign, the news media might have spearheaded Flippo's public defense. The absence of a credible insider meant that the reporters were as uncertain about Flippo's role in the letter as were some Flippo supporters. Word on the street and at the local political watering holes was that Flippo was probably not involved, but speculation persisted that the letter was the work of an insider. No doubt, it contributed to Flippo's defeat.

CONCLUSIONS

From the beginning, Flippo had faced an uphill battle to win the nomination. He had been willing to take a gamble on the election even though he had a secure position in Congress. However, Flippo had not hedged his bets.

Surrounded by whatever camp comprised the insiders on a given day, Flippo seemed blinded to the political realities. Even on election night he was touting the belief that his staff had voting results that would show him positioned for the runoff. Most news stations had already declared other victors, however.

Janis (1972) has explained how groupthink can lead to disastrous outcomes. He offered John F. Kennedy's failed Bay of Pigs invasion as one example. After that incident, Kennedy is reported to have taken aggressive steps to make sure that there was always someone close to him who would question his decisions. Thereafter he insisted on free and open debate on each important issue so that he could feel secure in making a decision.

The story has important implications. Rhetorical scholars instruct students to think critically about the various options and opportunities that lie before them. Part of that process involves open and honest debate, a strategy that stresses the inclusion rather than exclusion of people and their ideas. Even if there had been better debate and less infighting for position among the members of the Flippo organization, Flippo might still have lost. However, hindsight offers the hope that the flaw lay in the strategy.

The secret of building an effective campaign organization lies in weight and counterbalance. Politicians must consider ways of utilizing the best talents they can assemble while maintaining a clear perspective as to the effectiveness of strategies and tactics. The Flippo campaign never achieved that balance. To extend the analogy of the toy top, the Flippo campaign spent more time tinkering with the impressive adornments than in producing a balanced, spinning top.

Flippo is a man of integrity who has a deep sense of personal commitment to public service. However, during this campaign he lost control of his own campaign. At some undetectable point, Flippo began to believe the propaganda coming from his staff and, upon hearing it, chose to insulate himself in its deceptive warmth. I hope he will run again but with more awareness of the soothsayers and the limitations of their wares.

For an academic who studies and practices communication in campaign contexts, the 1990 Alabama Democratic gubernatorial election provided insights that are not usually available from a study of news clips and expost facto interviews. Having access to the decisions and accounts of events as they unfolded provided a picture of the campaign that an outside view would not.

PART II

"AVAILABLE MEANS
OF PERSUASION"

Chapter 5

Constructing Persuasive Arguments

Political campaigns are armed with a battery of research and data to help them understand the voting audience. They are often staffed by teams of experts offering advice on how best to tailor messages to fit the peculiarities of particular media outlets. However, without an understanding of the principles of persuasion that are active in our culture, the ultimate purpose of the campaign can be subverted.

This chapter is designed to review some of the principles of persuasion that have been derived through studies in a number of academic disciplines (for reviews of that research, see Bostrom, 1983; Gordon, 1971; Larson, 1983; Littlejohn & Jabusch, 1987; Petty & Cacioppo, 1981; Stewart, Smith, & Denton, 1989; Woodward & Denton, 1988). While these are not hard-and-fast rules, they should be viewed as guiding principles that may assist a campaign in understanding how most people react to certain stimuli.

In order to assess these tenets of persuasion effectively, the factors will be assessed in three categories: voter analysis, message variables, and candidate considerations.

VOTER ANALYSIS

One of the more difficult tasks in any persuasive attempt is to secure the audience members' commitment to action. That is not as difficult a job in elections as it is in other situations. The majority of the voting public has already made a commitment to action. By virtue of being registered, they have theoretically resolved to participate in the election.

The decisions they face involve determining who to vote for, who to vote against, and the races from which they will choose to abstain.

The last decision is particularly important to those involved in down-ballot races. Voting histories demonstrate that most people go to the polls to cast their ballots for the major contenders. In off–presidential election years, this may include the governor, a U.S. senator, or a candidate for the U.S. Congress. Occasionally other races will take on particular significance, such as a state's attorney general or lieutenant governor's race. Once votes are cast for the major races at the top of the ballot, there is a decided drop-off in voting.

There are various explanations of why voters tend not to vote for down-ballot positions. Some analysts claim that voters become weary of reading all the names, particularly because they know little about the issues and contestants. Others claim that it is because of a lack of specific knowledge that voters choose not to make a decision. In such cases, some people are content to let others make their decision for them. These analysts reason that people who are familiar with the specific issues and individuals are better positioned to make a reasoned choice. Still others hold that voters choose not to vote because they do not perceive a direct connection between the office and their personal lives. For example, a voter may abstain from voting on a coroner's race reasoning that the officeholder would have very little, if any, influence on his or her daily life. Yet another theory holds that voters are typically in a hurry when they vote. Those who work outside the home usually vote on the way to work, during lunch, or on the way home. As a result, they do not care to spend the extra time marking the bottom of the ballot. Whatever theory you accept, the fact remains that the farther down the ballot the race is listed, the fewer the people who vote.

Interestingly, the majority of candidates in each election cycle run in down-ballot races. An important task for them in the course of the campaign is to convince potential supporters to look for their name on the ballot. One successful strategy that assists voters is to provide them with a marked sample ballot. In this way they are able to see how far down the ballot they have to go to find the candidate's name. The ballot also serves an information function for all the other races. Voters can go home, study the ballot, and make decisions before they go to the polls.

Because one of the reasons why people fail to vote in down-ballot races is that they do not know the people involved, campaigns should concentrate their initial efforts on increasing name recognition. Name recognition is the single most important factor in voter choice for these races (Grush, 1980; Grush, McKeough & Ahlering, 1978).

Voters are also more likely to remember people with whom they have had personal contact (Cialdini, 1988, p. 168). In Laura Jo Hamilton's

1990 District Court Judge race in Alabama, her opposition in both the primary and general election ran admirable campaigns. What she accomplished that they did not was successful face-to-face contact with the ordinary voters. Each candidate showed up at major games, carnivals, and public meetings but Hamilton went further. She canvassed the county, dropping in for a chat at beauty parlors, mom-and-pop grocery stores, local restaurants, county sheds, fire departments, senior centers, and the like. Her primary campaign was built around the published meeting notices that appear weekly in the local paper. This personal contact, coupled with an effective media strategy, contributed to her win on the first ballot in a three-way primary and a decisive win in the general election.

Campaigns must serve an informational function. Voters must also sense that there is a need to vote in these races. A worker distributing materials for Hamilton at a tractor pull in the northern part of the county was asked by one man why he should vote for a judge. He claimed that he had never been before a judge, did not intend to go before one in the future, and would not know a good one if he saw one. The man had a point. However, the worker replied that he was just the kind of person who *should* be voting for a judge. Otherwise, the people making his choices would be the ones who do appear regularly before the bench. If the voter wanted tough, fair justice, the worker continued, he should make his vote count. As for not knowing a good judge if he saw one, the worker suggested that he review Hamilton's brochure. The candidate would be there soon, and he could talk to her if he wished. The answer seemed to satisfy this voter. Campaigns are full of these seemingly minor encounters. The problem is that so many of them are dismissed as mindless chatter.

The truth is that many people have the same question that this man did. Campaigns must provide answers to those questions in the voters' minds even if the questions have not been articulated. They must attempt to answer any conceivable objections in the minds of the audience that would prohibit their participation.

Once campaigns understand that most voters have made the initial commitment to vote, they can begin focusing their efforts on convincing voters to consider a particular candidate and on motivating voters to turn out rather than succumbing to apathy or allowing factors such as bad weather to keep them from voting.

Voter persuasion takes many forms. Given that each situation is unique, there is no ready recipe for the way in which a campaign should utilize its resources. Here again, understanding the principles of persuasion may be useful in determining the proper strategy.

One applicable principle of persuasion is that people typically seek out messages with which they already agree. If a voter makes a strong commitment to support candidates who are environmentally aware, then he or she will be drawn to a candidate who clearly articulates and supports such a position.

This is one reason why direct mail targeting is so effective. It allows candidates to reach a specifically identified group instead of broadcasting their message to hundreds of people who have no particular interest in a particular issue.

This principle of persuasion is particularly instructive if campaigns realize that their first priority is to attract voters with whom the candidate has a natural fit. To have a voter fail to support a particular candidacy because he or she was not aware of important areas of agreement is a shame. Persuasive attempts directed to voter awareness are more likely to succeed than attempts to persuade voters to adopt a new position. The former requires less effort on the voters' part to comply with the persuasive request. The latter requires most effort and concentration.

Two other implications can be drawn from this principle. First, not all voters are single-issue voters. Many people seek a general agreement with the candidate on a number of issues. Similarity with the candidate is critical to an acceptance of that person as representative of voter interests. In this sense, the candidate is literally the message. The candidate's values and approaches to governing are important ingredients for voter decision making. Therefore, campaigns should work to convey some sense of the person, and not just abstract images. Second, campaigns should consider the use of issues as introductions to the candidate. Contacting voters with whom a candidate has a particular agreement permits the candidate to ask for the voter's consideration. Starting a relationship off on a firm footing of agreement permits the relationship to be sustained even when the voter discovers other areas with which he or she has little or no agreement with the candidate.

Almost as a corollary to the principle that people seek out messages with which they already agree is another principle of persuasion. People tend to have greater resistance to messages from people they dislike. This has enormous implications for political campaigns. The one person the public needs to like is the candidate. Campaigns should be protective of their candidates to ensure that they are not put in a position in which they will unnecessarily offend voters. This usually means that someone else within the campaign must take the heat on certain issues.

For example, while the candidate hires paid staff, the campaign manager is generally responsible for firing someone who does not work out. The staff makes decisions about which printers to use or which businesses to frequent. If a business person contacts the candidate directly, the candidate can win favor by overriding the staff orders and directing the campaign to add the business to the supplier list.

This is particularly important on quality control issues. Brochures, palm cards, and printed materials have to meet certain professional standards. Occasionally, in the rush to get materials out on time, those standards are not met. The candidate cannot be placed in the position of fighting with a supplier over the acceptability and quality of a service. News of those feuds spreads across the grapevine and leaves lasting impressions on those who observe the fray.

The interesting point is that a candidate can have the right position statements and qualifications for the job and still not be able to persuade a voter. Impressions of the candidate make a difference in whether the voter will consider listening to the message. In one recent campaign, the opponent's sister-in-law who was serving in a major staff capacity went over to the other side because of her dislike for the attitudes of her brother-in-law. As in this case, once voters determine that they dislike a candidate, they are more resistant to the candidate's messages and may even commit to the opposition because of it.

Audience resistance to messages is not restricted solely to the dislike of a candidate. Others within the campaign also set the tone for voter relationships which may affect the election outcome. On numerous occasions volunteers show up at a campaign headquarters to work because the opposing campaign has been rude or thoughtless. Volunteers want to participate, but they also want their work to be meaningful. They expect to be respected and even praised for volunteering their time to the campaign. Paid staffers, in their rush to meet deadlines, often forget their influence on those around them.

Care must especially be taken in the selection of anyone who serves as spokesperson in the candidate's absence. Whether speaking to a local civic group or a news station, that person is representative of the campaign.

There are many opportunities in the course of the campaign for tempers to flare or for other unpleasant behaviors to emerge. Workers become tired and excited as they do their best to get the candidate elected. The bottom line in this regard is to make sure that no one within the campaign unintentionally sabotages the election efforts by giving the public a reason to dislike the candidate.

Many people remember that John Sasso, Michael Dukakis's campaign manager, was forced to resign after it was learned that he had secretly released the videotapes that brought about Joseph Biden's demise in the 1988 elections. Failure to demand Sasso's resignation would have been an indicator of Dukakis's character even if he had had nothing to do with the actual episode. No one likes a tattletale. Voters are particularly suspicious of candidates who attempt to undermine an opponent's campaign.

These attitudes of like or dislike are particularly important in the early stages of the campaign when the candidate is just surfacing. Early

impressions are lasting ones. This explains why some people who engage in attack politics generally fail so miserably. They often attack the
opposition before they have established credibility for themselves. As a
result, audiences develop low esteem for such candidates. Even if the
voters accept the attacks as legitimate, they may form lasting negative
impressions of the attacker.

In persuasive terms, how voters feel about themselves is just as important as how they feel about a candidate. Research confirms that
persuasion is more effective with individuals who have low self-esteem
than with those who have high self-esteem (see, e.g., Littlejohn & Jabusch, 1987, p. 107). Individuals with low self-esteem are not typically
comfortable with their decisions. They often look to others whom they
respect for guidance (Infante, 1976).

Interestingly, persuasion is even more effective when the speaker is
able to raise the listeners' self-esteem (Spillman, 1979). Candidates like
Ronald Reagan and Jesse Helms have made their reputations by making
some people feel better about themselves.

A commentator reviewing what many thought was a racist and di-
visive Helms North Carolina Senate race in 1990 noted that Helms made
a genuine appeal to a group that had felt left out by the system. In one
advertisement, Helms contended that working-class white people
should have just as much right to a good job as minority people, who
are protected by quota systems. The commentator noted that Helms was
reaching out to a population that was looking for someone to blame for
their predicament. Helms was successful because he made these people
feel better about themselves. Helms found a scapegoat for them and
assured them that the problem was not of their own making. He won
their loyalty by making them feel better about who they were.

Similar appeals could be offered to victim's rights groups such as those
that deal with battered spouses, child abuse, and alcohol or drug de-
pendency. People who are the victims of circumstance of abuse often
suffer from low self-esteem as well. Candidates who offer solutions or
support may find an audience that is receptive to their messages.

In order to learn how to develop arguments tailored to resistant audiences, candidates often go to college campuses to test messages directed to these groups. Students are willing to challenge statements and
test the candidate's reasoning. Particularly astute candidates utilize debaters as sparring partners before a public debate. In this way, answers
can be tested and strategies can be established. Moreover, logical claims
can be evaluated before undergoing an attack by the opposition.

One fundamental principle of persuasion of which campaigns must
be ever mindful is that once a voter makes a commitment, it is very
difficult to change that person's mind. The more public the commitment,

the more resistent the voter will be to change (Brockner & Rubin, 1985; Tedeschi, Schlenker, & Bonoma, 1971; Teger, 1980).

Campaigns seek to identify early supporters for just this reason. In the early stages of the campaign, the candidate must secure pledges of support. Whether through financial contributors or volunteered time, campaigns need to seek voter commitment as soon as possible. This is one reason why strategists go to war with fund-raisers. A hot dog fund-raising dinner may not earn the campaign much money but it can go a long way to secure commitments from a lot of people.

The biblical story of the widow's mite is instructive here. The contribution of someone who pays $5 for a hot dog is just as important to the campaign as that of the donor who gives $500. Professional fund-raisers do not always believe this, but in fact, what counts in persuasive terms is not the amount of money a person donates but the commitment that the money represents. In both cases, the contribution must be significant enough for the person to view the act of giving as a symbol of support.

Similarly, many media-driven campaigns eschew the use of bumper stickers and yard signs. They believe that these political gimmicks are worn out and useless in modern campaigns. Studies of persuasion do not support that thesis, however. People who place bumper stickers on their cars or put signs in their yards are making a public statement about whom they support. The objective of the persuasion has been reached when people make a public stand. Having made a stand, they are not likely to be swayed from their choice by future conflicts or information from the opponent.

One last audience variable should be considered. Even candidates with good intentions are sometimes neglectful in following through on their promises, creating voter apathy. Motivational appeals in the closing days of the campaign to help voters overcome their hesitancy are particularly important in close elections in which a few hundred voters can make all the difference.

GOTV (Get Out The Vote) segments of campaigns are designed to incorporate motivational strategies. An excellent framework for the GOTV effort can be found in the October/November 1990 issue of *Campaigns & Elections*.

There are several common practices that utilize motivational appeals in the closing days of the campaign. For example, campaigns try to make getting to the polls easy. They may provide voters with confirmation of their polling place, information on the hours of operation, and a sample ballot. Campaigns frequently offer rides to people, particularly the elderly or disabled. In recent campaigns, baby-sitting services have been offered at the candidate's headquarters. Phone banks are set up prior to election day for calling voters to remind them how important their vote is to the candidate. Postcard campaigns originating from people expressing their support for a particular candidate are designed to motivate their friends to consider the candidate as well.

Timing is critical in the GOTV effort. Voters need to be motivated on Election Day. Despite all the other valiant efforts, the actions of voters on Election Day are the only ones that count. Conventional wisdom among consultants today is that the motivational appeals should be executed during the last four days of the campaign.

There are several reasons for this limited period. The most important reason is that these appeals are short-lived. The longer the delay between the time the appeal is issued and the time the action is required, the less likely the voter will be to respond positively. Another reason is that GOTV efforts also require a great number of people. By the Saturday preceding the election on Tuesday, campaigns figure that the bulk of volunteer persuasion work is accomplished. Therefore, many of the campaign's regular volunteer staff can be concentrated on GOTV efforts during the closing days of the campaign. Finally, GOTV efforts are extremely successful in demonstrating momentum going into the election. The presence of people on street corners waving signs, phone calls reminding people to vote, last-minute door-to-door sweeps of neighborhoods, and the like foster the perception of a campaign on the move. Almost everyone likes to back a winner. Developing those winning perceptions may be very helpful in swaying a last-minute decision by the voters.

MESSAGE VARIABLES

Several principles of persuasion apply specifically to message construction. Each concerns itself with the way in which information should be arranged or disseminated in order to have its maximum effect.

Not the least among these principles is the concept of organization. Audiences are able to retain information better when it is organized for them (Larson, 1983, p. 203). Compare brochures for ten or twelve candidates running during any election cycle, and it will be relatively easy to figure out which ones people will read. Some brochures are so packed with information that reading them is like reading an academic manuscript. Most people simply do not have the inclination to sort through information in order to pick out the significant points and apply them to the emerging issues.

Voters read handbills like employers read resumes. They typically glance over them to see if there is anything of compelling interest. Those that are clearly organized and make the argument stand out will leave a more lasting impression.

The organization of a message also makes a difference in oral presentations. Candidates who ramble on will confuse an audience, particularly those individuals who do not have a prior interest in the topic. Candidates who have a limited number of amply expanded themes are better remembered by voters, many of whom may have low involvement with the message (Petty & Cacioppo, 1979, pp. 243–244).

Organization also alerts the audience about which arguments are most important. The laws of primacy and recency have been debated by academics for years. However, scholars corroborate the conclusion that messages placed either first or last in a speech are more likely to be remembered (Woodward & Denton, 1988, pp. 299–300). The current trend of scholarship tends to especially favor the importance of messages placed at the end of the address. Regardless of which theory is accepted, knowing that your most important arguments should not be buried in the middle of the message is critical.

In political campaigns there is an additional reason for using the laws of primacy and recency. News crews that cover political events do not typically stay for the entire event. Many reporters come early to get an interview before the speech and then leave after getting a few clips of the speech itself. Others come in late, hoping to get an interview and reaction interviews after the event. By placing the important messages first and last, the candidate assists the news crew in the selection of the themes it will broadcast to thousands of viewers.

The nature of the information conveyed is also important. One-sided information is effective when it is given to those who already agree with the message (Hovland, Lumsdaine, & Sheffield, 1949; Lumsdaine & Janis, 1953). In that case, the information serves as reinforcement for a conviction already held. At the annual dinner held to rally Democrats in Alabama, a lot of Republican-bashing goes on. People have fun, and the spirit is light-hearted. Speakers do not have to defend these claims. The crowd already concurs with the message based on their own experiences.

The problem arises when there is news coverage of the event. The same message that everyone readily accepted at the dinner table somehow seems more crass and jaded when depicted by the news media. One Republican acquaintance was very angry after reading some of Howell Heflin's remarks at one such dinner. She could not understand why Democrats like Heflin and Ann Richards (who spoke at the Democratic National Convention in 1988) were so offensive. The effect is that these speakers often alienate individuals who might otherwise eventually have been persuaded to vote for the Democratic candidate.

Determining the appropriate strength of the message is a matter with which all candidates and their strategists must grapple. One-sided information does not necessarily alienate people, yet in the majority of cases it may not be the most appropriate strategy.

The two-sided presentation of information has some strategic advantages (Faison, 1961). The most important advantage is that it permits the speaker to respond to audience objections to the message in a format best suited to persuasion. Questions and opposing viewpoints will emerge whether or not the speaker includes them in the presentation. With a two-sided presentation, controversial issues can be dealt with more thoroughly and the interaction will be less adversarial than in a question-and-answer format.

The two-sided presentation of information can also serve as an "inoculation strategy" for individuals who are leaning in the candidate's direction (see Pfau & Kenski, 1990). Knowing the objections that others may have to the speaker's message and hearing the speaker's response to them is instructive. It provides ready answers when supporters face similar challenges in their personal lives. Further, it prepares the voter for objections that the opposition is likely to raise.

A message cannot cover all areas of potential attack. It should, however, provide clues of upcoming criticism. Letting the audience understand the opponent's persuasive strategy can be as important as answering the opponent's objections. First, it prepares the audience for what is to follow. Second, when audience members hear the argument, they will be more resistant to it. Third, hearing the opponent retort just as predicted lessens the impact of the specific argument. Instead, the voters can focus on the strategy and motives of the opponent. Voters are, therefore, much more critical of the opponent's message than they would have been without such preparation.

As an extension of this principle, an effective two-sided message will demonstrate the weaknesses in the opponent's argument. The development of counterarguments is necessary, but it is a defensive strategy. The speaker should probe the analysis of the other side as rigorously as his or her own thoughts are challenged.

Message strategies in campaigns often focus on the adversarial nature of political contests. However, there are other issues of concern in developing messages designed to elicit voter support.

The message must be related to audience needs. Noted scholar Kenneth Burke (1969) contended that "you persuade a man only insofar as you can talk his language by speech, gesture, tonality, order, image, attitude, identifying your ways with his. True, the Rhetorician may have to change an audience's opinion in one respect; but he can succeed only insofar as he yields to that audience's opinions in other respects" (pp. 55–56). Even in introductory speaking classes, students are told not to move into the body of the speech until they have established some relationship between the speaker and the message, and between these two and the audience. Establishing common ground is essential before asking for compliance on some issue on which the voter has not yet decided.

Effective messages get audiences to think about the relationship of an issue to their own affairs. Many people may not readily identify how research funding for acquired immune deficiency syndrome (AIDS) affects them as they feel safe from the disease's consequences. However, demonstrating the impact of the disease on health-care costs, providing probabilities on the likelihood of these people or someone in their family facing the disease in their lifetime, or relating the topic to disease and suffering in general may get the listeners involved.

The AIDS issue in particular has been ravaged by half-truths and stereotypes. Many people still view AIDS as the disease of homosexuals and drug users. Their prejudices about the life-styles of the people in these two groups cloud their judgment about what should be done to lessen the suffering. A politician who takes an aggressive stand on such an issue must couch it so that voters begin to see its connection to their own affairs. For example, would this politician refuse to support research on Alzheimer's disease because he or she did not value elderly Americans? Couching the argument in the most human of terms permits audiences to unite with a common purpose.

The development of these human connections also aids in building a web of consistency between this and other issues on which voters have positions. For example, the AIDS issue may appear to conflict with a person's stance on birth control practices. Explaining the relationship between the suffering caused by AIDS with that of other diseases permits the person to see a consistency in the two viewpoints.

One of the more effective displays of this strategy was developed quite by accident in the campaign for the Alabama gubernatorial primary. As the candidate approached the lectern to speak, a man stopped him to question him on his pro-choice stance, asking him whether he believed that life began at conception. The candidate said that he did believe that but that he was not smart enough to know it with the moral certainty required to force that standard on others. In later discussions the candidate told me that his answer had not been planned, but rather came to him out of his own experience. The message was effective in demonstrating the consistency between his own personal choice and the choice he made as an elected representative of the people.

This story illustrates the necessity for politicians to be consistent in their private as well as their public lives. Those who seem to straddle the fence on every issue are not judged to be very credible. Instead, people view them as spineless individuals who will say anything to get elected. Whether or not the questioner accepted the candidate's position as his own, he was able to see that it was an issue about which the lidate had given enough thought to take a position with which the candidate was comfortable. He was not just taking an issue position in order to court the favor of a particular segment of the population. Explaining the internal consistency of the candidate's judgments gave the man a clue to his motives.

Consistency is an important message variable. Many times candidates are overwhelmed by a public gathering and try to cover all the areas of voters' concern. As a result, they do not develop coherent strategies. In the early stages during which name recognition and candidate identification are so important, the message should be focused on the candidate. Speeches are seldom more than elaborate introductions establishing a common ground with the audience. People want to know what candidates have to offer and why they want to hold a particular office. Once voters get to know the candidate, later messages are targeted to issue positions and arguments.

Messages should be consistent throughout the campaign. If the media message is about health care, speeches should be given to receptive groups advancing the same theme. In the event that there is free media coverage, it is useful for it to dovetail with the overall strategy of the campaign. Pressing certain issues at specific times is designed for a particular effect. Following through on that strategy in the various stages of the campaign helps ensure that the message will be perceived clearly and consistently.

This leads to yet another principle. In order to be effective, the purpose must be clear throughout the message. Strategists must determine the ultimate aim of the message. Whether it is to persuade them to show visible support for the campaign by donating money or time or to explain a candidate's position on a certain issue stance, audiences need to know what is expected.

Fund-raising letters are notorious for being confusing. Readers may not even realize that they are being asked to donate money until the request jumps out at them in the last paragraph. Candidates must be direct and specific in order to succeed.

Effective messages should also be constructed to use an appropriate amount of emotional appeal because research indicates that this improves the message effectiveness (see, e.g., Bailey, 1983; Minnick, 1968). Part of the reason for this is that emotional appeals build a relationship between the speaker and the audience that causes people to listen more closely and makes them less affected by outside distractions. Quite naturally, when people listen closely, they understand more of the message.

Of all the types of emotional appeal, fear is the emotion of preference for many political strategists. It is certainly an emotion that seems to warrant action (Boster & Mongeau, 1984; Miller, 1963). People who are given reason to fear for the future under an opponent's administration need only make their vote and voice heard to prevent this outcome.

Gun lobbies are particularly effective in perpetuating a bleak picture of a future in which the average citizen will have no means of defense. They then tie a particular race into the scenario. Voting for one candidate will create a bleak future, while voting for the other will preserve the citizen's right to self-defense. Similar fear appeals are used in almost every successful fund-raising letter.

A note of caution should be mentioned. Audiences have a limited tolerance for emotional appeals. Too much fear can produce a defensive response or an avoidance reaction. Some things are just too frightening to think about. Similarly, too much fear can also produce an aggressive attitude. People may actually become very angry at someone whom they believe is trying to manipulate them.

One of the more noted series of campaign commercials that overplayed emotional appeals was developed for Democrat Harriet Woods for the Missouri Senate race of 1986. The series focused on the hardships of one farm family. In each ad the farmer and his wife talked to Woods about some problem that they faced. The audience learned that this family, which had been named the Farm Family of the Year, was now bankrupt and was being forced to sell out. The turning point came when one ad showed the man breaking into tears as he expressed how hard it was to see his cattle sold. The producers had crossed the line of effectiveness. Instead of feeling supportive for the candidate who vowed to do something about farm foreclosures, voters became angry with her, describing the ad as "sleazy and shallow." Newspapers across the state decried the abuse of the family as a political token. The effect was overwhelming. Woods fired her media team but was never able to recapture the sympathy of the voters.

The appropriate use of emotion, like any of the other principles of persuasion, is critical to the success of a message. These message strategies are designed to provide guidance for the construction of persuasive messages. However, without an appropriate spokesperson, the message will not have the desired effect.

CANDIDATE CONSIDERATIONS

One of the more important elements for persuasion is the credibility of the messenger. Speakers with high credibility are able to change more opinions than those with low credibility (see, e.g., Anderson & Clevenger, 1963). While it is almost impossible to make someone credible to an audience by "smoke and mirror" tactics, there are some variables that the speaker can control.

One of the factors influencing credibility is the audience's perception of the speaker's status (Berlo, Lemmert, & Mertz, 1969). Candidates who have impressive credentials or titles generate a great deal of respect from the audience before they even begin to speak. Sometimes the status is projected by the office the person holds. When a U.S. senator or cabinet member appears before a group, the status of the office accompanies him or her. Similarly, a candidate may achieve status because of the boards or organizations on which he or she serves.

Importantly, a speaker's status is a matter of perception more than anything else. As with most matters, analyzing the audience carefully will provide important clues about what they think is important. It is also important to note that clues concerning status are assessed in the first few seconds of the encounter between the audience and speaker (see, e.g., Harms, 1961). This is one reason why introductions for the candidate should be prepared by the staff for the various people who may be introducing the candidate. In this way the campaign can make sure that the introductions contain information that may assist in raising the speaker's credibility.

First impressions matter. One variable that has received much attention in this regard is the attractiveness of the candidates (see, e.g., Adams, 1977). A quick survey of any legislative body reveals that politics is not a beauty pageant. While attractiveness involves issues other than beauty alone, a neat, crisp look will aid in the candidate's impression.

In Huntsville, Alabama, the city elections are nonpartisan. In order to maintain distance from party politics, the elections are scheduled in August. Anyone who has ever traveled in the South during the summer months knows the hazards of heat on personal appearance. Candidates who are mindful of their looks may change their clothes several times during the typical campaign day, particularly if the agenda takes them to outdoor meetings.

Attractiveness is also important in the way in which a message is delivered. Few people look attractive when they are extremely tired or angry. Care must be taken not to let behavioral attitudes influence delivery style. Hostile speakers are not only unattractive, the hostility also reduces an audience's willingness to consider other ideas.

This is one reason why candidates are grilled so heavily during practice debates. Even under the sharpest criticism, speakers cannot afford to lose control of the speaking situation. Speakers can be forceful and even display a broad range of emotions, including anger, without crossing the lines of propriety. Candidates must remember that they are asking to be representative of a particular public. They serve as mirrors to the population, and no one likes to see an unflattering reflection.

The message that should be continually on candidates' minds is how to establish a common ground with the audience. In this regard, sincerity is critical. Candidates who describe themselves as "just common folk" like the audience and then drive away in expensive cars to plush hillside homes do not fool anyone. It is possible that over the course of the campaign, voters may realize that they actually have more differences than similarities with such candidates.

There are other important variables affecting speaker credibility as well. Effective delivery of the message is one (Carbone, 1975). Speakers who know their materials well, whose pace is appropriate, and whose manner is energetic are perceived as more credible than those who fumble through a presentation. Contenders for president spend hours preparing for interviews and major public addresses so that they will appear confident. The same amount of preparation should be undergone by candidates on local levels who have major speaking opportunities.

Practicing a speech is essential to an effective performance. Speakers who are well rehearsed typically have good delivery. More important, practice provides them with a level of confidence that enhances audience perceptions of credibility. The term "confidence man" was coined to describe people who could trick people into poor investments by virtue of their strong, apparently trustworthy, personalities. Though I am not implying anything about the motives of candidates, I am suggesting that a person's confidence level has a big impact on his or her credibility.

Interestingly, another factor influencing credibility is the organization of the message. Audiences retain information better if it is organized for them, perhaps because the level of organization projects the amount of care that the speaker has given in the construction of the message. While we do not have information to substantiate the effects of good organization on credibility, studies have found that poor organization can actually lower a speaker's credibility (see, e.g., Sharp & McClung, 1966).

Assessing the relative strength of a speaker's credibility also provides insightful clues as to the use of information (Bostrom, 1983, pp. 143–152). If a candidate has low credibility, the use of well-documented evidence helps provide some credence for the message. By contrast, people who already have high credibility receive little benefit from carefully detailing their sources of information.

Challengers may find this information particularly useful since they often lack the credibility of the incumbent. If the challenger claims that there is little accountability in the budgeting process, that assertion will require more than just the speaker's opinion for audiences to find the message reliable.

The credibility of the speaker has much to do with the way in which a message is received by an audience. Candidates must be willing to take the time to explain to their audiences why they have a particular understanding of political issues. For example, a candidate with an accounting background may have useful insights into budgeting processes, while an entrepreneur may understand business development needs.

Credibility is not something that a person automatically possesses. Rather, it is determined by the speaker's relationship to the topic and the audience's understanding of that relationship. Once obtained, it privileges the candidate to speak with persuasive force.

It is critical that candidates take into account these speaker variables. Unlike other factors, many of these attributes are under direct control. Campaigns all too often lose sight of the fact that all persuasive messages revolve around the candidate. Since the business of political campaigns is to elect representatives, these factors play an integral role in the persuasive process.

CONCLUSIONS

This list of principles of persuasion is not intended to be exhaustive but rather to provide insights into some of the variables at work in the person-to-person political campaigns that dominate local and regional elections.

In the presidential elections, which receive much academic attention, the emphasis on coaching candidates to project pleasing visual messages may supersede the development of their interpersonal skills. Television coverage of candidates' every move places a primary emphasis on media performances that will translate well on the nightly news.

On the local level, audiences are much more intimate with the candidate, and news coverage is more scarce. This changes the very nature of the candidate–voter relationship. Candidates must project consistent images to a number of live audiences. Although they cannot neglect the impact of news coverage, they must be particularly sensitive to interpersonal skills which will mean the difference in electoral outcomes.

The study of persuasion is particularly important to down-ballot candidates. Most of these people cannot afford speech writers and strategists to help formulate their messages. They alone are responsible for the content of their presentations and the outcome of these encounters.

Chapter 6

The Torch of the Word

In the movie *It's a Wonderful Life*, the lead character, George Bailey, becomes embroiled in an argument with Mr. Potter, the richest, most powerful, and meanest man in town. Bailey scolds Potter, noting that the difference between his savings and loan and Potter's bank is that the S&L deals fairly with people whom Potter considered beneath contempt. As justification for his concern, he reminds Potter that those people are important to the community: "They are the ones that do most of the living and working and dying out there." They deserve a fair shake.

There is a lot to like about this movie classic, but what made it stand out is its ability to grasp some simple principles about human nature. Most people are not wealthy, nor do they have a lot of influence in the traditional sense of the term. Nonetheless, people do have a basic need to be treated with dignity and respect. Perhaps the movie's director, Frank Capra, had good instincts about the needs of the mass audience, having just directed a number of U.S. World War II propaganda films. Whatever the case, the movie projects a sensitivity to the issues and arguments that affected the lives of everyday people.

Years later, Tony Schwartz (1973) wrote his famous book *The Responsive Chord*, putting similar principles of human nature into a political context. What Schwartz offered was not new per se, but it was given a fresh approach. Schwartz believed that successful messages must touch a responsive chord within the listener. In that sense, the message is not constructed and forced on an audience. It is something already perceived and felt by the audience that the messenger stirs within them.

If voters are looking for a candidate who thinks like them and feels with them, then the candidate who can reflect the issues in terms that have meaning to the constituents' lives will stand a better chance of penetrating the marketplace than someone with only a lot of patter.

Understanding the needs of the voters is what enables a campaign to draw people together in a fragile alliance. Projecting that understanding is the obligation of the campaign. Learning to construct a political campaign within this context requires: (1) the understanding and articulation of an appropriate message, (2) given at the right moment, (3) through the most effective medium. These principles provide the framework around which political campaigns are constructed.

FINDING THE APPROPRIATE MESSAGE

The first task for viable candidates is to place themselves in situations that will give them insight into the data they have amassed. Once the polling data have been assembled and the campaign has some picture of the significance of the issues, the work begins to determine how these issues affect people's lives. This process begins somewhat clinically through thorough research of the key campaign issues. In well-funded races, research staffs are typically available to keep track of the latest developments on key issues. In local and regional elections, however, the campaigns cannot usually afford professional assistance. The research need not suffer as a result of this, however. In fact, high school and college debaters as well as other academically gifted students are frequently recruited to shoulder this task. In either case, the campaign must not give way to the temptation to proceed on knowledge that is readily available or already possessed. Doing so makes the candidate vulnerable to publicly revealed errors. Moreover, the errors themselves may serve as indicators that the candidate has selected an issue to represent rather than a cause that is believed and understood.

Campaign research can not be completed without moving beyond the library to talk with local experts. Among the first people with whom the candidate will want to talk in some depth as the policy statements are developed are the principal people involved with the issue. If education is selected as one of the issues, the candidate will need to know the current status and working of the school system, the problems, the pending solutions the controlling bodies have offered, and the public sentiments toward them. At that point the candidate can proceed to offer analysis with some sense of informed judgment.

Properly researched, exploratory interviews can be as insightful to the local or regional candidates as staff reports are to presidential contenders. Both have the potential to influence opinion leaders in a favorable way toward the campaign. For example, while campaigning for president Senator Al Gore (D-Tennessee) had occasion to visit the University of Alabama in Huntsville (UAH). This was one of the places

around the country in which significant breakthroughs on supercon-
ductivity had recently been announced. Using this as a press opportunity, Gore donned a white lab coat and had numerous photographs
taken while a UAH professor explained the significance of the findings.
Everyone was amused at the photo opportunity, but after Gore left no
one could stop talking about how informed he was on the topic. Everyone had assumed he was "just a politician" taking advantage of the free
press, but his visit changed that impression. Of course, Gore had a staff
that briefed him on the issues and ramifications of the experiments, but
the point is that he took the time to listen and to learn. He became
someone with whom the scientists and workers felt they could talk and
who was genuinely interested in their work.

Politicians on regional and local levels should be no less prepared.
Knowledge about the topics on which a candidate speaks is an indicator
of sincerity and trustworthiness. Candidates do not have to know everything, nor is that a realistic expectation, but they must demonstrate the
willingness to learn, the desire to be better informed, and the intuition
to ask good questions. Importantly, the way in which a candidate approaches the issues of a campaign is often viewed as the way in which
problems will be resolved once he or she is in office. The candidate who
demonstrates a desire to learn about a topic, to study it from various
viewpoints, to seek the counsel of those whom the problem directly
affects, and then to carefully construct a position is more likely to win
respect from others, even those who have reached different conclusions
on the issue.

Being knowledgeable about a topic also reflects the candidate's genuine degree of interest in the subject. The significance of this to an
audience is readily apparent. People rightly assume that if a topic becomes a personal concern to aspirants, once elected they will be more
likely to take timely action on it. Like most of us, politicians have a
choice of causes and issues that they can support. The order and priority
that an issue is given are usually determined by what interests and
intrigues the politicians most.

Using what is learned from interviews and discussions with voters is
not only prudent, it is sound communication strategy. Audiences are
not merely masses of people. They are publics—that is, groups united
in feeling and direction. Because they are listened to, they are made to
feel that they are participants in the formulation of policy decisions. In
this way, the public is drawn into a partnership with the candidate. The
ideas that the candidate articulates will no longer seem like abstract
platitudes; they will become significant reflections of public concerns.

If a message is to reflect the standards of the audience, the audience
must be understood. There is no substitute for placing oneself among
the electorate. No polls or formal research will be as insightful for can-

didates on local and regional levels. Well-financed campaigns are generally conducted by professionals who are adept at getting people to voice their concerns. They do this through focus group interviews, among other techniques. The job of these interviewers is to become familiar with the language and expressions of the voters toward particular topics. So critical is this process of localizing issues that the better pollsters conduct these interviews prior to conducting their public opinion polls. This process results in expert polling data which is more useful than the generic shopping-list approach used by many local polling firms. In part, these polls use specific, contextual language that roots out voters' preferences and passions. Once the poll has been completed, results not only indicate the public hot spots, they are also couched in language that the campaign can use in advertisements and brochures.

Whether conducted by professionals through focus group interviews or in the field by the candidate and the campaign staff, taking time to listen to voter concerns can only enhance the campaign. This is particularly true because steps that will contribute to the solution of a problem are typically not original to a campaign. They are ideas that emanate from those who face the problems and have put considerable thought into the methods of improvement. One Gallup study conducted several years ago indicated that as much as 44 percent of the average worker's time was spent thinking of ways in which to do the job better (Bowen, 1981). If that is true, there is no better way to discover those potential solutions than to talk to the people on the line who are working directly with the issues.

People who are immediately involved with the issues are not only important for the insight they provide on the topic but are also the voters to whom the issue will mean the most. This is a highly reciprocal relationship. When a candidate talks to educators and parents about the public school system and later advances their ideas along mass-mediated channels, these same educators and parents will reward the candidate with their appreciation and their vote.

Once the concerns of the public are well understood, the campaign must identify the issues for public debate. Issues are literally points of clash. They are disagreements that illustrate the differences between people or opposing points of view. In debate parlance, they are "voting issues."

Who determines whether points of clash constitute issues? Aristotle would contend that the audience is the judge. This perspective provides insight into one of the intrinsic factors of issue development: The audience must be able to distinguish between one candidate and another, hopefully interpreting those differences in the same way as the campaign.

In order to be effective, issue selection requires that the campaign find issues about which the public is concerned and that the candidate can effectively address. This critical match is imperative to successful message strategies. Unless the candidate has something to say, no amount of research will be able to fill the rhetorical void.

Campaign issues must also be expressible within a public arena. In one campaign the staff believed fervently that the opponent was a "spineless wonder," bought and paid for by the highest bidder. One government official who worked with the opposition daily in his current post contended that it was not a matter of getting him to vote a particular way, it was rather a matter of finding out who had to be called that day to pull the strings. These views were widely held by those who had even casual contact with the administration. During the next campaign, the opposition faced the problem of how to make this an issue. It was, in fact, a point of clash, one that clearly divided the candidates' approaches to governing. However, in order to make this an issue, it needed to be substantiated for a broader public. The voters would have to believe that the opposition was unduly influenced by certain parties and, consequently, likely to sell out their best interests. No one had ever proved graft, although there were numerous clear instances of poor judgment. Despite the best efforts of the candidate and the campaign staff, no one could come up with convincing evidence that would bear up to public scrutiny.

Some campaigns run on these issues anyway. It is certainly legal given that a candidate has the right to say that he or she believes the opponent to be a crook. Nevertheless, such campaign tactics work only by innuendo and implication. They are effective only if people read between the lines in the same way that the campaign does. As long as a cogent defense can be offered by the opponent, as was done in Richard Nixon's famous "Checkers speech" in 1952, the issue will be short-lived and will do more to tear down the campaign than to distinguish between alternative choices.

These "pseudo-issues" are frequently used in campaigns. They are the ones to which voters refer when they gripe about negative campaign tactics. Over the years, voters have expressed extreme displeasure over their use. Some strategists continue to use them, claiming that the tactics often work even without substantiation. They argue that they plant legitimate doubts in voters' minds and may well affect choices at the polls.

This marks the distinction between legitimate argument attacks and negative advertising. Although both may be based on fact, legitimate arguments, as used in political advertisements, have four characteristics. First, legitimate ads are based on provable arguments. Second, the information can be verified by an independent source. Third, they draw distinctions between candidates for the voter. Finally, even though they may be hard-hitting, they are generally viewed as accurate reflections of the opposition.

Even when these criteria are met, however, some issues do little to legitimize one candidate over another. In the 1990 Alabama Democratic primary for attorney general, the advertisements quickly moved into a mud-slinging contest outdone by few others. One candidate claimed, in essence, that his opponent was a crook. He revealed an FBI report that alleged that his opponent had been questioned for robbery. He also made other claims, including the assertion that his opponent had been reprimanded by the courts for illegal wiretapping. The tag line said that the opposition was "one step ahead of the law" and questioned whether that was the type of person the voters wanted for attorney general. The advertisement seemingly met the criteria for an effective attack ad. The problem was that the attack left questions about the ethical and moral judgment of the accusing candidate. The opponent's counterattack questioned how the campaign had obtained access to a closed FBI file. It was a good question. The rounds of attacks and counterattacks essentially left the voters with no viable option. They were simply angered by a choice between two "evils."

Effective issues, then, should not only distinguish the candidate from the opposition but should also position the candidate for the upcoming clash. If the campaign contends that the opposition is a crook, the voters will care only if they decide that the candidate throwing the punch is not. It is critical that an issue become an advantage for the campaign and not a potential liability. The Madison county, Alabama, Democratic party chair, Tom Woodall, cautions potential candidates to be aware of their own vulnerabilities before they make the decision to attack another candidate. He advises them to go into a quiet room and list ten things that would cause embarrassment or injury to themselves or their families should they come out in the course of the campaign. When they have drawn up that list, he advises them to consider that in a close and hard-fought election, half of those items will become public knowledge. Candidates must consider whether they can live with the revelations once such information surfaces. This is sound advice that should be heeded.

Campaigns have often been compared to battles with issues as weapons, and campaigners would do well to remember that weapons can be used against them as easily as against their opponents. The voter is the one who decides if an issue will cripple or disable the opponent. In some cases, an attack may have a boomerang effect and cut down the sender. In other instances it may be laid aside altogether. Good campaigns consider all possible scenarios before engaging in battle.

THE MOMENT

In communication studies, the concept of a rhetorical exigency is described as "a moment": a time when an audience is ready to hear a particular message and a speaker is prepared to deliver it. These moments do not occur in a carefully constructed fashion as specialists might have us believe. For example, there have been dozens of keynote speakers at major party conventions, yet there have only been a few that really stood out as exceptional: Mario Cuomo in 1984 and Barbara Jordan in 1976, to name two. The staging for the other speakers was just as well tailored to the event, but the chemistry of audience and speaker is unpredictable and difficult to orchestrate.

Rhetorical moments cannot be manufactured, but they will never occur unless the candidates are prepared to seize occasions that are presented to them. For example, Huntsville, Alabama, was struck by a devastating tornado that literally cut the city in two. The event occurred with little or no warning time. Almost as if by design, the National Weather Service was simultaneously undergoing a review of possible consolidations of their services. The reporting site located at the airport in Huntsville was targeted to be eliminated, making the closest facility some ninety miles away. Seizing on the public's need for security in such an uncertain time, a group began publicly arguing that the community needed to fight to retain the weather station and also needed to enhance its equipment by adding the new DOPPLAR radar system. This system is capable of detecting wind shears and assessing with more accuracy the conditions that might produce a tornado. Despite the fact that some had argued for the enhanced system for months prior to the tornado, only after that event was the public provided with a context through which to view the importance of the issue. Once the audience was ready to hear the message, the conditions were ripe for a leader to step forward, marshal the resources, and get the job done.

Rhetorical moments do not appear in a void, rather, they present themselves to candidates who have worked hard over the years on a particular issue. For example, District Attorney Bud Cramer was known as a leading advocate of children's rights. Throughout his tenure as a prosecutor, he actively tried cases that affected children's health and well-being. So significant were his contributions in this area that during his 1990 Democratic bid for Alabama's 5th Congressional seat, noted child advocate John Walsh, a staunch Republican, publicly supported Cramer's candidacy. As voters became increasingly aware of the approaching election, it was not unusual to hear people identify Cramer as the "one that does all that work for kids." Despite the fact that few people could recount with any accuracy what Cramer had actually done, they had a very acute sense of the type of person he was and some sense of his value system. Thus, Cramer's prior record became a useful issue in his present campaign.

The saying that great leaders are born, not made, may be true to some extent, but it is more accurate to say that great leaders cannot be created at the last minute, during the few weeks prior to an election. Issues like those for which Cramer stood were not exploitable opportunities that occurred just prior to the election. The issues reflected a pattern of concerns throughout his life. Effective rhetorical opportunities that may arise during the course of the campaign can only be seized on when they are extensions of behavior that has already been established by the candidate.

This again leads us to a distinction between local elections and those on the national scene. At the national level, politicians typically are already credentialed. They have usually held a major office or public station. There is a record of achievement on which they can run. Local and regional races are typically where politicians get their start. Often they have no previous experience on the job. Whatever the reasons for which they have decided to run for office, they now find themselves having to translate their experiences into campaign credentials.

First-time politicians in particular have a need to reflect on what qualifies them to represent other people. What is it about their character that is admirable? What issues stir their passions? Once these and similar questions have been answered, the candidate can then consider which issues are best suited to reflect those traits.

Perhaps the most frequent mistake of novices is the tendency to want to take the lead on every issue the public confronts and to exploit every available media opportunity. They attempt to position themselves as the leading advocate of environmental protection and the educator's best friend as well as the get-tough enforcer fighting crime and injustice. Frankly, the public does not believe that politicians are heroes. Fortunately, it recognizes that they are human. However, it is often this human side of the candidate that the novice most readily attempts to conceal in favor of a more idyllic persona which they hope to pass off as real.

For first time office-seekers and incumbents alike, seizing all the opportunities that present themselves is wise business practice. The challenge is to differentiate a real opportunity from one that may have negative effects. The dominant images that the public received from the 1988 presidential election were George Bush wrapped in the American flag, the Republican's Willie Horton advertisement charging that Michael Dukakis released dangerous felons, and Dukakis looking silly riding in a tank. Supposedly, each of these events was strategically masterminded. The first two had their desired effect. The latter was, for those who remember the shot, a disaster. If Dukakis and his staff had the opportunity to run the campaign over again, they would probably steer clear of tanks shots. Dukakis looked uncomfortable. The picture had an almost cartoon-like effect. One person noted that Dukakis looked more like Rocky Racoon than a presidential candidate. The illustration serves to reinforce the notion that campaigns can become too greedy for free media exposure. Effective campaigns must attempt to gauge the impact of an event before exploiting the opportunity and perhaps being exploited by it.

THE MEDIUM

The standard mode of political persuasion through most of history has been the public speech whereby candidates have laid out their case. Although modern political campaigns still rely on this mode of persuasion to some extent, the trend is toward electronic channels of communication and the compressed speech that the media requires.

The American public seldom leaves the living room to seek out advice or opinions any more. Further, it expects a capsulized coverage of events that can be quickly analyzed and easily digested. (Kathleen Hall Jamieson's 1988 book *Eloquence in an Electronic Age* describes in depth the transformation of the public speech into electronic patter.) Consequently, modern election campaigns have focused much of their efforts on preparing messages that will be transmitted through media channels. Much of that attention stems from the commonalty of experiences that people have shared as a result of television. At one time consultants could target the network channels and know with some degree of certainty that they could blanket a media market with a particular message.

However, with cable outlets providing sixty or more channels to choose from and with the growing number of videocassette recorders in people's homes, consumers are now able to construct their own media environments. These environments differ from the ones created just a few years ago when the networks dominated television programming. Some people choose to watch old movies, others watch music videos, and still others focus on political events through news programs and specialty channels like C-SPAN, which covers the U.S. Congressional sessions live and in their entirety. As a result, communities no longer share many of the common experiences that television was thought to provide at its zenith.

Targeting political messages via the mass media is much more difficult today as a result of these influences. The market is more diversified and the images more disparate. A political campaign today must, therefore, learn to be conversant in the many rhetorical forms that are tailored for the various channels of communication. Each has its advantages and limitations. Though there are similarities, there are also clearly specific differences in the style and depth of material as campaigns attempt to take a speech and summarize its impact in eight-second sound bites. Knowing how to tailor messages to specific target audiences is critical, but that awareness must also be accompanied by the understanding that the message and the moment require a means through which they can be joined.

Determining the most appropriate mode through which a message is to be presented to the public is not just a matter of knowing the capabilities of each medium. It is more often a recognition of the limitations that each imposes for campaigns conducted on local and regional levels. Learning to set media strategy from textbook analysis is instructive to beginning strategists. Several studies detail various formulas and strategies for choosing media blends (Bovee & Arens, 1982, pp. 166–194; Jewler, 1981; Sandage, Fryburger, & Rotzoll, 1988, pp. 200–334). However, this knowledge must be tempered by the capabilities of the local media market in which the election will take place, the media firm (if any) hired by the campaign, and the sophistication of media use employed by the opposition. These factors vary greatly from market to market and campaign to campaign.

Rather than attempting to provide a generic guide to media selection, a more appropriate understanding of local and regional elections can be gained by examining the limitations of each medium in instituting strategy.

Television

Television is a popular advertising medium. From its inauguration as a tactic in the 1952 presidential campaign to its spread to other major races, it has become the glamour medium of choice (Germond & Witcover, 1989, p. 55). Gradually, as the production technology has become accessible and local markets have become more competitive in rates, television has also become more prominent in lower-level state and regional elections.

Millions of dollars are spent each year in paid political television advertising. So important is it to modern campaigns that campaign managers in major races routinely allot 65 to 75 percent of the entire campaign budget for this one item alone.

The reasons are numerous. Television advertisements reach a large number of people for a relatively low cost per thousand viewers reached (CPM). Given that the goal of the campaign is to get the candidate's message to as many people as possible in a timely manner, this medium seems an appropriate choice. Second, voters rely on television to get information about candidates. A poll conducted by Roper (1985) found that three out of every four Americans say that television is their primary medium of information about the candidates (pp. 3–4). Third, given that voters depend on televised information to guide their choices, campaigns can use spots to present their case to the audience. This also provides an additional benefit. During the paid spot, the campaign can strategically package its message. By contrast, during debates, news interviews, or press coverage of campaign events, the news crews may edit a message in any way they see fit in order to construct their story. Particularly since the slant the news media takes on a story may alter the speaker's intent, many media handlers view candidate spots as a necessary means of self-defense. Regardless of how reporters choose to cover a story, in the paid political advertisement the candidate has the opportunity to get the message across in the form that best suits the given case. Fourth, spots are used because the public expects them and they are now a part of the political landscape as surely as yard signs and palm cards. Finally, part of the fun of running for office is to be in the spotlight. Politics is built on egos, and during an election, the candidate frequently needs a boost to compensate for the inevitable barrage of negativism. For some candidates, seeing themselves on television compensates for some of the harsher political realities.

Television ads in regional and local elections are problematic. One of the frustrating aspects of using television spots is to find a competent production firm that will take the time to do the job well. Typically, firms that specialize in production are sustained by nonpolitical clients. Politicians run only once every two, four, or six years. That is not a stable income for a production company. Moreover, most companies are not willing to drop other types of business to accommodate the needs of an occasional customer.

The major political consulting companies typically have in-house media facilities. Since they specialize in the production and distribution of spots, and since their primary clientele are politicians, they are better suited to handle clients. However, they do not typically take the time for low-level political races (and the campaigns could not afford them even if they would consent to assist). This marks one of the clearest distinctions between the major races and the majority of those run on the state and regional levels. Not having such facilities at their disposal, lower-level candidates are at the whim of whatever production company agrees to handle their campaign.

Some television stations will hire out their facilities to candidates, but this is also a chancy operation. The production and editing quality will only be as good as the people who perform those tasks. Though there are some highly talented people who work in the smaller media markets, they are often not the ones whom the station will assign to "job-outs" like these unless the politician has real clout. Even then, the first loyalty of the crew is to the news station that hires it. If a breaking story should occur before a shoot, the shoot may be canceled. If it occurs during the shoot, not only may the shoot be canceled but the crew may dub over the materials already shot if it is caught without enough tape to cover the news story.

Even under the most ideal circumstances, the length of time for which a station can spare a camera crew or editing facilities is limited. Most local stations keep their crews busy shooting and editing the materials used in early-morning, noon, early-evening, and late-evening news shows. Campaign production shots must be worked in around other, more pressing news schedules.

This often negates one of television's primary assets. The turnaround time in producing advertisements is a critical factor influencing the utility of television as a responsive medium. Given that one of the advantages to television is in getting a message to a large audience in a short period of time, a campaign can accrue those advantages only if the message can be produced in time to create the desired effect. The term used by many professionals for this turnaround time is "time fence." Because of their inability to respond to opponents within this critical time, the majority of local and regional campaigns without in-house media access are forced to rely on their opposition research and predictive prowess. Therefore, once a television strategy has been laid down many local and regional campaigns must execute it regardless of what the opponent may do. This places an enormous burden on the researchers and strategists. Shrewd campaigns also understand that it increases their reliance on other mediums as response devices.

On the local level, television is a stressful medium. Even when a qualified company agrees to shoot and edit the materials, campaigns still have to be able to specify what they want. Someone who has an ability to think visually needs to write the script and ensure that it blends with the other media messages. Even then, the best-laid plans are often subverted. During one campaign the producer attempted to find a video shot from stock footage. The script referred to drugs being sold on school playgrounds. Short of a copyrighted "48 Hours" special on "Crack Street," such footage is hard to find. After some time, a good shot was found. Then, much to his distress, the planner recognized one of the children in the footage as the daughter of a prominent local political figure. As it turned out, the material was shot for another election and the event had been staged. Consequently, he had to start the process over again.

While finding stock footage is not easy, there are ethical considerations to staging shots. Scholars of communications and journalism have been concerned for some time over the dramatization of news events (Bennett, 1988). Of course, the intent is to visualize for the audience something that has eluded the eye of the camera. However, using actors to recreate a story has the effect of blurring the distinctions between fantasy and reality. If politics has become too ethereal, perhaps it is in part because we have allowed candidates for major offices to wrap themselves in images and escape dealing with the issues.

One disturbing advertisement was developed for a state Senate campaign. The advertisement claimed that the education bill that the incumbent had passed had reduced the number of students per class and restored discipline to the classroom. That claim, though tenuous, was not a problem. What constituted a problem was the visualization of the classroom situation before the bill was enacted. The first shot showed students screaming and jumping around the classroom in a very unruly fashion. The teacher, in almost melodramatic style, turned to the camera, hands on face, as if to say, "What can I do?" Then the senator walked into the classroom, and order was suddenly restored. The effect was to trivialize the legislation. Because the visual aspects of the commercial lacked believability, so did the statements concerning the effect of the legislation on the classroom.

Local and regional campaigns also have greater difficulty in achieving quality standards. Political campaigns are mindful that presentation and production quality matter. They understand that an audience's daily exposure to Madison Avenue advertisements creates a standard by which they assess local advertisements. Sometimes the local ads become jokes, and so does the politician they were intended to help.

Television has become such a glamour medium that many local politicians never consider the basic question of whether they should use it at all. While television is a great choice for reaching large numbers of people quickly, not all campaigns have large numbers of voters that need to be reached. For example, the district for a city council race may cover an area that comprises less than one-sixth of the viewing area for local stations or cable outlets. While the televised message would be sent out to a lot of people, it would not do an effective job of targeting the specific voters in that district. Such media overkill is not cost-effective.

Further, not every candidate is capable of making a good impression on television. Usually people who hear themselves on tape or see themselves on a home video are shocked by the initial effect. Those pictures never seem to reflect the image that people expect to see. One of the determining campaign factors should be the availability of a director who knows how to present people in a favorable light and a candidate who is able to take direction.

Radio

Radio is the preferred medium in many local and regional elections for numerous reasons. Production time is relatively easy to get. Given the hours during which most studios are on the air, they can usually accommodate any candidate's campaign schedule. In some instances they will even permit the campaign to work all night to prepare a response ad that can be aired during the morning drive time. Additionally, radio personalities are generally easy to work with. Perhaps this is due to the fact that the job requires disk jockeys to be upbeat on the air (as opposed to television's "bad equals news" crews). This generally results in positive exposure for the candidate.

The down side is that radio stations are not usually willing to let their talent cut political advertisements. They typically view an on-air personality as a reflection of the station. Therefore, to have one of them cut a spot is viewed as an implicit endorsement by the station of a particular candidate.

The stations do, however, have a list of independent talent that can be hired for voice-overs. If the campaign is lucky, there will be demonstration tapes available so the voice can be assessed in advance of a call to contract the service. In many instances, that does not happen, however. In such cases, the campaign can request that it be able to talk to potential talent by phone in order to get some sense of the person's vocal impression on the hearer.

Voice quality is obviously important in radio advertisements. The spot may require the soothing quality of the announcer for the Gallo wine commercial or the news-breaking voice of an Edward R. Murrow. Seldom is one person's voice versatile enough to project all the qualities that an advertising series might require. Finding talent and tapping it when the campaign needs it is sometimes difficult.

In one advertisement, the campaign wanted a calm, mellow voice similar to the famous Gallo wine voice. They wanted the audience to be calmed and reassured by the message. What they got was Murrow trying to be mellow. The effect was disappointing.

Another problem in local radio is that little thought is put into the development of advertisements. This may result from the fact that radio is typically such a cost-effective buy that a campaign will unwittingly dismiss its impact. By contrast, campaigns will spend hours debating the appropriateness of a television ad.

Radio is clearly biased toward the imagination. Announcers must paint word pictures that the reader can see. The soundtrack backing, the special effects, and the words themselves are all integral to the success of the medium. Few people consider when they first decide to purchase media how much time is required for using it well.

Fewer people consider the impact of radio images on voters. During one election, a judicial campaign constructed a last-minute ad to respond to an opponent's "rumor mill" attack. The substance of the attack had been that the candidate would not treat people fairly. The wording was carefully prepared to respond to the attack, but the script was not specific as to the music it wanted to set the tone for the ad. It merely stated that the music should be "courtly." When the demonstration tape arrived, the campaign got a surprise. The music in the background was a beautiful rendition of "Dixie." This is not a song that brings to mind fairness and equality of treatment, particularly in a Southern Democratic election race.

Campaigns often rely on radio in local and regional elections, but this reliance may create problems. Campaigns must be careful not to overlook production flaws in this medium any less than they would in others.

Billboards

The single most important message of the campaign is the candidate. Billboards are very effective in building name recognition. They are large, they can be strategically located, and they are seen by viewers each time they drive past. However, the same elements that comprise their strengths are also their weaknesses.

Many people cannot envision the size of billboards. Looking over a number of sample boards printed on legal-sized paper, any number of designs may seem appealing. Seeing them larger than life-size produces a different image, however. One client told me the story of a candidate who had wanted to use a pencil-sketched portrait on a billboard. Against the advertising company's advice, the campaign insisted that it be used. Like any enlargement, flaws that were hidden when they were small suddenly became glaring. The resultant witch-like impression did nothing to enhance the candidate's image. Given the lag time in ordering another design, there was little that could be done. (Apparently, no one considered taking the sign down and going without the advertisement rather than having it hurt the candidate's image.)

Other people may overestimate the size of the boards, and fill the board with writing that travelers do not have time to read. Design and aesthetic considerations matter, as does size. This is particularly true given that billboards are up a minimum of thirty days and often as long as sixty or ninety days. The impression the advertisement creates will continue for the entire run of the board and may even linger afterwards.

A second common mistake is the location. Outdoor advertising companies, like other media outlets, use jargon that is often confusing. Their statistics are based on projections of how heavily traveled the roadways are. By strategically analyzing the traffic patterns, a campaign can achieve what is called a #100 showing, meaning roughly that 100 percent of the travelers in a specified region will be exposed to the message. Most campaigns do not buy that high a concentration of outdoor advertising due to limited financial resources.

Most of the problems occur when choices have to be made concerning which locations to use. For example, when eight strategically placed boards are required to achieve a #50 showing, it does not necessarily follow that *any* eight locations will produce that reach. Campaigns generally prefer to solve this problem by concentrating the boards within the voting district. Outdoor advertising companies are not receptive to these requests. Companies advance their sales to business clients by packaging board locations at various points around the region. They are reluctant to permit a candidate to buy all the boards within a district because it shuts out other advertising clients who might also want to target specific demographic groups.

A third problem is that not all companies maintain their boards well. If a board is damaged by wind or other weather conditions, many companies will just leave it. Sometimes, if the boards are not sold to another patron, the board will be left up too long. As a result, the paper begins to "flag" or tear off. There is no excuse for choosing someone who runs their business poorly, but buyers should be aware that when viewers see paper peeling off the signs, they do not remember the name of the company which is posted on a small placard at the base of the display; they remember the company whose advertisement is creating an eyesore. Most contracts have a replacement guarantee that specifies the time it will take the company to replace damaged boards. However, it is often the campaign's responsibility to report any damage and trigger that time-limit clause.

A similar problem with some companies is that they fail to maintain the area around their signs well. One may be hidden by a tree now grown too large while another may be virtually obscured by a building that has been built recently. Riding the route is the only sure way of knowing what the drivers will see. Buyers should also insist on a "strike list" of unacceptable locations, thus avoiding the waste of limited advertising resources.

The final consideration concerning outdoor advertising is that people who drive these routes will inevitably see the message over and over again. The advertisement must stand up to repeated viewing. Elements that may not annoy the first time can become increasingly troublesome. Outdoor advertising companies urge clients who use photographs of themselves for billboards to consider using makeup for the shoot. They are fond of pointing out that if a person's face is shiny on the picture, the billboard will make him or her look effusive, while if a person is pale, it will make him or her look anemic. Be careful that the image you desire is the one you convey.

Newspapers

Newspapers vary greatly in their editorial policies. The only way to know for sure what will not be acceptable is to ask. Often that requires the campaign to show its ad strategy to someone who may not support the candidate. That constitutes a major liability. The alternative is to delay submitting materials until just before the final deadline in hopes that there will not be a problem or that the piece will be pushed through under pressure of getting the paper to press.

In the 1989 Alabama state Senate campaign, a comparative advertisement was constructed to run on the Sunday before the Tuesday election. There was no dispute about the factual content of the advertisement. The person who received the advertisement for the paper, however, was concerned because it was very hard-hitting. He determined that the ad could not be run unless the opposition had time to respond. That meant running the ad on Friday. The stipulation was agreed to, and the ad ran in both the Friday and Sunday papers. At that point, the campaign had to consider how to handle any response the opposition might make. The next day the procurement agent talked to the advertising manager at the newspaper office to find out when the last chance to submit a response ad would be. The deadline was less than an hour away. That would mean that the deadline for response would be Thursday at noon, a full day before our opponent would see the advertisement. In addition to charging the campaign for running the ad another day as well as the liability of exposing an attack before it was scheduled, the paper still did not provide time for a response.

Each newspaper is different. Each editorial and advertising staff makes decisions with different value criteria in mind. Sometimes the advertising policies vary greatly from the editorial policies. The rule of thumb is to try to nail down these policies in writing before the campaign is waged and then hold the newspapers to them. Knowing deadline policies right from the start will give the campaign the advantage of timing.

Newspapers are also problematic in terms of the placement of advertisements. Sometimes an ad is placed in a particular position because it fits with the available space after the news and features stories have been configured. However, there are also other variables at work. Some politicos claim that whom the paper endorses is the greatest determiner of advertisement placement. Still others believe placement is directly corrolated to the amount the campaign spends on newspaper advertising. The possibility for this type of checkbook journalism certainly exists.

Checkbook journalism is a fact of life that campaigns must consider. Advertising dollars may have news implications. One editor told a campaign official point-blank that the amount of advertisement space the campaign purchased had implications for news coverage. He said that although they would cover any legitimate story, a reporter was assigned only to their "more important accounts, if you understand what I mean." This may seem like an atypical case, but my colleagues in various parts of the country have confirmed that such practices abound, particularly in the smaller media markets.

Of all the public media, newspapers are the only ones that routinely endorse candidates. The important aspect of the endorsement process is the implied favoritism that the news treatment receives and whether this comes out in the actual reporting of campaign events. By itself, an editorial endorsement is not critical to a campaign's success. Not every reader subscribes to the paper's editorial recommendations. In fact, an endorsement from some newspapers can be the kiss of death. However, endorsements generally do have some limited positive effects (see Robinson, 1974; Roshwalb & Resnicoff, 1974).

The question of how newspaper advertisements fit into the overall media plan must reflect an understanding of the way in which people read newspapers. Readership patterns indicate that most people read through the paper only once. The campaign needs to consider that its message must attract attention on the first reading. Buying a very small ad in order to save money may not be astute. Another consideration is that newspaper readers are biased toward information. They read in order to become better informed. Newspaper advertisements should attempt to fulfill that expectation. Furthermore, newspaper readers seldom read the entire ad (or article): They skim. Their eyes jump to what attracts them—which is, often (and surprisingly) white space.

CONCLUSIONS

Political campaigns must forge alliances between candidates and their publics. In order to accomplish this communication objective, they must be aware of the principles of message development, timing, and media selection.

Just as Capra was able to address audience needs in his movies, Schwartz (1973) contends that politicians must concern themselves with the needs of the voting public. In the final analysis, voters place their faith in candidates in order to secure a more certain future. During an election, average citizens are asked to consider the merits of conflicting proposals that will literally affect their lives. They do not possess a crystal ball that would enable them to know with any certainty what will happen. Choosing among candidates is a statement of faith, a way of making choices about the future.

Despite the limitations and constraints of the particular medium, candidates must be responsive to both the message and the moment in order to demonstrate the kind of leadership that voters seek. The communication environment in this sense both provides the framework for interaction with the voters and becomes a symbol of the candidate's relationship with them.

Chapter 7

The Climate for Image Campaigns

Every good campaign knows the importance of voter impression. Whether through dress, choice of color combinations for campaign literature, quality of print in brochures, or a variety of other "telling" features, images have much to do with the perceptual base of a campaign (see Edelman, 1988; Nimmo & Combs, 1990).

Until recently, many scholars viewed image variables as interesting communication phenomena but did not acknowledge the intrinsic importance of political images to campaigns. Many researchers have now reevaluated the significance of these variables. Salmore and Salmore (1985) have contended that in addition to party-centered and issue-centered strategies, there is now a clearly defined "image strategy" utilized by campaigns. Whole campaigns are often centered on image qualities of the candidate such as leadership, experience, integrity, independence, honesty, intelligence, and trustworthiness.

These characteristics may be either intentionally or unintentionally projected by the candidate and the campaign. Taken to the extreme, they are the substance of the "smoke and mirror" issues that scholars of politics detest. Many object to image campaigns based on their perception that image campaigns are pseudo-campaigns without substance or real issues. However, even in campaigns that are characterized by serious issues, politicians are not immune from the effects of the images they cast (Rudd, 1986).

On the other hand, some people claim that these character traits are more stable than issues, and should, therefore, count for more in the decision-making process (see Hahn & Gonchar, 1972). They reason that the issues a candidate will face in upcoming years in office are not likely to be the ones that surface during the election campaign. What voters need, then, is a sense of how a political leader will approach issues in the future. If voters think of some candidates as too hot-headed and too quick to advocate military solutions to problems, then they may reject their candidacies even though they agree with them on other significant issues. In such cases, the candidates' images are perceived as more telling of how they are likely to react in the future than are their statements about their stand on a particular issue.

One reassuring attribute of image campaigns is that regardless of how fervently a campaign may attempt to sell an image to the public, the audience is still the final arbiter. The audience determines which images count and interprets their significance. As with many other campaign issues, there are typically a number of plausible interpretations of events that cause voters to react in particular ways. Gary Hart, for example, undoubtedly lost some votes in his 1988 Presidential race due to morality issues because of his alleged affair with Donna Rice. To other voters, who knew of Hart's reputation for "womanizing," the Rice incident may have indicated that his attempts at self-reform had failed. Still others may have determined that he had contradicted his own heritage as a post-Watergate politician who would keep things open and aboveboard. In this scenario, the affair was not the issue. The issue was the audacity of Hart's challenge to the press to catch him and his stupidity in being caught. What seemed clear at the end of the episode was that regardless of how voters interpreted the meaning of the events, there were very few positive interpretations that could salvage Hart's voter base. Consequently, his decision to withdraw was probably well founded.

Regardless of voters' personal taste or distaste for image campaigns, they are here to stay. What should be addressed is what we know about the way in which images are formed and utilized as political leverage.

IMAGE DEVELOPMENT

Much of the research investigating the way in which we process information demonstrates that to analyze information people require two variables. First, the person receiving a message must have the desire to want to process the information. Second, the person must have the ability to analyze the information once it becomes available.

The desire to learn is an interesting variable. To many naive politicos, the voting public is comprised of thoughtful voters who stay abreast of the issues and truly want to make a reasoned choice. Because of their own interest in political events, these politicos automatically assume that other intelligent people will share a similar interest. The reality is wholly different. The number of people who can correctly identify their own district's city council member—let alone recall in which district they vote—is dismally low. That is not to say that these voters are unintelligent, but only that they do not have the motivation to sort through a host of political information or to commit such information to memory (McGuire, 1969).

Given the massive amount of information available to us on all kinds of subjects, some selectivity is necessary (Cohen, 1978; Milgram, 1970). Even people have a genuine desire to want to know more about politics, they may not succeed without some basic analytical skills. Consider the number of illiterate and functionally illiterate people who comprise our population. Without basic reading skills, what sources of analysis are available to them? They have access only to the oral mediums such as television, radio, and personal encounters with interested parties in which the information is analyzed for them.

Image campaigns become particularly important to those who lack the desire to sort through the mass of materials or the ability to do so. However, that does not imply that the voter does not have a valid basis for decision making. Voters may choose candidates for their stand on particular issues or for the behaviors they display that reflect values that voters believe the candidate will apply while in office (Husson, Stephen, Harrison, & Fehr, 1988). Others may vote for a candidate whom they perceive to be similar to them, reasoning that such a candidate is most likely to represent their best interests.

A major determiner of how much any campaign is analyzed by a voter is whether the campaign is viewed as directly affecting the voter's life or well-being. Studies have illustrated that when an issue is important to a person, the arguments supporting it are more carefully analyzed and evaluated. When voters do not see a direct connection between an event and their own personal interest, nonrational appeals such as image issues are viewed as more important (see, e.g., Petty, Cacioppo, & Goldman, 1981; for a review of the literature on response cues, see Chaiken, 1987; Petty & Cacioppo, 1986).

While the rational paradigm is favored by scholars as the preferred method of decision making, nonrational appeals clearly dominate the political media market. Although it seems clear that the political system is strengthened by campaigns that attempt to provide motivation for voters to become active, educated participants in the political process, there is some doubt as to how much a campaign can motivate and educate an electorate in a relatively short election period if voters do not already have those inclinations. Moreover, it is doubtful that voters could retain detailed information on each of the competing candidates running for the host of offices that appear on the ballot. Based on available information, it would appear that even "informed" voters are selective about which candidates and races they spend time analyzing. Again, the rule of applicability holds true. The races that the voters see as having the most impact on their own lives are the ones to which they will be most attentive.

THE TREND TOWARD IMAGE CONTROL

Given the proclivity of nonrational appeals, some campaign managers rely on their ability to control images via the media (Arterton, 1990; Germond & Witcover, 1989, p. 55). By necessity, in this strategy, they keep their clients away from unstructured public events. Their actions stem from the fact that they consider images as having a greater impression and eventual impact on the voters than arguments.

Many seasoned political advisors concur that nonrational appeals dominate public rhetoric. Raymond K. Price served as a major speech writer in Richard Nixon's 1968 campaign for the presidency. In that capacity, Price was at least partially responsible for Nixon's mixture of rhetorical arguments and stylistic images. Price explained why nonrational appeals are favored:

The natural use of human reason is to support prejudice, not to arrive at opinions. Voters are basically lazy, basically uninterested in making an effort to understand what we're talking about. . . . Reason requires a high degree of discipline, of concentration; impression is easier. Reason pushes the viewer back, it assaults him, it demands that he agree or disagree; impression can envelop him, invite him in, without making an intellectual demand. . . . When we argue with him we demand he make an effort of replying. We seek to engage his intellect, and for most people this is the most difficult word of all. The emotions are more easily aroused, closer to the surface, more malleable. (cited in Mc-Ginniss, 1969, pp. 37–38)

Regardless of how offensive some people might find Price's analysis, the truth is that his viewpoint is considered to be conventional wisdom by many political consultants.

Picture this scenario. (This is, by the way, a common event that is being played out in elections across the nation.) A candidate running for Congress faces the physical, mental, and financial challenge of running for office every two years. One campaign is barely over before the next one begins. After several terms in office, the candidate is persuaded by the advertising firm to run a media-intensive campaign. Essentially, the campaign spends all its resources on mass-mediated messages. No campaign headquarters are opened, no position statements on issues are mass-produced, no bumper stickers are printed, no buttons are handed out, and campaign rallies are limited to those that double as fund-raising events. The assumption is made that because the incumbent is viewed favorably by the constituents, and because the opposition is not viewed as someone who can threaten the strategy through a grass-roots campaign, all that is necessary to win is to bolster the perception that the incumbent is serving the people well and ought to be reelected. In such cases, issues are rarely discussed in open forums. Instead, the battleground of the campaign centers on the narrative fidelity of images and themes.

Media firms perpetuate this kind of campaign for obvious reasons. One of the more motivational reasons is that the greater the media share of a campaign budget, the more money they make. In addition to their retainer, expenses, and production costs, such firms also hope to gain some, if not all, of the 15 percent media commissions. The larger the media buy, the larger the kickback. Although shrewd candidates usually negotiate the discount with the media firm, the firm still stands to gain from a media-intensive campaign.

Additionally, the candidate's only campaign responsibility is to raise money. Given the expense of these campaigns, the candidate's primary targets will be the constituents who have money or influence, or, as happens more often, the candidate will court political action committee (PAC) support. As a result, the candidate is further shielded from personal contact with the mass voting audience.

However, perhaps an equally compelling reason for media-intensive campaigns is that controlled messages preclude opportunities for major mistakes. Due to stress and exhaustion, candidates working the campaign trail do make noteworthy errors. Because of an off-hand remark (for example, Jimmy Carter's "ethnic purity" statement in reference to the acceptability of segregated neighborhoods), a poorly chosen description (Jesse Jackson's reference to New York as "Hymie Town"), or an inappropriate gesture (Spiro Agnew's flipping the finger at reporters), the campaign may suddenly find itself spending countless hours attempting to rectify the situation. While on the surface it makes sense to avoid unnecessary work for the campaign staff due to some out-of-character response by the candidate, the effect is also to mask other actions that are true indicators of character and that might help the voters make a better decision about the people running for office.

Media-intensive approaches, while the current trend, must be viewed with some skepticism. They are at least partially responsible for the negative campaigns that voters claim they dislike. When a field of candidates is forced to press the flesh during the campaign, people can view firsthand how the candidates deal with sensitive public issues, hostility, or praise. For that matter, thousands of other people who are brought to the event through news coverage can also witness the candidate's natural interaction patterns. However, when the public has only the formally controlled mass-mediated channels of information that commercials provide, they are less effective arbiters of character. They cannot ask probing questions nor view the candidate's reaction to issues that

they deem important. Voters are left to choose between carefully constructed mediated messages from opposing sides. How do they get the
information to distinguish the candidates? They often get information
from the candidates attacking each other through yet another series of
mass-mediated messages.

The specific images used to create negative impressions are often
determined by two factors. First, if an issue is not surfacing during an
election and it is deemed an important decision factor, the campaign
will advance a claim concerning that issue against the opponent. Second,
attacks are chosen because of their ability to play well through media
channels. In a recent campaign the opposing candidate had some negative attributes that were judged to have a potential effect on the voters'
choice. The question that inevitably emerged was how to get that information to the voters. Certainly, the opposing candidate was not going
to display that information himself. Accompanying any decision to run
an attack that highlighted these attributes was a question of how to
convey those images so that they were honest and believable to the
audience.

Information was given to the campaign regarding newspaper coverage
of the candidate during an earlier term in office. The paper had once
printed a picture of the opposition candidate sleeping during one legislative session. Several other "compromising" pictures had also appeared. The effect on those people who remembered the shots was to
feel that the candidate was not conscientious about the job he had been
elected to do. In reaction interviews, several people recalled the photographs but could not remember who the elected official was.

This could have provided an opportunity for the campaign to project
an image of the opponent that might become a voting issue. The power
of such pictorial images cannot be easily dismissed. Whether or not the
public would draw similar conclusions about the candidate's behavior,
in a close campaign the information might be significant enough to let
the voter decide at the ballot box. To fail to mention these behavioral
tendencies might mean that voters would never see the other (non-
packaged) side of the candidate. Unless the campaign undertook the
responsibility to disseminate this in addition to the more substantive
issue objections, vital information that might provide the basis for a
decision in their favor would be suppressed by the process. In a media-
intensive political environment, the issue projected by an image may be
more significant than issues based on reasoned appeals.

The strategy of using media campaigns exclusive of other channels of
persuasion is suspicious. Polling companies sometimes become over-
zealous in interpreting their findings. Just because a potential challenger
is not viewed as a serious threat six months out from an election does
not mean that he or she cannot subsequently build a movement. In the

description of the mayoral race presented earlier, the winning candidate was fourth in a field of five only four weeks out from the election but finally won the seat by a 68 percent margin. Underdogs can win. As sad (and unprofitable) as it is for a media consultant to lose a client by losing an election the firm thought was a sure winner, they may forget that in the process of maneuvering they are gambling with someone's career. Inadvertently, they are also preventing the electorate from reanalyzing the suitability of the candidate for office.

Yet another reason why media-intensive campaigns should be viewed with skepticism is because of their potential effect on the political process. Many people view such campaigns as politically abhorrent and strategically unsound. The effect is to limit political involvement by the average voter and, by doing so, to have a significant impact on the health of the political system. After all, if winning is what counts, a media-intensive strategy is certainly a feasible one which can produce results. Nonetheless, any time the involvement of the voter is limited to pulling a lever on election day, the effect is inadvertently to increase voter apathy in the electoral process and to move farther away from reasoned discourse.

Some people might argue that the news media provide the necessary balance to image campaigns in political elections. Perhaps other supposedly unbiased sources of information could serve as a balance to the candidate's own paid media efforts, but such circumstances are not likely to be present in the current media climate. Kathleen Hall Jamieson, a professor of communication, appeared on numerous news shows during the 1988 presidential elections contending that not only were campaign images flooding the public airways, but that the news media, long thought to be a Fourth Estate to balance the coverage of elections, also failed to cry foul when erroneous messages were shown (see also Germond & Witcover, 1989, p. 183). Numerous examples were given demonstrating that the commercial messages broadcast by one campaign or the other were not completely truthful in their reporting. In some cases, the information was simply false and misleading. Since to date there are no laws that cover truth in advertising for political candidates, if the media does not serve the role of arbiter, no other effective alternative source of information can credibly offset the errors.

Fortunately, in the 1990 elections, some newspapers like the *Miami Herald* began ad-watch columns that served this function. If more journalists take up this cause, the public may at least see more honest advertising.

Some members of the press have told me frankly that they consider themselves to be somewhat bound in their reporting during political campaigns. The organizations for which they work want the candidate's advertising revenues. Consider how much money is spent on media during an election year. It is easy to see how much additional revenue can thus be pumped into a news station without having to do much selling. The resulting fear is that if they attack a candidate's advertisements, the candidate will pull all business from that station. In competitive media markets, that can be important to the bottom line. Moreover, the stations are afraid to offend candidates who could potentially win the election. Officeholders are a great source of news information. The threat of being shut out by a vindictive candidate while other, more amicable news media scoop a story may also have an impact on the organization's bottom line.

The other factor restricting the news media is the myth of objectivity. After all, in following standards of objectivity, they do not want to unduly influence the outcome by privileging one side over another. However, this does occur (see Alger, 1990; Morello, 1988). Supposedly, the news services want to be objective. They purport to be fearful that once they cry foul about a particular advertisement, their comments will be interpreted as lack of support for the candidate in general—a perception that might bias the outcome of the election. Other journalists question whether the press has the right to simulate issue discussions. If, for example, a reporter uncovered some questionable associations between a candidate and certain key contributors, the media would be reluctant to carry the story. Failing to provide evidence of wrongdoing, the report could only lead to the inference of guilt by innuendo and implication. If, however, the opposing campaign revealed the information to the press, the press could justifiably investigate the claims and report on their validity.

The apparent argument is that if the press will not challenge candidates about disseminating false information, it will certainly be reluctant to cover other potentially crucial angles unless first prompted by some other organization (which may include, but is not limited to, an opposing campaign). With no checks on the content of media messages, the voter will continue to be justifiably distrustful of all advertising claims.

The similarities between product advertising and candidate advertising are significant. People have a general distrust of all types of commercials because they recognize that the motivation of the advertiser is to sell the product. They recognize that the seller will attempt to stress the positive attributes of the product and downplay its weaknesses. Voters regard candidates in the same way. As a rule, they believe that candidates are neither as wholesome as they portray themselves to be or as wicked as their opponents make them out. Nonetheless, voters still have to make a choice, and information gleaned from advertisements is their primary source of guidance (Luntz, 1988, p. 231).

Voters are also willing to suspend rational paradigms of judgment, preferring to believe in miracle solutions (Larson, 1982; Schwartz, 1973).

People buy into the visions of some candidates in the same way that they purchase pills to solve weight problems. In their hearts they know that there is no simple cure. The resolution of problems requires hard and often dedicated work. However, sometimes the burden seems too great and they prefer instead to escape into some wish-think scenario.

Voters also respond like consumers in that they are committed to taking some action (whether buying a product or voting) but do not give careful consideration as to how those choices are made. They may use Tide detergent because their mothers did, and they may grow up to be Democrats because they were raised in Democratic families (Kinder & Sears, 1985).

In truth, the climate is riper for propaganda than for persuasion. Edward Filene's Institute for Propaganda Analysis, which was formed in 1937, recognized that propaganda has "twin foci of inquiry—on the motives of the communicator and on the key symbols composing message content" (see Nimmo & Sanders, 1981, p. 19). Note that message content is subjugated to motives and symbols. Recognizing the motivations of the seller is easy, but understanding the symbols and recognizing their effect, is more complicated (Kern, 1989; Larson, 1982).

One particular advertisement used an elderly schoolteacher as its spokesperson. Although the audience might not have known her, each viewer probably had a teacher like her. She appeared to be the most strict, and fondly remembered, instructor of our childhood. (Trigger: She would not lie to us; she never did.) As the teacher speaks, the audience watches her play a hymn on the piano. Her husband sits nearby reading. (Trigger: This is a wholesome family; they have good values.) A moment later, the hymn becomes recognizable. The words, although never sung, float through the viewer's head: "And He walks with me, and He talks with me, and He tells me I am his own. . . . " (Trigger: He cares for me, savior and candidate alike.) The teacher tells of a school that burned down and the congressman who got the funds to rebuild it. She is grateful. (Trigger: A charitable act like this should not go unacknowledged.) A warm and fuzzy feeling develops for a candidate whom the audience may never have met and whose picture flashes across the screen only in the final seconds of the ad.

The impact of the ad cannot be judged apart from the lasting images it conveys. An audience is left with a predisposition to like the candidate (see Cialdini, 1988, pp. 2–7). The emotional evidence is much more compelling than the argument in favor of the good deed.

IMAGE DEVELOPMENT STRATEGIES

Aristotle in *The Rhetoric* defined the three types of proof as ethos, logos, and pathos. Ethos, the power derived from the personality and reputation of the speaker, is considered to be the most effective means of persuasion that a speaker possesses. To that extent, it provides guidance to the development of public arguments via the media. The first questions that the voters must ask are "Who is running?" and "What kind of person is this?" Therefore, one of the first tasks of the media campaign is to help build hard name identification. Put succinctly, voters must recognize the candidate's name and realize which office the candidate is seeking.

Simultaneously, the campaign must attempt to convey something about the character of the person who is running. This can be accomplished in a number of ways. Often the first series of messages are biographical in nature. (For an analysis of commercial sequencing, see Diamond & Bates, 1984.) They tell the candidate's history in a kind of visual resume. Character traits can also be determined by the candidate's associations. Wyche Fowler (Democrat, Georgia) ran a name-recognition advertisement in which a teacher helps students learn the correct pronunciation of the candidate's name. She says, "Wyche. 'C' 'H' as in church." The effect was not only to teach the candidate's name but also to associate the candidate with a positive (in this case, religious) value system. The candidate was also associated with educational concerns by the presence of the schoolteacher as spokesperson. Moreover, the advertisement also served to dispel the connotations of the incorrect pronunciation, "Witch," before they became seated in the voter's mind.

Early name-identification advertisements also serve as preemptive arguments against future claims. In a 1988 Maryland race, Republican candidate Linda Chavez used the tag line, "Made in the U.S.A." The advertisements sought to depict her as a person representing traditional American values. Also implied, however, was a defense against those who might vote against her because they thought she was "some foreigner" who was trying to get elected to office.

The early phases of image development in a campaign begin by establishing a rapport between the voter and the candidate. The character issues provide the bridge of common experiences and values that lays a foundation for the development of a relationship between the voter and the candidate.

Establishing speaker ethos also requires an understanding of the candidate's motivations for running. For some it is a call to public service, while for others it is to repay support that was once granted them in time of need. Other candidates may want the job because they feel they have been properly educated, either formally or through personal experience, in such a way as to provide perspective to a government in need of becoming a better reflection of the voters' wishes. In any case, the voter must be able to detect some understanding of the speaker's motivation. Speakers who appear to be self-serving are not good prospects.

Conveying a sense of the person who is running for office can be one of the more critical campaign tasks. People generally prefer to know what candidates feel, not just what they think. In the days of the civil rights movement, for example, the following theme emerged: "If you talk the talk, then walk the walk." The meaning, of course, is that if a person claims to support equal opportunity, that will be demonstrated through that person's actions. Similarly, expressions of feeling are used as indicators of the strength and depth of a candidate's commitment to an issue.

Importantly, images are also developed quite by accident. The key issue is to consider the images that stick with people but that were projected unintentionally. A former press secretary to Alabama Governor George Wallace recounted one such incident regarding Wallace's famous speech at the schoolhouse door, where Wallace formally barred blacks from entering the University of Alabama. During the early days of televised news coverage, cameras required setting the f-stop as they do now for film coverage. Generally, that meant determining certain variables based on the distance between the camera and the speaker. In order to help the camera crews determine the appropriate distance both to get a good shot and to accommodate each member of the camera crew, the press secretary drew an arch on the cement to represent the camera placement distance to the lectern. Unfortunately, the line was drawn in white chalk. The image conveyed to some spectators and analysts was that Wallace had drawn a white line around the schoolhouse door, that no black was to cross. Although that was clearly not the intent, the image blended with the message to add a more powerful visual descriptor to the event.

Images are influenced by a host of variables, but one that deserves particular attention in political research is what some call the "waffle phenomenon." Research has concluded that "individuals who change their attitudes [are] generally evaluated more negatively that those whose attitudes remained stable" (Allgeier, Byrne, Brooks, & Revnes, p. 170). Further, even when the attitude change results in greater similarity between people, the person will be viewed as "less decisive, less reliable, and a worse leader than was an individual with stable attitudes" (Allgeier et al., 1979, p. 170). Nonetheless, change is inevitable in politics.

Each election year a number of attack advertisements utilize the waffle phenomenon to argue that the opposition is too "political"—meaning, of course, that judgments are made in order to placate the constituency rather than because they are correct. The issue appeal that is typically used touches some vulnerable class such as the elderly (Social Security) or working families (day care, taxes).

THE STRUGGLE TO DEVELOP IMAGES

The reader might assume that image campaigns are easily developed. However, nothing could be further from the reality of the situation. While it may be true that major advertising firms that typically handle the wealthier political races are unusually adept at creating image campaigns, in politics on the state and regional level it is quite different. You have only to watch the local television spots for used car dealers or carpet companies to verify that many local companies are short on creativity and imagination.

The truly weak firms copy the major firms. They take their ideas from coffee commercials or even, at times, from political commercials that they have seen the major firms use for other candidates. They offer a look-alike campaign with no sense of the uniqueness of the communication situation before them.

Whereas the larger firms hire specialists in artistic design, copy work, layout, and research, small firms are typically comprised of generalists who do everything. Problems arise when the campaign rejects a proposal. Although a firm's work may be substandard, certainly no professional intends it to be that way. They generally consider their work to be pretty good. If the campaign has difficulty in relaying its concerns, this can result in reduced quality in other areas as well. In the smaller communities, other firms may already be committed to other candidates. The options are to take the business out of town (and the campaign's money out of the local economy) or to hope for a reconciliation of ideas.

There are, however, some extremely innovative and insightful people who do more to influence the future of political campaigns than we might imagine. Small regional firms are generally hired by political newcomers (the truly wealthy contenders usually reach for a major Washington, D.C., or California firm). Newcomers, by contrast, are typically the underdogs and are being outspent and outmaneuvered by those currently in office. These are the candidates who are the most willing to take risks, try new campaign tactics, and experiment with the democratic process. Interestingly enough, they generally do so at very cost-effective levels. A few instances of creative advertising strategies may help illustrate how regional firms can strategically gear their techniques to the audience.

During one election cycle, a number of news stories had surfaced about political corruption. Although none of the attacks were specific to particular candidates currently running for office, the climate was certainly right for them to question each other and ride along with the public disillusionment with politicians. Sensing that people were getting tired of the mudslinging, but also cognizant that everyone likes good gossip, a brochure was developed by one candidate to twist the topic around. The front of the brochure read in bold headlines, "Which candidate for [office] committed these acts?" The teaser got people to pick up the brochure and open it. Inside, the copy told of the "acts" the candidate had sponsored and passed while in the legislature. All of them constituted positive issue positions on such topics as crime, environmental protection, and education. The effect was to draw attention to one candidate's positive record while simultaneously poking a little fun at the "nattering nabobs of negativism" who had been slinging mud.

Another firm faced the challenge of working with a candidate in a special election scheduled in early January. The customary campaign period was a nightmare. With the financial drain of Christmas and New Year, family outings, and an excessive number of parties held to satisfy the socialites, the typical campaign messages were difficult to finance. Further, research indicated that it would cost considerably more to penetrate the market during this season than was normally expected, and that even if the messages could be financed, they would not be particularly welcomed. Given the spirit of the season, the company proposed a number of innovative ideas. One was to give large, sturdy shopping bags away to help people carry their Christmas purchases. In addition to the candidate's logo, a message on the bag was to read, "A candidate who will be there when you need him." (The idea was vetoed since the local shopping mall would not permit distribution on the premises.) Another idea was proposed for radio advertisements. The spots would serve as promotions for the local Christmas activities that were open to the public. During regularly scheduled times, the announcer would list whatever church activities, lighting ceremonies, or public festivities were scheduled for the week along with the tag line, "Vote for [candidate's name]: A candidate who keeps you informed." (This idea was also rejected since the media firm recommended television spots instead.)

The basic theme in these and other campaign ideas is to find a way first to penetrate the market and then to establish evidence that the candidate is a person of action who can act on the public's behalf. This image formation is particularly crucial to first-time officeholders who have not yet had the opportunity to do things on a grand scale in the public interest.

CONCLUSIONS

Packaging candidates is not a new concept in political marketing. Campaigns traditionally attempt to control as many variables as possible in an attempt to secure favorable outcomes (Jamieson, 1984). The attention that political packaging receives in the current advertising market is due to a suspicion that voters are being overtly manipulated.

Jamieson (1988) has argued that scholars should teach the ways in which messages can be manipulated in order for people to learn to defend themselves from such appeals. She has argued that too much of our scholarship focuses on the techniques of manipulation without the accompanying strategies for subverting those attempts.

However, understanding the tension created by candidates who truly want to be effective public servants in an era dominated by deceptive media claims must be the first step. Armed with that understanding, campaigns need no longer perceive themselves as helpless in the face of adversity. Instead, they can begin to focus more judiciously on the means of self-protection that are available.

Chapter 8

The Shot: Constructing Persuasive Images

Consider for a moment how people who are interested in political careers get started. Many times they begin preparing themselves by getting involved in a political race for a candidate whom they perceive to be a role model. In hopes of observing the successful development of a campaign, they work hard to develop credentials as team players. Most of the time they stuff envelopes, run phone banks, and put up yard signs. Other, usually older individuals who are interested in political careers work to position themselves in some campaign job of rank. Though the jobs are different, workers still have the same basic intent of learning the tools of the trade before they begin a political career themselves. However, despite their observations and the lessons they learn, approaching and working with the media is an ongoing and difficult task.

Few people ever find themselves under the watchful eyes of the press until they enter the public sphere. Suddenly, everything they to have say—whether in anger, frustration, or fatigue—must be accounted for. Basic decisions about who the candidate sees or has dinner with can become political fodder. Behaviors and attitudes toward other people that previously went unquestioned may suddenly be discussed in the afternoon news.

Watching first-time candidates attempting to learn how to give interviews is instructive. They struggle to say something meaningful while they feel nervous and intimidated by the media. It is no wonder that most novices are frightened by these opportunities. As consumers of television news and occasional radio interviews, we have witnessed numerous examples of people who have embarrassed themselves—and amused us. When political figures face the media, they realize, perhaps for the first time, that as spectators, Americans have become keen, and sometimes brutal, media critics. They often fear being on the receiving end of such evaluations. Further, they recognize the importance of seizing the moment. What is said and the impression the message and the messenger foster are events that are suspended in time, recorded by an electronic device for others to witness.

There is, of course, no substitute for natural performing talents and abilities. Nor can the possessors of these skills hone them without considerable practice. However, there are some tricks of the trade that can help campaigners improve their performances and become better media personalities.

PRESENTING AN IMAGE

In national politics, media images are thought to be carefully constructed. In the later stages of the primary process, candidates are shielded from one-to-one contact with the voters, placing a greater emphasis on the perceptions we obtain by observing them interact with the media. In presidential elections, for example, few of us will have ever seen the candidate for whom we vote except through the media. We have no way of personally verifying whether the person resembles the image we have witnessed.

On the local level, the scenario is markedly different. The politicians at this level live next door, not in Washington. They may attend the same church, have children who play with ours, or work and conduct their business in the same way we do. For these reasons, the public in a local or regional race is able to sense with more accuracy which candidates are role-playing or pretending to be something they are not. A good image requires sincerity. Although intended to stress campaigners' positive attributes, it must actually be viewed as an honest reflection of their character.

The character of the speaker is considered by communication scholars today as it was by Aristotle in his treatise on *Rhetoric* in the fourth century B.C. It is the most effective means of persuasion that a person possesses (Aristotle, 1984, p. 25). We are more likely to believe what people have to say if we trust them. Even when we disagree with their interpretation of events, we acknowledge the sincerity of their opinion. The problem for many first-time politicians is learning how to go about projecting an image of themselves that reflects their admirable qualities while not losing a vision of what makes them unique individuals.

The first rule of thumb is for people to learn to be themselves. Roger Ailes, an advisor to Ronald Reagan and numerous other successful individuals, has co-authored an insightful book that stresses this notion. The book, *You Are the Message: Getting What You Want by Being Who You*

Are (Ailes & Kraushar, 1988) stresses the importance and necessity for clients to overcome their tendency to act cool and aloof. Ailes noted:

Many people, particularly business executives, freeze their faces regardless of the emotional state they are in. They believe a poker face is a strategic advantage. Sometimes it is. But often, you only gain complete credibility with an audience when they feel you're completely open and not masking anything from them. The viewer generally perceives the warmer, more vulnerable personality as being stronger and less afraid. (pp. 7–8)

People change their behaviors in front of a camera even when they know only a handful of people will ever see the tape. This scenario is magnified when the person realizes that news cameras will carry these shots to a substantially larger, and probably less forgiving, audience.

Many people change their behaviors because they want us to like the image we see on the screen. We have become such tough critics of others that we are also extremely critical of our own performance (Ewen, 1988). People are aware that television personalities are different, and often bolder than the average person. In an attempt to "measure up" to those standards, they mistakenly believe that it is necessary for them to become actors, taking on attributes that they would not normally possess. One of the secrets of an effective image is the honest portrayal of a person's own, naturally intriguing, personality traits.

While some people become actors, others become machines, donning a poker face in an attempt to hide their nervousness. The CEO for one of the leading contract manufacturing companies openly proclaimed at our first meeting that he would rather chew nails than give a speech. After reviewing tapes of speeches he had recently given, I believed him. He did not seem comfortable with the situation, and the result was a dull, almost lifeless presentation. At the end of a taped session with his senior management team, he said something to the effect of, "Now that is over, let me talk to you about something else I've been thinking about." He proceeded to undergo a personality change. Suddenly, he was animated, relaxed, communicative, and even dynamic. Why did the sudden change occur? There were at least three reasons. First, the client did not view this second message as part of a speech. He was just talking to people he knew, a situation in which he was obviously skilled and comfortable. Second, he was conveying his message in the form of a story. Over the next few sessions, I began to realize what he had never acknowledged about himself: He was a consummate storyteller. Perhaps it was part of his Tennessee background. Many of the lessons he learned, and the lessons he was attempting to impart to his managers, came in the form of stories. Often he would leave the moral of the story dangling, as something for the listeners to think about and absorb. A third reason for this change of attitude was that the message was more important to him than the previous topic. He clearly had something he wanted to say, something he wanted understood. By changing his mental picture of the speaking situation and by realizing that what people wanted was to listen to him, and not some "ideal" speaker type he had envisioned, he made a dramatic improvement in his presentation. For the first time, he capitalized on his own unique speaking style, one that reflected the essential character of the man.

The development of an effective communication style is not done through acting or poker-playing deceptions. The objects that comprise the backbone of any effective media image are a desire to communicate, a strategic way of telling, and an important message.

DESIRE TO COMMUNICATE

People enter political life for numerous reasons. Some feel they are uniquely qualified to perform a job. Others think they have some particular insights into the way things ought to be regulated or some problem that they envision themselves solving. The list of reasons is endless. What some politicians fail to realize, however, is that these reasons are significant to the voter. They should comprise a basic component of the overall campaign theme.

One potential client gave me a carefully worked out pattern of why voters should elect him to office. I listened for a while, and then asked why he was really running. A slow smile crossed his face, and he replied, "Because I am the best qualified person to do the job," and went on to explain why. I suggested that he tell people that in his next speech. He looked shocked. "You mean *tell* them I'm the best qualified, just like that?" I suggested he do so only if he truly believed it and wanted others to know it. If he did not he should drop out of the race. With much trepidation, he presented his case in the next public speech. When the crowd broke into spontaneous applause, he looked back at me and shook his head. Later, he commented on how good it made him feel that other people seemed to view his abilities in the same way he did. All along he had wanted to tell the voters that he believed in himself and his abilities to do a good job for them, yet he had chosen instead to tell them what he thought they wanted to hear. Until this point, he had failed to recognize that he was not communicating effectively, in part because he was concealing his real message. He lacked interest in just mouthing words. He became enthusiastic only when he had something worthwhile that he *wanted* to say.

After years of teaching introductory speaking classes, I have still not figured out a way of convincing students that audiences are keen judges of sincerity. Almost without fail, an audience can differentiate between a speaker who is enthusiastic about a topic and one who has chosen a topic in order to fulfill an assignment. One thing is certain: If the speaker does not care about the subject, the audience will have little interest in it either.

Too much of the time public speakers throw a speech together in just the same way in which they quickly used to snatch an article to present at show-and-tell in grade school. Any object or subject will do as long as they have fulfilled the assignment. The results are always less than satisfactory, but the speaker has given him- or herself an excuse to fail. Since I was not prepared, the rationalization begins, I did not do as well as I could have. By contrast, effective speakers not only hold a genuine enthusiasm for the subject but also find it necessary to share with the audience the reasons for their interest in the topic. Their enthusiasm is contagious. As a result, audiences often find themselves engrossed in a discussion of ideas that they might otherwise have dismissed.

Unfortunately, challengers often dismiss the importance of the message that they truly want to share. Sometimes they feel overshadowed by more practiced incumbents. As a result, they provide themselves with dozens of reasons to excuse sloppy performances. They are not usually provided with many opportunities to speak to crowds. They are not generally asked for television interviews. They may not have a staff at their beck and call. However, challengers have unique opportunities to change the political landscape. Quite frankly, challengers usually lose (Howell & Oiler, 1981). For example, in the United States Congress, 98.6 percent of the incumbents retained their seats in the 1988 elections (Cook, 1990, p. 8). These statistics are not atypical. The figures are not as clearly tabulated at state and regional levels, but the wisdom holds true. However, the important point is that even those who do not attain office are often successful in changing the political agenda. The programs and ideas that they mold into arguments during the course of the campaign are often adopted by the victor. Whether motivated by a desire to regain a constituency that was lost during the election or a genuine wish to utilize good ideas, victors cannot fail to notice the issues that drive campaigns and establish a constituency for their opponents.

Some first-time politicians make the mistake of copying the seasoned opponents they are challenging. However, by doing so, they lose a major advantage. In fact, challengers typically attract attention by their differences and legitimize their campaigns as outsiders who have not been corrupted by the system. Given that case, why would they adopt the behaviors of those whom they are trying to defeat? Instead, they should have bold messages delivered with their own unique spark of enthusiasm (for a review of challenger strategies, see Denton & Woodward, 1990, pp. 96–99; Trent & Friedenberg, 1983, pp. 105–113).

The desire to communicate, to win an election, is the fire in the belly that many consultants look for before determining for whom they will work. Consultants with impressive win–loss lists are not just successful because they are talented advisors. They also know how to pick winning clients. Without fail, consultants can increase their win–loss record by working for those people who truly have something to say and are eager to say it. However, even with these skills, politicians sometimes need help in learning how to convey their message to the public.

WAYS OF TELLING

Whenever we attempt to convey a message to an audience, we must consider how to do that most effectively. These message strategies comprise the ways of telling. Included are rhetorical choices such as the format through which the message will be conveyed, the people with whom the speaker must publicly interact, and the characteristics of the audience receiving the message.

Before any of these choices can be addressed, the speaker should assess the purpose of the communication. Does the speaker hope to inform the audience, persuade them, or build a case for his or her position? Who is the audience that is being addressed? What does the speaker want from the audience? These are all basic questions that are asked in preparation of any communication event. However, they are easily forgotten in the fray of the campaign. In traveling with one candidate around several cities, before each stop I asked what he wanted from his audience. He shot back the obvious response, "I want everything." That is great for a wish list but hardly acceptable for an effective presentation. When he did specify his intent, the message became much more directed and unified. For example, in one community he wanted to make sure that the voters understood his work on their behalf in getting major capital funding for a public works project. In another meeting with a group of working women, he wanted to demonstrate his empathy for their concerns. He decided to tell them about the challengers his widowed mother faced thirty years ago with a house full of young children. His singleness of purpose helped drive these events and increased the likelihood that his objective would be realized.

Once the intent is clear, the medium must be considered. Since the most predominant and widespread images of candidates are mediated ones, these channels deserve the primary focus of the campaign.

Television audiences may be exposed to at least four formats of messages: new stories, advertisements, talk show interviews, and debates. Given the visual bias of the medium, each of these formats has a key concern how to "tell" the message in an eye-pleasing way.

THE VISUAL COMPONENT

The visual component is particularly crucial in the news and advertising formats (see, e.g., Germond & Witcover, 1989, p. 55; Jamieson, 1988, pp. 59–60). National campaigns are instructive for local races in this regard. They have mastered the art of staging photo "ops" (opportunities) so that the cameras have something to shoot in addition to talking heads. If a candidate is going to speak about slope development, the talk should be illustrated by photos of a visually compelling location, perhaps at the top of a mountainside or at the site of a mudslide, which permit the viewer to "see" and feel the problem in the same way the candidate does (see Gronbeck, 1989). This becomes important in getting the message across, in part because it pictures the scene being described.

Good visuals are the substance of effective television (Cundy, 1986). In either news or advertisements, the reason why campaigns spend so much time considering the visual elements is that visuals have the power to compel people to listen, if only for a moment. The same visual criteria that apply to news formats also affect the production of political advertisements. Ads that are visually interesting command greater audience attention.

In addition, people are able to retain information better when it is visually reinforced. Since one of the goals of effective advertisements is for viewers to recall what they have seen, the time spent finding compelling visuals is justified. Several years ago, when I lived in Texas, I attended the mandatory driving safety course required of those who used university vehicles. Most of the presentation was lifeless and uninteresting. Then, two railroad engineers came in to speak about train hazards. Few of us were initially interested, arguing that this was not a common traffic problem. However, we found out that in states where the railroad is still a major transportation source, the situation was more severe than we had imagined. The engineers impressed on us the imminent dangers of accidents involving trains. In one compelling illustration, they argued that the impact of a train hitting a car was approximately the same as that of a car running over an empty Coke can. Some eight years after hearing their story, some of the specific details have been lost, but I still remember the visual impression of that Coke can. I can assure you, I never take a chance by crossing the tracks as a train approaches. Since part of the success of advertising is its ability to stimulate consumer recall at the time of decision, the attention to visual impression is useful.

Another argument for the careful use of visuals is that they provide the speaker and the message with a sense of place (see Jamieson, 1988, pp. 57–61). When Abraham Lincoln gave his address at the Gettysburg cemetery, the fact that the crowd was surrounded by the graves of the war dead could not have gone unnoticed. The impact of the place—the emotional and reflective atmosphere it provided—contributed to an interpretation of the message. Today, audiences also interpret messages that provide a sense of place. A candidate may talk about the dangerous erosion of our hillsides, but when we see homes in danger of a slide downhill during a rain storm, the message takes on new meaning. Statistical descriptions of costs, numbers of people affected, or other measures of significance are helpful in one sense. However, as Lowell (1913) said, "The mass of mankind has more sympathy with the fortunes of an individual than with the fate of principles" (p. 53).

"Place" may also be an evocative ingredient (Blumenthal, 1988; Edelman, 1964; McDonald, 1969; Nimmo & Combs, 1980). McDonald's hamburger ads often take us back to events in our childhood where McDonald's provided the place. Ronald Reagan's campaign visuals similarly took us to a mythic mainstreet America that many of us would like to believe still exits. The visuals provide a context for the narrative. They are, therefore, an integral part of the argument the candidate is making, and not something that simply makes it more attractive.

Visual proof has the power to validate the speaker's claims if the images are concrete and specific. I remember reading a passage that said that you can tell people that there are 10 billion stars in the universe and people will look to the heavens in amazement, but tell them that a park bench has just been painted and everyone wants to touch it to see for themselves. The essential message is that visuals provide a sense of confirmation for the words a candidate expresses. The use of visuals to enhance the message should be considered integral to message development.

Some campaign formats—interviews and debates, for example—do not permit visual diversion. In fact, these formats typically require what most producers deem dead air time: the talking head sequence. The cameras shoot people talking: That is all. In such cases, the physical appearance of the speaker and the words the speaker uses to paint mental pictures assume vital importance.

Ever since the study of the John Kennedy–Richard Nixon debates of the 1960 election, scholars have examined the importance of physical appearance variables on viewers (Kraus, 1962; Mayo, 1962). Some contend that height is a factor. In numerous debates, negotiators have won the right for one candidate to stand on a raised platform in order to appear similar in height to another candidate. Other researchers find clothing color and style to be factors (see, e.g., Bassett, Staton-Spicer, & Whitehead, 1979). Consultants possess detailed information to help form positive images of their clients (Martel, 1983, pp. 78–84). The foundation for many of these claims is that if each candidate is unique, visual factors and audience taste may have a significant role in decision processes. If, however, the candidates are similar in dress, then these trivial matters are less likely to unduly influence electoral outcomes.

Although some people smirk at the attention that consultants pay to these details, many of the same principles apply in courts of law. Defendants are routinely told to shave facial hair; get a short, business haircut; wear a nice, clean suit; and watch their posture while in the courtroom. Lawyers do not want their clients to look guilty before the jury has had an opportunity to hear the case. The same is true in politics. Consultants often help to neutralize the negatives and allow more substantive issues to be focused upon.

Visual elements often comprise the substance of image issues. A person's image is affected by a number of factors, and physical attractiveness certainly plays a significant role. Studies confirm that people are more responsive to those whom they find attractive (see, e.g., Berscheid & Walster, 1974). Personality traits help in determining a candidate's likability, another factor that increases our attention to certain people over others (Joslyn, 1986; Woodward & Denton, 1988, pp. 169–173). Audiences are often drawn by the charisma of the speaker. For example, on nationally syndicated talk shows, the term "host" has been replaced by "personality." Successful interviewers like Johnny Carson, Oprah Winfrey, Phil Donahue, and David Letterman are effective because their personalities serve as a kind of magnet to audiences. Some candidates have that kind of magnetism as well. Mario Cuomo, Ronald Reagan, and Jesse Jackson are perhaps the most noted political speakers of our day because of those traits. However, even though some may never make it to national prominence, local personalities can be just as compelling to local audiences. Projecting the personality of a winner can be an important consideration in the election of a candidate. Because appearance is so important, candidates can be either helped or hurt by situations that permit close visual comparison with their opponents.

Voters' perceptions are often changed or solidified when they see both candidates side by side in debate. In the 1990 general election congressional race between Bud Cramer and Albert MacDonald in Alabama, polls revealed that every time the two appeared together in the media during the last few weeks of the campaign, Cramer won a few more votes. Cramer looked vibrant, healthy, and polished. These characteristics appealed to voters who were conscious of the fact that he would soon be filling the shoes of Ronnie Flippo, a very popular and polished legislator. MacDonald, who had been agricultural commissioner, looked more suited to that role than to a role in Congress. He looked, in the words of one voter, "tough." For a lot of voters concerned about stereotypical perceptions of Alabamians, Cramer projected the better image.

SELECTING MEDIA OPPORTUNITIES

Candidates can also be affected by visual or nonvisual comparisons that audiences make between them and persons in media. One feature segment on a local Huntsville station is hosted by Jamie Cooper, "The Country Rover." His stories are typically witty and focus on local people and simple values. Recently, he and some of his colleagues hosted a morning wake-up interview show. They enjoyed poking fun at each other and engaging in raucous laughter. For those guests who felt comfortable kidding around with them, the format was successful. Occasionally, however, they would get a guest who, for all their efforts, just could not think fast enough to get into the foray of quick verbal exchanges. The result is that a person who might in another format have come across as reasonably competent and sincere appeared lifeless and dull-witted. Sometimes, these guests would become irritated in their own defense. The hosts were gracious enough to attempt to modify their style in these cases, but by then the damage had been done. First impressions do matter. What is of particular importance is the fact that not everyone is a media personality. For this majority, interview opportunities must be chosen with care.

The task of selecting media opportunities is relatively simple for those who work and live in the market area. The interviewing style of most local personalities is well known. Candidates should consider how they would feel interacting with these moderators. Campaign managers should realistically assess whether the candidate would be overshadowed or have negative perceptions bolstered by comparison. Campaigns must be careful not to accept invitations to appear merely because the opportunity of addressing a rather sizable audience at no expense to the campaign has presented itself. In an age of media spins and image campaigns, detail can be very important.

This discussion should not leave the impression that appearance itself is the only thing that matters. The reason why all these visual and nonverbal elements are important is that they provide informational clues to the audience. Research tells us that we are more apt to be persuaded by people who we determine are similar to ourselves (see, e.g., Infante, 1978; Infante & Gordon, 1981; McCroskey, Richmond & Daly, 1975). In part, this is due to the fact that people believe that they know what to expect from others whom they perceive to be like them (see Berger & Calabrese, 1975).

In elections, the much-overlooked fact is that voters are asked to vote on candidates as if the electorate had a crystal ball that would tell them how the candidate would respond to future key issues. Elections are about the future. The past is only an indicator of patterns of behavior that guides audiences by virtue of establishing a chain of probability based on a candidate's past known actions, behaviors, and statements.

These projections may constitute good reasons or may be as spurious as the ones used by amateur betters at a horse race: the name, the rider's colors, or the "look" of the horse. Regardless, these images may affect election outcomes.

Images are illusive, they are sometimes misleading, and they are often trivialized. Campaigns can quickly become engulfed in image battles by virtue of the fact that they can have so much influence on outcomes. Constructing positive associations between the candidate and the issues is difficult to accomplish. This is compounded by the fact that campaigns have so little time in which to do it. With the exception of paid television advertisements, the format of media opportunities does not favor the candidate.

Unlike national races, candidates at local levels may have difficulty luring a camera crew to some unique visual location unless the story to be covered is deemed significant. Often, the story is not compelling enough to meet news criteria. The result is that candidates frequently release statements to the press only to discover that the story is not picked up. If the candidate has chanced upon a slow news day, the station may still cover the story using file footage while the candidate is left tromping through the wetlands unfilmed.

Even when stories are covered, candidates have to remember that television news is a form of entertainment in which the anchors are the stars. Other personalities are subjugated to the anchors in part by the way in which the story is told. More often than not, the newscasters are the focus of newscasts. According to one estimate, a candidate's words accompany the pictures only 37 percent of the time; the rest of the time the reporter talks the viewer through events. When candidates are permitted to speak for themselves, the average sound bite is only 9.8 seconds long (Cunningham, 1990). Of perhaps greater distress to the campaign is that it has no part in determining which 9 seconds will be used.

Politics is replete with examples of news stories that distort a candidate's message. After a public meeting with a candidate, one newspaper may carry a feature on the candidate's view of the economy, another on the campaign reform issues, and another on the candidate's ability to draw a crowd. Those who actually attended the meeting may find all these accounts to be distortions of the event that they witnessed firsthand. Nonetheless, more people will see or read the news accounts than actually attended the meeting.

CANDIDATE ANALYSIS: HOW TO PLAY BEFORE THE HOME CROWD

Knowing and working the audience may be the only safety valve that campaigns have with which to try to keep the campaign on track. That is one reason why audience analysis is so important.

When I think of audiences, I am not limiting the term to the audience that watches once the program is aired. I also refer to those who are present when the message is delivered. In that case, the camera crew, the interviewer, the campaign staff, and the curious observer are all part of the audience. During each campaign I remind candidates that for media stories, the most important contact they have is the camera crew. These are the folks who lug the heavy equipment around but get none of the glory. They are typically underpaid, yet they are responsible for a major part of the story production. They determine the shots, the camera angles, the background, and the visually compelling addendum. Most of the time, however, the camera crew is ignored by the candidate and the campaign staff. A few words in personal greeting to all those present is not only a common courtesy but, in the case of camera crews, may actually influence the quality of the shot. It only makes sense that people will perform their job better when they feel that their work is appreciated.

Another segment of the audience is comprise of reporters. Their job is to report the news, of course, but it is also to analyze what they observe. Those observations begin from the moment when they arrive (Germond & Witcover, 1989, pp. 59–61). Candidates who ignore the press and then suddenly become warm during the interview are viewed as insincere actors. In larger campaigns, a press secretary briefs the reporters, gives them copies of the candidate's statement, and works with the crews to set up the shot. Giving reporters the necessary tools with which to do their job well is not only productive for the campaign, it also helps them do their job better. Handing them copies of the script is not only polite, it also gives them time to think about questions they would like to ask and to phrase them appropriately.

I remember one incident during which a novice reporter had trouble asking a question. The candidate gave a perplexed look and then smiled at a staffer who was similarly chagrinned at the reporter's trouble. That night on the news, the segment was edited with a more succinctly phrased question, but the footage showed the same puzzled and chagrinned politician. In effect, the politician looked confused. Most people have a strong eye-for-an-eye defense system. When politicians make reporters look bad, they should be ready for the tables to be turned.

Campaigns also do well to remember that reporters are no different from anyone else. They would like to sound reasoned and intelligent to their audience. Candidates who hold successful news conferences are often those who provide reporters with potential angles for addressing the stories. Professional journalists will not need these aids, but it gives novice reporters a way in which to think about the issues. The bottom line is a trade-off of favors: The reporter is given a good story and the campaign gets fair coverage of an issue it deems important.

The other part of the audience that should be remembered is the staff. I urge clients to be careful about who goes along on the press conference. Anyone who is on the staff of a candidate is fair game for reporters. Staff members must know the substance and intent of the message. Reporters may ask questions about strategy (a favorite question). They may probe for information on how the campaign is shaping up. They may ask apparently innocent questions about the internal power struggles of the campaign. Each of these probes has implications for the slant that the story will receive.

Despite the potential liabilities of staff attendance, these workers can be of great service in keeping the tone of the conference centered on the issues and the candidate. In recent years national campaigns have begun using spin control: a formal effort at determining how a story will be told by the media. The tactic is very strategic. It was born from the idea that the news likes to get reaction shots from people after a major event. They particularly like to cameo prominent persons who attend. Given that perspective, handlers reasoned that if key leaders whom the campaign was sure would give position reactions to the message were present, the campaign could exercise some control over the way in which the message was reviewed. Though staff members are rarely interviewed about their reactions to their candidate's statement or position, they do have an opportunity to help reporters to find positive reactions instead of just negative ones and thus to control the spin of a story.

Staff members can also be of invaluable assistance in evaluating the process once it is over. Despite the fact that campaigns would like every press conference to go smoothly, they do not. Candidates get tired and are sometimes sloppy. They need to be reminded of bad habits that are reentering their behavior. Constructive criticism helps candidates stay at their best. Moreover, candidates cannot indulge themselves in the luxury of having a lot of yea-sayers surrounding them. They need a few realists on their side to keep them in check. The other audience that is present is the unseen audience watching the event at home on the news. A large, multi-interested group will never be fully satisfied with a candidate who favors one position over another. That comes with the territory. Candidates have to be careful that in their attempt to satisfy everyone, they may end up satisfying no one. It is far better to have one side mad at you than having both sides mad because you failed to say anything of substance. Looking uncertain is far worse than taking a less-than-popular stand.

Campaigns must also consider the types of people who might be watching (see Martel, 1983). Debate audiences are different from any others. Some people watch because they truly want the information, and others because the story is interesting to them, perhaps because the problems being discussed are ones they are experiencing. Sometimes people watch out of amusement. More often, however, people watch candidate debates and talk show interviews because they are rooting for the candidate of their choice (and perhaps simultaneously hoping that the opponent will stumble). The primary objects of persuasion for these events should be the home crowd who supports the candidate and the fence sitters who probably tuned in with the intention of letting the debate guide their decision.

The issues that aided in the development of a core constituency need to be reinforced in the debate. However, it should be remembered that these people will become supportive with minimal effort. Messages are tailored to those who have yet to make a decision and who are watching in order to get substantive information that will led them to a conclusion. This type of audience generally likes to perceive itself as being rationally led to a decision. Consequently, these individuals demand fact-rich materials. They are capable of following detailed arguments, and their interests should be cultivated by careful reasoning and analysis. Candidates should not spend an inordinate amount of time preaching to those who are already in their camp. Nor should a lot of time and energy be spent trying to convince the hard-core opposition of issues with which they will never agree. The words of debate coaches around the country are instructive in message construction for these unique audiences: "Debate the proposition, not the opposition." Since these audiences are not composed of the typical "sound bite groupies," persuasive efforts should be directed toward more substantive analysis. This does not mean that the speaker should avoid good lines for sound bites on the evening news. It does mean that the more persuadable audience demands closer analysis.

These audiences stand apart from those who only catch images that are flashed in advertisements between their favorite shows—if they view political commercials at all. They regard politics as another form of entertainment (Kern, 1989). They like the conflict of people embroiled in a great battle with one another. They enjoy the dirt, the scoop, and the drama that soap-opera politics provides.

This audience type comprises the largest target group for political messages. Most of their information about political races comes from the television, which is entertainment-oriented. People can be informed and entertained simultaneously. The strategist's job is to make sure that substantive information is conveyed through a medium that is largely concerned with entertainment. This can be accomplished only through careful visual message development.

CORNERING: THE EFFECTIVE SELECTION
OF MESSAGES

Candidates know that they must take stands on the central election issues. These are the handful of themes that have specialized constituencies and that divide major groups of people (usually Democrats from Republicans). However, the more persuasive messages are those that lie beneath the surface and receive much less attention.

These image issues are frequently personal to the candidate but also have important implications for the public. Often these issues arise out of personal experience. For example, one candidate's father died while he was still a child. He grew up in a household in which his mother was the sole supporter of the family, and remembered the hardships she endured in raising her family alone. As an adult in a world quite different from the one in which he grew up, the circumstances surrounding the breakup of traditional family structures may have changed, but his understanding of the plight of single parents did not. The candidate argued passionately for after-school programs to reduce the number of latchkey kids in the community. He spoke about job-training programs that enhance skill levels beyond minimum-wage–bearing status. Through these and similar issues, his personal values became public arguments.

In the sometimes plastic world of razzle-dazzle politics, campaigns often forget that these genuine issue concerns have powerful effects on a candidate's image. Everyone believes in better education, decent health care, and well-paying jobs. Candidates who mouth the obvious seem lifeless automatons to the watching public. Personal expressions of attachment to issues are what help define the turf for campaigns and establish credible candidacies.

In the 1990 Alabama governor's race, Guy Hunt had a unique opportunity that should have been better developed. He came to office on a fluke. After a heated election, the duly elected Democratic candidate in 1986 was ruled ineligible according to party rules and the election was overturned in favor of his opponent. The mudslinging that had been a part of the Democratic primary only escalated after the party's ruling and lasted well into the general election period. People became so fed up with the Democrats that voters elected the Republican Hunt. This was quite a feat for a state that had been solidly Democratic since the Civil War. Despite his election, people were wary of Hunt's ability to do the job. Many publicly hoped that he would not make any serious blunders until a new governor could be elected. Surprisingly, after four years they discovered that he had performed quite nicely. He had not been an extraordinary leader; Alabama had not experienced unprecedented growth or significantly changed its public perceptions under

Hunt's administration. However, Alabama had not noticeably suffered under the Hunt administration either. As one "good ol' boy" put it: "He cleaned up real nice."

In the general election period, Hunt initially attempted to pass himself off as a governor who had accomplished great things. The message fell on deaf ears. Next, he attacked his opponent Paul Hubbert's stand on education issues. Hubbert, a former lobbyist for the Alabama Education Association, was too closely aligned with education issues to be harmed. Hubbert was even able to withstand the antiunion sentiment that Hunt tried to exploit. Finally, the Hunt election team seemed to recognize the fact that Hunt's best argument was himself. As a former minister, he stood for decent, honest government. Although Hubbert could find a few chinks in the armor, people basically had no trouble believing that Hunt was an honest man. Hunt was also likeable; people felt good about him. A series of testimonials from citizens around the state played well.

Hunt had done a remarkable job of growing into the job of governor. Although he probably was not the choice that voters would have made had they had found a better alternative in 1986, he had managed to perform admirably. The theme of "growing with Alabama" was alluded to late in the campaign but was never fully developed as a warrant for Hunt's return to office. Hunt offered stability. His next four years might not be progressive or dynamic, but people knew what to expect based on his past four years of service. Sometimes the security of a sure thing is comforting. When Hunt allowed himself to advance the issues that more naturally fit into the public perceptions already held about him, his campaign became infinitely more successful.

Issues like abortion, gun control, or an amendment to the Constitution on flag burning have what communication scholars refer to as high issue saliency (see Infante, 1988, pp. 111–113). They quickly come to mind when people think of election issues. These are the issues on which every candidate is expected to stake a position; however, as Hunt found out, although these issues are important, they are not the only salient issues that may have importance to election outcomes. Less salient issues constitute swing issues by virtue of their importance to an uncommitted segment of voters whom the candidate needs to persuade. In the Hunt–Hubbert race, Hunt's implicit argument was for voters to bet on the known, sure thing. During a time when international tensions over the possibility of war in the Persian Gulf were high, when the budget problem could not be resolved on Capitol Hill, and when economists predicted an upcoming recession, Hunt offered stability. Because such issues are less volatile and controversial, and because they directly affect our future well-being, they command greater persuadability potential than more volatile issues do.

Just as finding the right message is import in constructing a viable, believable image, so is the way in which the message is told. Some communication scholars believe that audiences assimilate information best when it is presented in story form (see, e.g., Deighton, Romer, & McQueen, 1989; McGee & Nelson, 1985). The elements of the story hold the disparate details together in a fashioned unity. Most of us grew up listening to bedtime stories and learning the lessons of our culture via such tales as George Washington and his cherry tree. We are accustomed to filling in gaps in detail and discerning the implications for our own lives from such stories.

In much the same way, campaigns may be viewed as a contest between competing narratives. The campaigns attempt to tell the story, the voter fills in the gaps based on familiarity with the story form, and eventually voters make choices based on their perception of the implications of accepting the story as operative in the governance of their lives.

If we accept this theory, then we can understand why some campaigns are less successful than others. In some cases, campaigns may not provide enough framework for a story. As a result, they fail to provide a sense of unity for the various issue positions (see Smith & Golden, 1988). For example, a voter may not be able to reconcile a candidate's pro-life (antiabortion) position with his stance on the death penalty. Without some understanding of the principles that would permit the candidate to judge one circumstance as acceptable and the other as unacceptable, voters are left to their own devices to determine the saliency of the claims.

In other instances, voters may understand the story but not accept the implications as guiding principles for their own lives. For example, a candidate may portray himself as a real scrapper, willing to fight for the causes in which he believes. Voters may appreciate the story but may philosophically believe that they need a leader who is less testy and more willing to sit down with others and work out solutions.

In other cases, voters get to choose between two or more narratives. Perhaps this can best be illustrated by discussing three stories that were tested for Ronnie Flippo's race for governor of Alabama. After reviewing Flippo's record and talking with him at length about what he believed were the crucial elements of his campaign, his analysts tested three differing stories, each of them true but each with different implications.

1. Ronnie Flippo is a U.S. Congressman from Northern Alabama. He was a construction worker until he was injured on the job at age 23. He then worked his way through college, becoming the first member of his family to receive a college education. Flippo started his own successful business, and later was elected to the Alabama State Senate and eventually to the U.S. Congress. Flippo says that because he has worked for a living and struggled to raise a family as well as working in both state and federal government, he would

be able to understand and respond to the needs of Alabama's working families, if elected Governor.

2. Ronnie Flippo is a U.S. Congressman from Northern Alabama. Flippo says that for the last 25 years the same old crowd has been in control of Alabama. By electing him, Flippo says we can put an end to business as usual in Montgomery. He says we need some fresh ideas and new approaches to the state's problems that would include cutting waste and overhauling the state's revenue structure to make sure that everyone pays their fair share in taxes. Flippo says that only by redesigning the state's revenue structure and closing tax loopholes can we guarantee Alabama's financial security and improve state programs like roads and education.

3. Ronnie Flippo is a U.S. Congressman from Northern Alabama. Flippo says that at present the state does not have the resources needed to achieve economic growth. Flippo says that the state must have a better educated work force, a better system of roads and services, and more decisive leadership in order to take advantage of economic opportunities in the 1990's. Flippo says his record of bringing jobs and economic growth to Northern Alabama shows that he knows how to provide the leadership to improve education and roads, as well as bring jobs. He wants to use his knowledge to improve the state's image and make the changes necessary for statewide economic growth in the 1990's.

Pollsters Mark Mellman and Ed Lazaras tested the effects of these different story lines on voters to see how they accepted them. What they found was that voters liked each of the stories but were particularly persuaded by the second and third ones. The fact that Flippo was not a political insider made him seem more credible as a person who might have new ideas about how to change things.

In this case, the campaign was able to assess the way in which voters would judge three stories, each with different implications for a voting public. The more typical example is the choice between the competing narratives offered by opposing candidates. These judgments similarly require voters to decide which approach is most relevant to their own judgments and values (see Kirkwood, 1983). Just as Flippo tested different stories, each of which was accepted as valid by the audience, so opposing campaigns can offer equally valid but competing story lines to voters.

Voters have other ways of assessing the validity of a candidate's story. One method of evaluating the stories being told during the election is to assess them for their veracity. The narrative fidelity of the story is very important to its potential success. Voters have to believe in the truth of the portrayal in order to accept it as a warrant for their vote. To maintain fidelity also demands that the candidate and the campaign pay close attention to details.

This is another case in which the visual elements of the campaign compel close scrutiny. For example, in one campaign for state representative, the candidate ran an advertisement that was particularly unsuited to his claims. As the grandson of a former senator who was one of the revered political figures of his state, people compared the candidate to his grandfather. He, like his grandfather, was a successful attorney and active in the community. However, unlike his grandfather, the average voter would not consider this man to be a "down-home guy." He had lived a life of privilege. Pictures of the candidate in his home showed him, even as a child, seated with some of the nation's greatest leaders. He had received an exceptional education. He now was employed by a prestigious law firm. When the campaign commercials attempted to portray him as one of the crowd, the voters knew better. When the words he spoke voiced his concern for his child's future, no one could believe that the child whom they viewed on the screen dressed in an expensive coat would ever face the same challenges as their own children. The inconsistencies of these messages concerned the voters. They had to doubt the sincerity of his claims.

Details are important. In part, they lend credence to the story line. Details also provide additional bits of information that help to establish a total picture of the campaign. There must be a sufficient number of details to permit the voter to validate their conclusions.

In 1990, Laura Jo Hamilton ran for district court judge in Madison County, Alabama. She truly wanted this job because she believed that as a judge she could have a positive impact on juveniles who were brought before the court. She had experience dealing with these youngsters and their families because as a prosecuting attorney, she had tried some 4,000 juvenile cases. On almost every occasion she shared with potential voters her concern with upholding community values. The law for her was more than just the legal yardstick of what was right and wrong; it was a means of sustaining the fabric of the community. She argued that a judge's most important responsibility was to take whatever legal action was necessary to help the offender understand the standards of the community. Further, she contended that she understood those values better than her opponents. She was a descendant of two of the community's oldest and best-respected families. She had held offices and memberships in at least fourteen key civic, social, and philanthropic organizations since graduating from law school. She had served the public as a prosecuting attorney for nine years. These were not just isolated facts to her: They were intrinsic to the telling of her story.

Hamilton could have fallen prey to the political wisdom that urges people to avoid specifics. Some pundits hold that name recognition alone is sufficient to win down-ballot races. This logic has two flaws. First, the further down the ballot voters go, the less they tend to vote. This drop-off in overall voter participation leaves these lower-level races more influenced by those who are more familiar with the candidates. Second, in local and regional races, competing candidates may be able to achieve equally high name recognition. Something else must account for why the lever is pulled in one candidate's favor.

The Hamilton campaign believed that the specifics of Hamilton's life and career were central to an understanding of the value system she would put in place if elected judge. Voters might not know the law or how Hamilton would sentence a person on a given offense, but they did come away with a sense of what standards of judgment would be operative.

The narrative format just described may lead the reader to believe that from beginning to end a campaign is orchestrated. In some cases, it is. More often, however, the elements of the story line and plot emerge like a music video. If the pastiche of images in music videos has demonstrated anything, it is that people are quite capable of interpreting messages and determining themes even when they do not follow traditionally organized patterns. The more central element of effectiveness is that all the ingredients are there or that they are omitted with intent for strategic effect.

The danger for campaigns of permitting pastiche images to remain unstructured for long is that they become overly subject to personal interpretation. Campaigns that do not provide audiences with enough information to construct their own stories may have one defined for them by the opposing campaign if it offers a plausible scenario.

In politics, conflict often begins over definitions. The outcome may very well be determined by who defines the opposition first in ways that stick with the voters. In the 1990 Democratic primary for Alabama, one analyst was able to accurately peg the four front-runners as they portrayed themselves to the voters: a lawyer, a lobbyist, a football linebacker, and a legislator. Which role carried the least political baggage and which offered the most potential from which to stake a claim was the subject of some debate.

In the early stages of the election season, comments about these chosen roles were bandied about. The lawyer was portrayed by opponents as slick and manipulative. The lobbyist was viewed as beholden to special interests. The linebacker was considered addled from too many hits. The legislator was thought to be jaded by the political system. The campaigns sought to define the candidates in other terms. The lawyer was not just any lawyer but the state attorney general. He was educated, dedicated to upholding the law, and protective of the rights of the people. The lobbyist was the head of the Alabama Education Association. The PAC money he controlled was an accumulation of the ten- and fifteen-dollar contributions of schoolteachers, not fat cats. If he spoke powerfully for them, it was because education deserved a strong voice in the legislature. The linebacker was not just a piece of flesh but the pride of the state football team. He was portrayed as a leader both on the field and off, a person with skills that exceeded those of the average player. He was better for the job by virtue of his innate gifts. The legislator was a veteran congressman with fourteen years of experience behind him. He knew how to work with the federal government and how to attract federal dollars to the state. He could do for all of Alabama what he had successfully done for his district. Each candidate attempted to define himself while pointing out the negative attributes of the opponents' definitions of themselves. The battle over these descriptions centered on the various interpretations of those images.

Perhaps campaigns are more like music videos than strategists care to admit. The public seems to have an uncanny ability to structure meaningful stories out of isolated details. Although these interpretations are often contradictory, the public is the final arbiter of their meaning and significance.

CONCLUSIONS

Campaigns are comprised of hundreds of images, each flung before the public like flash cards to children. They are generally projected with intent and with the hope that the audience will understand the identifying words written on the back of the image card. When those interpretations are not forthcoming, more clues are given in order to draw the conclusion from the learner. However, politics confuses the simplicity of meaning these childhood games taught us. Just as we think we understand their significance, competing campaigns call out differing interpretations of the images we thought we knew. Each vies for our agreement.

Campaigns will continue to research image variables and attempt to better understand the illusive nature of image interpretation. Campaigns will also attempt to package images in ways that simplify the voters' task and call for their agreement. However, campaigns will be well served to remember that the final arbiter of meaning is the audience. The voters alone decide a candidate's—or an image's—fate.

PART III

THE FACULTY OF OBSERVING A CAMPAIGN'S CRITICAL JUNCTURES

Criticism, Co-optation, and Cynicism: Response Strategies for Handling Hostile Situations

Participants in every campaign hope that the voters and the media will extol their virtues and overlook their flaws. That rarely happens. Most campaigns come complete with a set of dirty laundry. Even when it is not aired in public, it is the source of much internal trepidation and external speculation.

The key factor in how well any campaign can sustain a hostile situation is how well the candidate and public relations team have performed their tasks. The better the public knows a candidate, the better it is able to assess the believability of claims made against him or her. Effective campaigners are ones with whom the audience becomes familiar and whom it comes to view as similar to itself. The candidate who has established this relationship benefits from a more benevolent response. By contrast, a loss of identity with the voters inevitably ensures that when rumors and issue attacks begin, even the more loyal followers have to check in to ask about their validity.

Another critical element in evaluating a campaign's ability to sustain attacks is the ability to foresee potential problems and inoculate the public against spurious claims (see, e.g., Pfau & Kenski, 1990). For example, if a candidate is primarily funded through PACs, the campaign should foresee potential claims of undue influence or vote peddling. Being prepared to respond to negative comments enables the campaign to frame the issue for the public. The facts do not change but the interpretation and significance of the argument can be structured so that the candidate's position is more favorably received. Further, knowing about the nature of pending attacks empowers the campaign to rejoin in a timely manner. Candidates may be able to disarm the negative assaults and perhaps even put a positive spin on the issue.

The bottom line in any campaign is that given the relatively short periods of time during which elections are waged, a campaign cannot afford to stay on the defensive. This is particularly true during the closing days of the campaign. At a time when fragile swing-vote coalitions are beginning to lean toward one candidate or another, campaigns cannot afford to have outcomes affected by matters that should have already been settled. Negative factors should be acknowledged and the substance of the arguments addressed in the early stages of the process.

The question that inevitably arises during each election cycle is why campaigns have to be so negative. In part, the answer rests with the nature of the event. In political affairs, public criticism of incumbents and acute appraisals of challenger appeals are necessary ingredients of effective decision making. In the current political climate in local politics, voters are rarely provided with information that distinguishes candidates except as instigated by the campaigns themselves.

In truth, issue debates and positive campaigns do not generate the public interest required for responsible decision making. Many voters are either not willing or sufficiently competent to research candidate claims themselves. Unless these claims are challenged by the opponents, news media decline to cover positive issue debates in favor of more stimulating news items.

A headline in the *Washington Post* (2 June 1990, p. A6) provided evidence for this claim. Just four days before the Alabama gubernatorial primary, the headline read "Clean Campaign Proves Duller Than Dirt." It discussed the standing of four leading contenders who were running relatively positive campaigns. None was able to break away from the others. Each held 20 to 24 percent of the vote. Using a traditional "news" criteria, no compelling issues emerged to foster public reactions to issues. The polls still showed that 15 to 20 percent of the voters were undecided.

Similar patterns are observed in smaller campaigns. One state senator prepared for a positive free-media blitz by visually demonstrating the kinds of work he had been performing for the citizens of his district over the last four years. He had state appropriations money ready for dispersal to numerous worthy civic groups. However, press releases, photo opportunities, and personal solicitations could not stimulate media coverage. After hours of long work, the only coverage was one picture buried in the evening newspaper with only a short caption. The media judged his "good deeds" as politically motivated and, therefore, as suspect. The use of positive press events is often viewed as an attempt to manipulate the press, yet the press does not make a similar claim when one candidate calls the other a liar or a cheat.

Roger Ailes called this phenomenon his orchestra pit theory of politics.

"If you have two guys on stage and one guy says, 'I have a solution to the Middle East problem,' and the other guy falls into the orchestra pit, who do you think is going to be on the evening news?" (as cited in Runkle, 1989, p. 136).

Such examples provide support for the theory that political campaigns work, for better or worse, as dramas in which a real-life conflict unfolds before a public and is resolved by the voters. People are not content to watch an uneventful show. They seem to have a need for controversy to make the story interesting, if nothing else.

No less an issue is the fact that a campaign, as the military term implies, is based on winning and losing. Both teams will make errors. The outcome is often determined by the team that commits errors that are then capitalized on by the opposition. Given this perspective, many campaigns use whatever strategy it takes to get coverage and exploit opponent weaknesses.

In order to understand the strategic nature of criticism, two areas must be addressed. First, candidates must understand the impact of implied criticism that arises out of rumors and inuendo. Second, candidates should understand the use of issues as weapons. Given this perspective, an analysis of response strategies can be discussed.

THE NATURE OF EFFECTIVE RUMORS

Rumors are typically initiated when other channels of communication are closed down. Four factors typically affect the choice to disseminate information across these more informal routes. First, the attacks may not be able to be substantiated well enough to avoid legal repercussions. In this case, the information being circulated may be reasonably accurate but derived from sources that refuse to go on record. Without that documentation, the campaign cannot take the issue public.

This happens so often in political campaigns that it provides an almost irresistible opportunity. Information just appears at the campaign's doorstep—information for which no one asked. The nature of the information is often so compelling that it spreads even when the campaign would prefer it not be disseminated.

Frequently, the information comes from highly credible sources. Sometimes the source may be a relative, a disgruntled client of the opponent, the opposition's business partner, or, amazingly, someone on the opposition's own strategy team. Assessing the motives of these sources is difficult. However, without confirmation from reliable sources that are willing to verify the claims to the watching public, the chances for becoming engaged in a lawsuit are greatly increased. As a result, the rumor circuit is the preferred tool.

Second, almost as an outgrowth of the first factor, rumormongers love to spread information in cases where the nature of the communication is privileged. The emergence of the information means that either someone close to the person being attacked has leaked confidential information or that the information was obtained through illegal means. Police records, college activities and achievement scores, and medical records inevitably find their way into the opposition's possession. When this information provides insight that voters can use to make a decision, the rumor mill is the chosen channel of dissemination because of its ability to achieve the objective and yet protect the source.

Sometimes even privileged information on the rumor circuit is magnified by the press because the leaks constitute good news copy. In the 1990 Alabama governor's race, one headline received a lot of local attention. The Huntsville *Times* (30 September 1990, p. 5E) noted in its headline, "A Fiasco for Hubbert: GOP's Folmar Steals Democratic 'Bombshell.' " The Democrats had been leading an attack against Governor Guy Hunt that raised "serious questions" about his finances. They had called for Hunt to release his income tax returns—if he had nothing to hide. In one particularly damaging attack, the Democrats produced a check from Hunt's 1986 campaign written to a bank that held the mortgage on some Hunt property. Using campaign funds to pay off personal debt is, of course, a serious charge. However, the Republicans were able to alter the public perception of events through a combination of timing and opportunity. Emory Fulmar, Hunt's chief fund-raiser, produced a document prepared by a consultant for the Hubbert campaign. It detailed a number of "press hits" against Hunt. One was particularly relevant to the Democratic attack. It said that if the Democrats hoped to win, they had to keep the focus on one central question: "Is Hunt a crook?" The Hunt campaign made the consultant's report public and then argued that this whole attack was nothing more than a dirty campaign strategy by the Democrats and warranted no response.

As shown in this example, rumor circuits may be used to let opponents know the kinds of materials that are available about them. The confidential nature of privileged information poses an implied threat. Even if the information only circulates across the rumor circuit, it can have devastating effects on a campaign. If a candidate knows that the opposition has information reaching into the most private aspects of a person's personal life or confidential campaign materials, the campaign has to realize the potential for the opposition to use that information if the campaign gets too heated or close. As the Hunt case demonstrated, campaigns are perfectly willing to use that information when they find it necessary to do so.

A third factor influencing the use of the rumor mill is that the nature of the communication is considered to be in poor taste via more public channels of communication. People are often quite comfortable telling dirty jokes or making off-color remarks among friends in a one-to-one setting, things they would be embarrassed to do in public. Rumors are no different. Spread along formal channels of communication, a backlash would occur. Spread informally among friends, however, the information is juicy enough to warrant deliberation.

A fourth factor that encourages the use of the rumor mill is that the information is spread from friend to friend. As a consequence, it is given the same reliability and credibility as the person who spreads the rumor. In some ways, using the rumor mill is preferable to making charges in a more public way, sometimes even when the charges can be verified. In a public channel the information may be discounted since the obvious motive of the communicator is to discredit the opposition. In the rumor mill, however, those motives are concealed.

In political campaigns—particularly on the regional and local levels—rumors are not something that strategists can ignore. They are of critical importance to the opposition since they can quickly undo months of good work. The rumor mill is used for specific reasons. The information that is disseminated across rumor circuits may also be strategic in character.

Typically, strategic rumors flow out of accurate perceptions. There must be some grounding in reality that gives credence to even the most spurious claim. Huntsville, Alabama, Mayor Steve Hettinger and his wife, Bonnie, have faced the same problem almost since Hettinger began his political career. The rumor stems from two accurate claims. First, the couple has always kept matters about their personal lives private. Families of major public figures often live in a fishbowl, and the Hettingers have always been concerned about the effect of public life on their two children. Bonnie overtly shields their two girls from some public gatherings, preferring them to engage in other activities in which they can have more fun and just be themselves. By contrast, the very nature of the mayor's job requires him to be out among the public and to attend the numerous functions at which his attendance is expected. As a result, the public does not see the whole Hettinger family together very often.

The second factor in the development of the rumor is that both the Hettingers are attractive. These factors have provided the truthful basis for a vicious and hurtful rumor. Almost inevitably, whenever the mayor is riding a wave of popular approval, a rumor develops that he is having an extramarital affair. The person with whom he is purportedly having the affair is always attractive and competent, and typically serves in a position in which she must work closely with the mayor. The rumor mill stokes the fire with "insider information" about fights between Bonnie and Steve which, because of their private nature, no one can really verify nor deny. The rumor always suggests that proof for the claim can be demonstrated by the fact that the couple rarely appears in public together. Those who know the couple immediately dismiss the rumors. In fact, when the rumors started during his 1988 campaign, defenders became so outraged that they extolled the virtues of the Hettinger marriage to the point where the Hettingers became viewed for a time as an idyllic representation of the American family.

Rumors are rarely true, but they are designed so that they weave the truth in and out of the story line. Similar rumors abound when an attractive, single female rapidly rises to a prominent corporate position. The rise is rarely attributed to competence but rather to some licentious behavior.

Effective rumors also characteristically have a built-in argument that, *if understood*, unifies people in some perception of the candidate. In a sheriff's race, copies of legal documents circulated stating that the incumbent had fathered an illegitimate child after a tryst in the back of a car. Another document detailed the events that lead to a divorce from his first wife as a result of his physically abusive behavior. The rumor mill failed to note with equal vigor that the events took place some thirty to forty years ago or to mention his current attitudes and behaviors.

There was clearly a moral argument evident in the dissemination of this information. There were also implied arguments that were far more intriguing, though in this case they were never sufficiently clarified to damage the incumbent's campaign. The implied arguments were that the sheriff did not respect the law and that he did not respect women. Consequently, as a leader of the police force, he did not set an appropriate example for his staff to follow.

These issues were particularly significant at the time of the election. The area had recently undergone a series of problems in police handling of some explosive situations. The news stories stressed abuse-of-power questions. One might reason that perhaps the strong-arm tactics used by the police were condoned, if not perpetrated, by a boss who himself had a violent nature.

Another event in the headlines alleged that a police officer had, on at least two occasions, pulled a woman over for traffic violations and then raped her. Again, the implied argument was that such activity was not outside the moral boundaries of the sheriff and might even be privately condoned. Given the increasing numbers of women voters, pulling them together to create a gender factor for the race would certainly be to an opponent's advantage.

Was it coincidence that these headline events correlated with the rumor mill's dissemination of information about the sheriff's personal life? Even though no connection could be made between the events and any of the sheriff's employees reporting directly to him, the potential for such violation was a focal point for the rumor mill.

Had these arguments ever developed across more public channels, they might have been strong enough to pull away would-be supporters who expected the law to be tough but also required it to be practiced ethically and fairly. Some people made the connection between the news events and the rumored information on their own. Most people, however, were not well enough read on current events to make the connection. Whether or not they understood the full implications, the rumor met its fundamental goal by serving to drive a moral wedge between the candidates. The rest was media baiting which, in this case, was not responded to.

Effective rumors are also spun out of fantastic situations. Like the concept of "Ripley's Believe It or Not," people are always quick to disseminate information that is too bizarre to be true. This strategy is the implementation of the "big lie" theory. People will not typically believe the little lies; they can be verified or denied too easily. A big lie, by contrast, leads people to the assumption that no one would invent something so incredible. Therefore, they reason, it must be true.

Consider this example. Undercover police officers working a neighborhood street witnessed a woman jump out of a car, pull up a yard sign, and throw it in a drainage ditch. There had been a rash of yard sign vandalism recently so the officers stopped the car in which the woman was riding. The officers then called the candidate whose sign had been destroyed. The candidate had expected to find juveniles who were just being mischievous. When she got to the scene, however, she found four very prominent citizens of the community. Even more fantastic, the woman who had actually committed the offense was the opposition's daughter. This scenario is every campaign's dream. It hints of dirty tricks or foul play, and it is rather funny to see the opposition put in the hot seat because of its own actions. Moreover, it creates a political wildfire on the rumor circuit.

Rumors about such behaviors spread amazingly fast—sometimes told in outrage against the perpetrators, and sometimes told tongue-in-cheek as a "Can you believe this one?" event. The substance of such fantastic rumors usually occurs by accident. Nonetheless, this is the stuff on which reputations are built or destroyed.

Effective rumors also spotlight a specific, narrow area that is hard to defend and easy to exploit, and that makes a lasting impression on the hearers. Information leaked throughout one campaign attempted to portray an opposition candidate as a liberal. Circulating newspaper clippings showing the candidate in 1960s protest marches and pictures of him with long hair and the ragged clothing of the day helped bolster the perception. The crowning bit of information alleged that he had also used illegal drugs. Given what people had already seen, the use of drugs would not have been a surprise. There was no evidence that the candidate had ever been arrested on drug charges, nor was there any corroborating evidence to strengthen the claim. Nonetheless, the information did not seem sufficient to sway their vote to the other side. The more significant damage occurred when a barrage of advertisements combined with the rumor circuit in asking how effective a candidate would be in leading the war on drugs when he himself had been a part of the drug culture.

The attacked candidate was in an awkward position. Even if he was innocent, it would be almost impossible to prove that he had never taken drugs. If such a denial were offered, given the pictures and other supporting circumstantial evidence, it would be viewed as suspicious. The rumor was easy to exploit. Further, it had real implications for a race in which issues of drug control were a major voter concern and one on which the officeholder would have enormous impact. The rumor also helped to nurture a lasting impression that labeled the candidate as a liberal, a druggie, and a renegade. In a conservative era, those images sounded a potential death knell.

Often campaigns find that responding to a rumor can make things worse. Suppose a judicial candidate is, according to the opposition, not qualified to serve because he lacks keen legal insight. Rumor supports the assertion, claiming that the candidate graduated last in his law class. After checking, the candidate learns that he did graduate in the lower half of the class but not nearly at the bottom. The campaign persuades the candidate to stay quiet and to refrain from defending his honor. The rumor mill steps up the assault, claiming that the candidate failed the bar examination the first time and had to retake it. Most lawyers know that this is not an uncommon occurrence, but the public does not seem to grasp it in the same way. The accused has little room in which to make a stand. To go public would be to admit that his grades in law school had not been stellar. Anything less than outstanding academic qualifications would support the contention that the candidate did not possess a keen knowledge of the law. It would further cause the candidate to publicly admit to failing the bar exam the first time. Essentially, this is a no-win scenario. A candidate cannot strengthen his position by denying that he was last in his law class and proving instead that he graduated in the bottom half of the class. Nor will he make a strong case to be a judge by publicly admitting that he failed the bar exam.

Used offensively, part of the strategy of an effective rumor is to provoke the opposition into publicly defending a claim that only the candidate can verify or deny. In such cases, a candidate will shoot him- or herself in the foot by publicly airing information that the opposition was gracious enough not to publicly address. If a candidate makes it seem as if he or she has been forced to make a statement regarding the issue, things will only look worse. The public may speculate that the information must be true since the candidate addressed the issue only when forced to do so. On the other hand, if the public has not heard the rumor, it may assume that the candidate's claims that the charge was being perpetrated by the opponent are unfounded. Without direct proof, the audience is more likely to believe that the rumor surfaced somewhere other than in the opponent's camp.

What voters will believe is that the candidate was looking for a scapegoat. To have a skeleton in the closet and then make it look like the opposition's fault is to misdirect the issue. The public is pretty astute at perceiving that tactic.

Another characteristic of effective rumors is that they leave a path for people to follow. In the case in which the rumors spoke of the candidate's involvement in 1960s protest marches, a quick check of news clipping files revealed several pictures of the candidate participating. The press chose to broadcast the evidence to support the rumor but without counterbalancing information about the circumstances in which the demonstrations were held.

Effective rumors typically have solid information to back them. They lead the press and other people who are trying to do good work to uncover materials that are juicy enough to print. The rumor mill is a valuable tool for reporters to supply tips to potential stories. Reporters are constantly fed information by the competing sides in the race. Each campaign hopes that it will be able to attract a good reporter's research efforts. As much as anything else, campaigns are aware that any time that crack investigative reporters set out to conduct thorough research, they will inevitably find something, even if it is not proof of the original rumor. Rumor mills only serve to whet the investigators' interest and provide them with a direction.

Those bits of uncovered information serve to legitimize the information on the rumor circuit, making it more effective for those who would pass along as credible information that has no basis in fact. This is perhaps the most damaging aspect of the rumor strategy. The rumor circuit is typically pretty accurate because its initial screening of information is thorough. Following a series of reliable tidbits of information, new information is passed along with less scrutiny. Harmful, deceitful information can thus be passed along by people who have no intention of spreading fallacious data.

Conversely, information can be planted with the intent of ruining a reliable information-gathering chain, much as a computer virus affects computer networks. Planted information can then be proven false, thus thwarting future attempts to disseminate information along the same routes.

Effective rumors are used to inflict damage on the opponent, even though some will never reach the public. Rumors cut to the deepest realms of our emotional well-being. They often concern issues that are too sensitive for public dissemination. Frequently, they are intended to disable the opposition at a critical time in the campaign process. Candidates can spend so much time feeling hurt and angry that they abandon the business at hand.

Rumors work. Regardless of how much we may wish to ignore rumor strategies, they are part of the political landscape in local and regional elections. They will continue to impact the candidates, their families, and their campaigns, sometimes with devastating results.

Rumors even work on national candidacies. Most people can recall the impact of leaked information just after Tom Eagleton's vice presidential bid in 1972. Quite simply, the fact that he had been under medical care for emotional problems was the crowning blow to his candidacy. The Democrats may have been able to overcome the perception, but they realized that it would consume all their time and energy while they simultaneously let other issues slip away. Other candidates make similar choices, virtually withdrawing from the campaign in order to prevent further attacks, sometimes leaving their names on the ballot but otherwise closing down their campaigns. They are simply not willing to put their family and friends through more emotional stress.

Rumor mongering does occasionally backfire. In the 1988 Huntsville, Alabama, mayoral race, the persistent rumor of Steve Hettinger conducting an extramarital affair surfaced once again. Friends defended the Hettingers. Simultaneously, the campaign launched an assault to provide a glimpse of the private lives of a relatively normal, happy family. In commercials, public appearances, speeches, and even on the rumor circuit, family themes were clarified. Survey results showed that the image of Hettinger as a stable family man was readily accepted.

Whether or not the affair rumor was started by the opposing candidate, it *was* started by someone who wanted Hettinger to lose. The ironic consequence was that while Hettinger was able to overcome the initial negative story, his opponent was not. His opponent was a single father with two young boys. The more people viewed the classic family portrait of the Hettingers, the more they became aware of the hardships and responsibilities of a single parent facing a very demanding public role. The issue clearly hurt Hettinger's opponent.

As this example illustrates, strategic rumors often affect both candidates. The rumor mill initially attacked Hettinger but ended up hurting the candidate whom it was designed to help. Understanding the consequences and long-term scenario of a rumor is critical to its effective use.

Of all the things that concern me about the nature of the rumor as a political tool, one stands out. During the heat of a campaign, it is almost impossible to assess who has started a rumor or with what intended purpose. The ultimate arbiter of who gains or loses is the public.

During one Huntsville election season, my husband and I were surprised by a flier that had been placed on our windshield during church. It compared Christian teachings and doctrine to that of the Mormons. Initially this was confusing, but a section at the bottom of the flier held political implications. It noted that of the two candidates running for a particular office, one was a Christian and the other a Mormon. We were outraged, as were a lot of other people who discovered the message.

There was no source of information cited on the flier, so it is hard to determine who sent the material out. The first conclusion was that it was disseminated by the Christian candidate, who was hoping to exploit prejudicial feelings and augment value differences in regard to his opponent. The majority of people to whom I spoke interpreted the materials in this way. They were outraged and vowed to vote against any candidate who would stoop that low. The thing that has always puzzled me is that the timing could not have been worse for an audience to receive such a message. When received after church, in which the typical message is to love your neighbor, such a blatant message of hatred seemed so incredibly stupid that I began to wonder if it had been put out by the Mormon candidate in order to achieve just that effect. The third possibility is that it was put out by some party acting independently with either these or other motives. The truth will never be known, but the effect of the message was overwhelming. The attacked candidate became the beneficiary of an enormous sympathy vote.

People will inevitably comment on the appropriateness of using rumor mills and negative attacks. While those debates are raging, however, the tactics are being effectively utilized to provide a winning edge for one candidate. Whether or not a campaign chooses to use these tactics, planners should be aware of the potential for their use and abuse, because without understanding how the rumor mill works, a person cannot hope to defend against it.

Not all attacks use the rumor mill, however, some devastating attacks use issues as weapons.

ISSUES AS WEAPONS

Many people do not understand what an issue is in a campaign context. Taking a stand on something like abortion or gun control does not mean that these will be issues for the campaign. They are only potential issues. A topic achieves issue status only when it becomes a point of clash between the opponents.

There are several ways of finding out what topics might make interesting, and winnable, issues. Polls are effective tools for finding out what is on voters' minds. Even candidates who cannot afford to commission their own private poll can get some assistance by studying the results of national polls. These can be found in almost every university library. *Editorial Research Reports* and Gallup polling results provide a rich source of data. However, it must be remembered that in order to be effective, the topics must have significance to the candidate and the local constituents.

For example, education has been a national priority throughout the 1980s. During that time, the public has been calling for an improved educational system. Typically, voters want better results on student exit exams. However, the problem has a slightly different focus when examined in terms of changes in the local school system. In one area it may be teacher salary increases, and in another, better discipline. Each school system and community is unique.

There are numerous ways of identifying these localized concerns. In Huntsville, Alabama, the Vision 2000 Policy Board conducted a series of hearings on local issues. This citizen panel also recommended the goals and objectives that should lead the city into the year 2000. Anyone who attended those hearings could get a pretty clear picture of the topics on people's minds.

Localizing issues not only demonstrates the candidate's knowledge, it also helps establish proof for the argument that the people want something done. It assures the voters that the campaign is paying attention to their unique problems. Candidates should remember that successful campaigns develop accurate portrayals of voters' passions and concerns. These issues are persuasive because they reflect issues that voters believe will directly affect their future well-being (see Lang & Lang, 1968, p. 16; Petty & Cacioppo, 1981; Schwartz, 1973).

Issues are important for obvious reasons. They receive a lot of media attention. In part this is because people like a contest. News organizations capitalize on hotly disputed issues to foster the competition. Some strategists speculate that challenger-led issues attract media attention because news ratings increase in a close race. As a result, the news covers underdog attacks in order to help even the odds, foster competition, and augment their own profits.

Whatever position a person accepts as true, the bottom line is that issue clashes provide major news coverage. Every campaign has to be concerned about the free media licks that the opponent is able to get. No campaign can afford to give the opposition free media time by responding to charges that would otherwise dwindle away without comment. Neither can it constantly play catch-up by defensively responding to the challenge of the day. Issues in this sense are the media-driven weapons of campaigns.

More important, issues serve as ways of distinguishing one campaign and its accompanying value structure from another. They are symbols of the political order, representing value systems and approaches to governance. In this sense, when news organizations cover political issues, they convey a lot more information to the public than simply informing them who stands for what.

An issue may also serve as a constituency-building tool. It is a rallying point around which people may gather, and represents a public's values. When a campaign loses an issue in a campaign, it also loses real votes and numbers of supporters.

There is another class of issues that I refer to as pseudo-issues. These are used as bait to draw media attention and lure the public away from the opposition. Suppose there is a race in which neither candidate has a strong environmental stance. The polling data indicate that voters who hold strong environmental positions do not have a viable representative. Cross-tabulations indicate that they are leaning toward the incumbent because of other issues that also guide their choices. If the incumbent is vulnerable because of environmental votes or positions, a challenger may very well launch an attack for the purpose of siphoning away those voters. Importantly, the goal of this strategy is not to win voters by virtue of the challenger's strength but on the basis on the opposition's weakness.

The use of pseudo-issues is an opponent-based strategy that requires some consideration. Many voters have become cynical because they no longer believe a politician's motives to be honorable. Pseudo-issues are largely responsible for this perception. Candidates may take a stand or launch an attack against their opponents on a controversial issue not because they are committed to the issue but because they are attempting to broaden their electoral base. We have all heard people comment that politicians will say anything to get elected, especially when they take a stand on some issue late in the campaign. To some extent, these perceptions are correct. Once a candidate's core constituency has been defined, polling data will divulge whether that public comprises a majority of the voters. If it does not, the candidate has to broaden the base of support by reaching out to those who have not yet found a suitable representative. If that still does not produce a majority, the candidate is forced to consider ways of taking voters away from the opposition.

These pseudo-issues work more effectively when certain conditions exist. First, the candidate should have made every attempt to win through a combination of the core constituency and appeals to undecided voters. Campaigns that are successful in creating a winning coalition on this basis are freed from the encumbering stigma attack to dirty politics. They can take the higher moral ground and contend that personal attacks are not necessary in political elections.

Second, the nature of the issue attack must be analyzed for any potential vulnerability it may cause in the candidate launching the attack. For example, a candidate with a poor environmental record will not be able to serve as a viable alternative once the environmental voters have been drawn away from the opposition. This is particularly important during primaries in which there are multiple contenders. The number two candidate may draw away a number of voters from the front-runner only to discover that those votes went to another candidate who was third or fourth before the attack was launched. This leads to the third condition.

Attacks should not be launched until the candidate is positioned to reap the benefits from the attack. In Mayor Hettinger's election, we had an effective way of lumping the three front-runners together as insiders who had created many of the problems that the city faced. However, before that attack could be launched, voters had to be convinced that even though Hettinger was an outsider, he was not inexperienced. We had to be able to demonstrate that he had the know-how to do the job or else no winner would emerge from the attack phase.

Fourth, attacks should only be launched in areas in which the opponent has "high negatives." No candidate is perfect. Just because an issue weakens a candidacy does not mean that it will affect the outcome. Attack strategies can be very successful when the data has been carefully scrutinized. In order to determine a candidate's strength, polling data are analyzed. One method, for example, measures hard name recognition by tallying those who not only recognize the name but also have valuative opinions on the candidate's job performance. The ratio between those who think the candidate is doing a good job and those who think the candidate is doing a poor job is calculated, and the contenders with low ratios become the target of the attacks.

In Congressman Ronnie Flippo's 1990 race for Alabama governor, the initial statewide poll showed that Flippo had hard name identification among 36 percent of the state's voters. He was viewed favorably by 31 percent and unfavorably by 5 percent. Thus, his favorable to unfavorable ratio was an impressive 6.2 to 1. Any candidate who falls below a 2 to 1 ratio is considered vulnerable.

Analysis such as this provides valuable information as to how attack strategies can be directed. Opponents with high positive–negative ratios can be attacked with good results only by directing the attacks to the issues, not the person. Disagreeing with even the most highly regarded and prominent statesman on issues is not unpatriotic or demeaning. However, care must be taken not to attempt to disgrace the person by discrediting some issue stance. Otherwise, voters may become hardened against the attacker.

Attacks often center on issues other than an opponent's character. Positive–negative ratings can be broken down by demographics and issue positions. From this research, a voter profile begins to emerge. "Typical" supporters can be identified in terms of their characteristics. Campaigns can learn the profile of those voters who are their hard-core supporters, those who are adamantly against them, and those who lean in one direction or another. Using this information, the candidate can begin to determine how coalitions can best be built or how wedges can be placed to keep coalitions from being formed by the opposition.

The old adage contends that knowledge is power. In political campaigns, that is decidedly true. Campaigns no longer need to rely purely on speculation about which strategies will work. They are armed with audience analyses that guide their choices and increase their chances for success. The question is whether the campaign has the ability to follow through and act on that information. Having a powerful tool is unproductive unless the campaign is willing to use it and knows how to use it well.

Much time is spent analyzing specific races on the basis of issue analysis. Analysts may claim that the race was won or lost because of a candidate's stand on a certain issue. That is a simplistic analysis of the persuasive process. It is more accurate to say that a particular issue served a critical function in the campaign.

Remember that issues can either unite publics or siphon them away from the opposition. Opposition camps cannot control the first type of issue. The concerns of candidates and their core constituencies define them and their value systems. However, candidates do have some input into the pseudo-issues that are designed to draw voters away from their campaigns.

Pseudo-issues are generally taken very personally by the candidate who is attacked. Their intent is to pull away people who were at least leaning in favor of the candidate. People who have made tenuous commitments require more than information that highlights a single issue discrepancy. Compelling information must be produced that will first create doubts about their choice and ultimately provide opportunities for persuasion that will change their opinions of their candidate.

There are numerous strategies for using issues as wedges against the opposition. Four of them merit significant attention. They are built on fundamental principles of persuasion. Given this framework, issues must be considered in light of the principle they employ, not on the merits of the issue itself.

One type of wedge is developed by demonstrating through issue attacks that the relationship between the opponent and the voting public is an inequitable one. Relationships are built on premises of give and take (see Cialdini, 1988, pp. 20–29). People have obligations to one another that they are expected to fulfill. This strategy seeks to demonstrate that the opponent has not kept good faith on a promise of service.

In Bill Smith's 1990 Alabama Senate campaign, the opposition made the argument that Smith had not represented his constituents well. One man testified in a commercial that he had tried to reach the senator by phone fifty-one times and that the senator had never responded. Failing to return phone calls is hardly a crime. Messages are often lost or displaced. Fifty-one unreturned calls, however, is not a normal behavior. It implies that the calls were intentionally not returned. It makes people question why this happened.

The attack in and of itself was not critical. Many people regarded it as a nuisance tactic. However, if the public believes that their elected representatives have an obligation to hear their points of view, as most of them do, then the attack takes on new significance. It serves as one illustration that the senator was not willing to enter into a reciprocal relationship with his constituents. If the voters accept this analysis and can support it with other corroborating evidence from their own experience, they have good reason to withhold their vote from Smith and look for another choice.

Voters elect officials with the understanding that in return for that vote, the official agrees to represent their interests. It is a mutually beneficial relationship. Once a compelling argument is presented stating that the exchange is inequitable, there is little need to sustain the relationship.

A second wedge between opponents and their constituencies can be created by demonstrating that the opponent has inconsistent behaviors on important issues. Inconsistency is not considered to be a desirable personality trait (see, e.g., Allgeier, Byrne, Brooks, & Revnes, 1979). Voters dislike politicians whom they view as two-faced or spineless (Allgeier et al., 1979). A challenge of this sort leaves doubts in the voters' minds about the opponent's motives and reliability. By contrast, a consistent person is viewed as more trustworthy (for a review of research on consistency, see Bostrom, 1983, pp. 88–107).

One of the standard television commercials explicates this technique. The formula for the ad documents what a candidate claimed to believe and then shows that he acted in a manner inconsistent with that belief. The claim is made that the opponent is willing to say anything to get elected. Voters are, in essence, urged not to regard the opponent as honest or forthright. At the end of the ad, the voters are offered a more honorable alternative. The ad thus raises provocative questions. Can the opponent be trusted? Is his word good? Who influenced him to change his mind?

A third tactic for driving a wedge is achieved by demonstrating a developing trend of voters who have broken away from the opponent. Social proof is a powerful took (see Cialdini, 1988, pp. 108–155). We learn from those whom we trust. We seek others out to confirm or deny our perceptions or events in order to see if we have a similar reading of the situation (Noelle-Neumann, 1974a). This strategy seeks to amplify the viewpoints of people from within the opponent's camp who have decided to seek another choice. Testimonial devices are frequently used in the early stages of a campaign to build social proof in favor of a candidate. This strategy can also be used to tear people away from the opponent.

In one particularly competitive primary election, the contestants developed an assault mentality. Every day the headlines were filled with charges and countercharges. The public wearied of this rapidly. For a time, no one seemed to recognize that one candidate had refused to play the game. Two things happened. First, the other campaigns left that candidate alone because he was not considered a threat. Consequently, he was not muddied by the "assault brigade." Second, he launched his strategy in the closing days of the campaign when his opponents had already been bloodied and had little chance to recover and no time to effectively respond. The advertisements showed people who echoed the public sentiment. They stated that they were tired of the constant negative attacks, including those by candidates for whom they had originally intended to vote. At the end of the ad, each person vowed to vote for the one candidate who had maintained his values, and thus had risen above the crowd.

Had the candidate made the same claim himself, the message would not have created the social proof needed to give the perception motivational force. It took others with whom the voter identified and who were perceived to have no biasing stake in the election to give the message its persuasive power (Arnold & McCroskey, 1967). Moreover, because they were once in an opposition camp, their credibility is viewed as higher than that of other people. In the particular case cited, the strategy worked. Voters swarmed to the candidate.

A fourth method of creating a wedge is to demonstrate the dissimilarities between opponents and their constituencies. People like those who are perceived as similar to themselves (see, e.g., Byrne, 1971). In the early stages of a campaign, constituent-building efforts focus on demonstrating the commonalities between candidates and their publics. Attempts are also made to familiarize the voter with the personality and reputation of a candidate. Political figures must be viewed as sufficiently similar to their public to be considered representative. Further, people tend to make assumptions about others based on their level of familiarity with them. In fact, familiarity serves as an indicator of voting behavior (see, e.g., Grush, 1980; Grush, McKeough, & Ahlering, 1978). One method of disrupting that relationship is to present sufficient information to show that opposition candidates are poor representative choices because of the difference between them and their respective publics.

U.S. Senator Howell Heflin had been attacked by his 1990 opponent for being a Washington politician, too distant from Alabamians to represent them well. Heflin replied by providing evidence of the number and frequency of visits and speaking engagements within the state. Following that, Heflin countered with an attack against his opponent that illustrates the use of dissimilarity quite clearly. Heflin's ads visually portrayed his opponent Bill Cabaniss as a very wealthy member of Birmingham's elite. In both verbal and visual claims, Heflin was able to show that Cabaniss was not the "good ol' boy" that he wanted people to believe he was. In fact, the more the public saw Cabaniss, the less they seemed to have in common with him. While there may have been some truth to Cabaniss's claim that Heflin had become part of the Washington corps, polling data indicated that he was still viewed as more like the people of Alabama than was Cabaniss.

Although these are not the only methods of dividing publics, they are four of the more prevalent strategies used. Understanding the purpose of the attacks makes the choice of response easier to make.

RUMOR AND REMEDY

Once attacks begin to saturate the circuit, the object of the attack must determine the appropriate response. In every campaign that I have been associated with or read about, some crucial point has emerged. How the campaign handles an attack may be more significant than the attack itself. It is as if the campaign is a small recreation of a larger world stage. If George Bush cannot respond effectively to rumors of an extramarital affair (a rumor that actually did surface and quickly died in the 1988 election season), how will he be able to cope with rumors of U.S. covert operations abroad that supposedly attempted to unseat a duly elected leader?

Voters seem to realize that people will make mistakes and that campaigns will face unexpected problems. Many of the voters will face some of the same dilemmas themselves during their lives. The critical question then is not who chopped down the cherry tree but how that person responded when the act came to the attention of others.

There are numerous approaches that a campaign can take in response to a hostile attack. None is superior. Each situation calls for clear, level-headed thinking. Each attack is unique and requires strategies tailored to fit the specific circumstance. In each situation, it takes time for rational thinking to emerge. The first reaction is shock, the second is anger, and the third is to fantasize about retribution. This is followed by a calm, after which some sense of rationality takes over and a more effective strategy can be established.

The immediate chore is to allow this scenario to run its course. Campaigns that are too quick to respond may end up sabotaging themselves. They must take the time that is necessary to understand the attack, its intent, and the probable effects and outcomes.

Much time is wasted in the initial hours following an attack by guessing who is to blame. The more important question to address is whom the public perceives to be behind the slur and how it will respond to the substance of the attack. I recall a line in a play entitled *Mary, Queen of Scots* that says something to the effect: "It is not what happens that matters. Nay, not even what happens that's true . . . but what men believe to have happened. I control that, being who I am." This is the sentiment that campaigns should echo in the early hours of strategy setting. An accurate perception of the public's interpretation of the events is critical.

Further, getting an assessment of who currently controls an image is crucial in determining an appropriate response. Sometimes the information remains in the sole possession of the rumor mongers. Once the information becomes more public, the press may control an image. Sometimes control lies with a specific group or individual. In order to intercede effectively in the process, a campaign must know what (or who) the public believes the campaign to be up against.

Also critical to the process is an accurate reading of the candidate's involvement with the issue. No one likes to admit to having acted irresponsibly or having made mistakes in judgment. Candidates are no different. The worst thing a campaign can do is to mount a full-scale rejoinder to demonstrate the candidate's innocence only to discover later that there is incontrovertible evidence that proves the candidate's guilt. Truth has a way of coming out. Moreover, attacks are not usually built on only a single case. Had Joseph Biden (D- Delaware) been found to have quoted text without properly attributing the source on only one occasion, the charge during the 1988 election that he had plagiarized portions of a major campaign speech would have been regarded as an unfortunate mistake. Substantive attacks are those that aim at the heart of a candidate's character and methods of approaching ethical issues. They become substantive because the behaviors around which the attack centers have occurred more than once. Even the most groundless attack must be assessed to find the one scintilla of truth on which the claims were founded. Armed with that information, the choice of strategy options is clarified.

The two over-arching strategy variables are defense and offense. It is not unusual for campaigns to attempt to control the situation through defensive efforts before turning to the more aggressive plans.

The first defensive strategy is merely to watch the drama play itself out. When rumors or issue attacks do not merit a campaign's attention or response, the matter will sometimes fade away on its own. This requires the campaign to fight the immediate impulse to respond, retort, or make some defense. This is a viable approach unless the nature of the criticism has calamitous implications for the fate of the campaign. Attacks that do not die out require further action.

The most common defensive response involves damage control. In this scenario, the campaign attempts to limit the extent of the damages incurred. Prominent leaders, and sometimes even press contacts, are reached. Explanations or accounts are offered. Efforts are made to hold together the public that has been supporting the candidate and ask for others to grant a fair hearing regarding the substance of the claims before rendering a verdict.

Depending on how publicly the attack was made and how much visibility the race has, the campaign may issue a press release. Typically, a press conference will not be called until all the facts are gathered and the strategy for handling the attacks has been laid. Press conferences are not very predictable, particularly in this context. Once the cameras are rolling, the candidate may be asked any number of questions. Even though the candidate may choose not to respond to questions, they will be asked. Responses may open up new areas of discussion for which the candidate is not prepared. Failure to answer smacks of guilt. Press releases via fax machines and E-Mail (electronic mail) is a much quicker and more effective way of handling the initial press comment.

During this phase, the candidate and key campaign officials are in containment, isolating themselves from the public. Events may be canceled in order to keep the candidate out of the public view and away from press scrutiny. If there is psychological or emotional damage inflicted on candidates or their families, those issues need to be addressed in private. They should not be worked out on a public stage unless there are special circumstances that warrant them.

The Gary Hart incident was well handled in the sense that his wife almost immediately came to stand with him. Her presence greatly helped in persuading people to suspend their judgment temporarily. After all, if the injured party can suspend judgment until all sides are heard, what good reason does any one else have to hold a grudge?

Importantly, candidates and their families cannot be viewed as being out of control. One of my earliest memories is of Jacqueline Kennedy at the funeral of her husband. She appeared to handle the situation gracefully. I was moved by her ability to deal so well with the tragedy when the nation at large seemed so grieved. Years later a playwright and director told me that the secret of portraying tragedy well is the actor's ability to take the audience to the threshold of emotion. Actors who break down and lose control become pitiable, while the ones who stop at the edge of emotion permit the audience to experience the emotion with them. Although I do not mean to suggest that Jacqueline Kennedy was acting, I now understand better why her contained emotion elicited such a profound involvement from me.

The same premise holds true in political campaigns. Even in times of tragedy or hardship, candidates must permit their publics to share in the experience. Leaders are representatives of a public's concerns and should be aware of their constituents' involvement with the implications and repercussions of events. If the voters are not connected to the events, the leader will be ostracized as someone whose reality is wholly different from their own. A barrier is thus created, and the leader will be viewed as being significantly different from the public. Once that occurs, there is little hope in unifying a public with the candidate.

Another defensive approach used to manage attacks is to address the criticism and then attempt to reduce its significance as a campaign event. Nothing plays as well as honesty. If a campaign has been involved in some inappropriate behavior, admitting it and then indicating the steps that have been taken to address the issue and prevent its recurrence is a sound strategy. It permits the campaign to move on to other issues. Simultaneously, it transmits a clear signal about the status that the campaign has given the situation. This matter-of-fact approach to problems is refreshing to people who are concerned about traditional political cover-ups. It is also disarming to those who had hoped to interfere with the opponent's campaign.

Another tactic is to expose the injury done by a fallacious rumor and shift the attack to the opponent. People enjoy a soap opera. This strategy provides for the open display of emotion. If a candidate truly feels outraged, the public display of that sentiment can be powerful. Members of the viewing public usually respond positively, noting that if they had been dragged through the mud in this way, this is how they would have responded. As long as the emotion is honest and forceful but tempered, the campaign has much to gain.

Any expression of emotion must be considered by the public as appropriate for the situation. Candidates who openly break down and weep make others feel uncomfortable, while those who display their anger can be perceived as too threatening. Control is the key. At the same time, the public needs to see the more sympathetic side of the candidate occasionally. Candidates are too often judged as people with no feelings, morals, or personal concerns. People who exhibit cavalier attitudes when faced with a challenge to their integrity may very well be assumed to be guilty simply because the public dislikes them. Quintilian (1977) rightly pointed out that "proof may induce the judges to regard our case as superior, but an appeal to the emotions will do more—it will make them wish our case to be better—and what they wish they will believe" (VI 2.5). Exposing the natural passions can at times bond the speaker to the public. Once the injury incurred by the attack has been exposed, the campaign can begin shifting the responsibility back to another party. The hurt that the criticism was designed to inflict is acknowledged while the method of attack provides the capital for supplanting another focus for the charge.

One motive for instigating criticism is that the opposition may be attempting to "get your goat," a phrase that has interesting political implications given the common horse-race reporting style affecting campaign reporting. Thoroughbred horses are high-strung, nervous creatures. In earlier days when they were transported from race to race via rail, a goat was placed in their stall to soothe them. The goat served as a calming agent. Unscrupulous betters would sometimes steal a horse's goat on the eve of the race. The horse would become so fretful that it did not rest for the race. Thus, the expression "get your goat" came to represent events in which a person was flustered by some action taken by another person with the intent of changing the odds in the race.

At times during political campaigns, the opposition similarly attempts to agitate a candidate in an attempt to change the outcome of the race. Redirecting the attack toward the source publicly acknowledges the disruption of the campaign efforts that have been caused by the opponent. At the same time, it raises issues of fairness. In political races, as in horse races, people prefer contests to be waged on equitable grounds. Shifting the ground back to the opponent attempts to reestablish campaign equilibrium to the situation.

These and other defensive strategies are designed to prevent candidates from becoming bogged down in constantly defending against claims while failing to establish their own agenda. Defensive strategies, however, do not always have the desired outcome. At times, offensive strategies are necessary.

One of the more prevalent strategies is an attempt to establish standards of judgment by which attacks can be measured. Olson (1988) explicated this as a strategy of definition and redefinition in her analysis of Ronald Reagan's controversial dedication to the brave soldiers who fought on both sides of World War II in his Bitburg cemetery address in the spring of 1985. Those making the charges lay down, at least implicitly, the standards by which a situation will be judged. If campaigners are successful in changing those standards, they can control the way in which a situation will be adjudicated. Of course, campaigners will attempt to make sure that the standards that are initiated permit them to bury the specific attack against them under weightier issues.

One example of this tactic was during the 1990 U.S. Senate race between Bill Cabaniss and Howell Heflin in Alabama. Cabaniss launched an attack claiming that Heflin was controlled by special interests. His advertisements offered evidence of questionable campaign contributions that could easily permit the voter to conclude that Heflin may have been influenced by concerns whose priorities were at odds with those of his constituents. Heflin's campaign did not address those charges. Attempting to deduce a person's motives on the basis of who has access to a candidate or who contributes to a campaign is almost impossible. Even if Heflin had attempted to prove the charges wrong, he could not have offered objective evidence for verification. Using the standard implied by the attacker, it was one person's word and intuitive judgment against another's. Instead, the Heflin campaign established a more accountable, less inferential scale of judgment. Heflin's campaign contended that if the voters wanted to know how well someone represents them, they should consider the behaviors of their representative. It then offered an example of how that could be measured, pointing to Heflin's attendance record. The evidence clearly proved that he was doing the job that he had been sent to the Senate to do. Whether or not people agreed with all his decisions, he was on the job every day. Once the criteria had been established for measuring effective representation, the campaign could follow with a counteroffensive.

In a second stage of the attack, the Heflin campaign charged that as a state senator, Cabaniss had been so concerned with his own personal interests that he had failed to show up for work a great percentage of the time. Whereas Cabaniss's argument rested on inferential claims, Heflin offered more direct evidence to corroborate his charges. On the weight of the evidence presented and the criteria of judgment established, voters were more likely to see Cabaniss as the greater offender. These issues contributed to Cabaniss's defeat.

Another strategy that is frequently employed is to meet power with power (see Miller, Boster, Roloff, & Siebold, 1977). This principle is explicated in the philosophy that drove the Cold War era. World War II established the United States and the USSR as international powers. Both sides demonstrated their ability and willingness to exercise force. Once both had been established as powerful, the arms buildup was justified based on the argument that parity prevents combat. Equality of strength would mean that in the event of confrontation, there would be a costly and bloody war. Neither side would benefit from such a conflict.

The same philosophy drives many political figures. Candidates who demonstrate their ability and willingness to use aggressive campaign techniques will ward off future attackers who are not willing to enter into a bloody combat. Many political figures ride for years on a reputation established early in their career. Others face decisions about the aggressiveness of their campaigns once in office.

Several features of this strategy should be evident. The first punch is typically thrown by a challenger. Those in control have no motive to attack the newcomers without cause. Unless there is a threat, there is no reason to respond. In fact, conventional wisdom states that unless there is some threat or potential threat that would arise out of an unanswered attack, challenger assaults should be met only with defensive strategies. To answer the attack is to elevate the issue to a level of public scrutiny that the challenger probably could not otherwise afford. In essence, the incumbent makes it an issue that is worthy of press scrutiny.

Because issues are so highly visible in news channels, incumbents have traditionally avoided responding to challenger claims. Once elevated to issue status, the incumbents are on tenuous grounds. Obviously, challengers will not launch charges unless they are convinced that it was an issue on which the incumbent could not win. An incumbent response means that the challenger has successfully set the agenda and positioned the incumbent to lose on at least one issue.

Second, before a full-scale public fight is enjoined, every conceivable measure must be taken to ward off a confrontation. Power confrontations are rarely waged without high human costs. Even those who win come away scarred and weakened. In the best interest of all parties, candidates attempt to avoid public confrontation. However, there are numerous power options short of political battle.

Power may be exercised by force or by *threats* of force (Bandura, 1973; Zillman, 1979). As many of us remember from our own childhood, the threat of punishment can sometimes be much more devastating than the actual event. Our own imagination leads us to fear the worst-case scenario. Similar exercises of threats works in political campaigns.

The challenger in one recent campaign launched an early offensive against a well-entrenched incumbent. His timing was poor. His intent was to garner a number of voters by establishing the public perceptions of the incumbent before the incumbent could set them for himself. The strategy seemed to have merit at first. The incumbent had not been very visible in the media over the last few years. Many voters did not know enough about his record to know what kind of job he had been doing although the assumption was that he was probably doing a good job. In order to make an inroad, the challenger put forth his strongest attack at the beginning and left nothing of significance in reserve.

One failing of this strategy was his inability to recognize the strength of the incumbent or his own weaknesses. The incumbent waited, all the while accumulating a healthy war chest and an immense research file on the opposition. In the final days of the campaign, the challenger got an understanding of what money and research can do. During the counterattack, voters could not help but become aware of the challenger's vulnerabilities. The message was amplified through radio, television, and print media. Unlike the opposition, the incumbent also had information in reserve. If the challenger had responded and upped the ante, the next round of counterattacks would have been ruthless. No one wanted the attacks to escalate to that level. The incumbent allowed information to leak back to the challenger as to the nature of the upcoming attacks should he pursue this line of attack further. Meanwhile, the incumbent used the interim time to recover from the early attacks and position himself before the critical time when voters were ready to make a commitment. The challenger broke off the attacks.

As this case illustrates, the incumbent never used the force of his best attacks, which were intended to be severe enough to damage the challenger's political career. However, the challenger was led to believe that the incumbent would escalate the use of force to whatever level was necessary in order to stop the attacks. The only thing that the public saw, however, was a single round of quid pro quo.

The word among political insiders was different. Other potential challengers saw a powerful incumbent who had systematically shored up his weaknesses once they had been spotted. There were not many areas of public vulnerability. Further, they were able to reevaluate the commitment of someone whom conventional wisdom had held was too nice a guy to play hardball politics. This was a person who clearly intended to keep his office.

Third, threats often work based on the knowledge that once a fight has been enjoined, it will only escalate over time until there is a winner and a loser. People who engage in this sort of power clash understand that there will be heavy casualties, that the cost will become heavier over time, and that once the fighting begins, there will be no way to stop it until the election is over except by admitting defeat.

The display of this kind of open warfare can be found in the more hotly contested media races. Each round of attacks becomes more vicious and personal. Unless both sides are careful, the end result will be that the voting public finds both candidates unworthy of the office for which they are running. The whiplash effect of negative campaigning often occurs when the attack phase of the campaign is long (thus allowing for more rounds of attacks). Toward the end of the prolonged media races, the attacks are generally based on such loose arguments that they carry very little credibility. The public may even come to question the validity of earlier claims.

Fourth, this strategy quickly hardens lines of support. In some elections, voters seem to put off making a decision. The number of undecided voters then indicates that no candidate has emerged as a strong choice. In such cases, attack campaigns are used to sway the voters and break the stalemate. Timed appropriately and amplified through the right channels, the results of an effective attack strategy can establish a voter preference trend for one candidate.

Finally, perceptions of power matter. Political figures cannot be placed in the position of constantly having to prove their strength. Politics concerns perceptions. Power can be attributed to a candidate either because the candidate has demonstrated its use in the past or because the candidate is perceived to be willing to use sufficient force to make the challenge untenable.

Perceptions of power are intriguing. There is an implied belief that powerful people only respect those whom they perceive as similarly powerful. By contrast, people who are viewed as weak are sometimes defeated just for sport.

The theory exists that if powerful persons permit others to publicly challenge them with no rebuttal, a climate will be established in which future attackers will not fear launching a challenge. Eventually, there will come a day of reckoning when the powerful person will have to exercise extreme measures to handle a situation that should never have emerged. Powerful people are not thought to be tolerant of those who would attack them. Any sign of provocation from a weaker party is sufficient to warrant a counterattack. Given this perspective, rumors, inferences, or direct attacks are addressed with the same severity.

Though each of these strategies can assist in determining the appropriate course once charges have been made, the best defense is a good offense. Foreseeing potential problems and inoculating against their negative effects is by far the best choice (see Pfau & Kenski, 1990). However, no campaign can foresee all the turns that the road may take. These strategies are designed to assist campaigns in becoming prepared for the unexpected.

CONCLUSIONS

Most people would prefer not to think of the strategic use of rumor and innuendos. Many elect not to acknowledge the seamier side of human nature which uses important issues as political weapons. These are the people who are not prepared for political life. Many of them lose.

Just because a campaign understands the strategy options available does not mean that it has to use them. One should note, however, that the morality and ethics of these strategies are much easier to judge in the calm periods between elections than during the heat of battle. Politicians will want to consider many of these issues before they enter a race.

Similarly, strategies cannot be determined outside the context for their use. Each campaign offers its own set of unique challenges and circumstances. As with most things, hindsight offers a better vantage point for evaluating the successes and failures of strategies than can be had at the time when the plans are laid. Our knowledge of politics and human decision making is still evolving.

Knowing the mechanics of how to assess strengths and protect vulnerable areas of defense provides the best chances of producing a positive outcome. Knowledge of these strategies is a critical component in modern elections. West Point and other U.S. military institutions specialize in training people who will think strategically. Political warfare requires no lesser understanding.

Chapter 10

The Spin: Public Relations
and Elections

There can be no question that public relations campaigns work in part by presenting information about the client in the most favorably possible light. Such efforts are overt attempts to establish public perceptions about the client in a manner that will establish similarity with the voters and expand the scope of the client's influence (for studies supporting the effectiveness of similarity on persuasion, see Berscheid, 1966; Byrne, 1971).

Whether it is intentional or not, campaigns have propagandistic tendencies. I know of no campaign that would not like the public to view its candidate as a unique representative of the citizenry. Campaigns attempt to project the associated positive images of this relationship through every reliable means to perpetuate and reinforce favorable perceptions. The one-sided nature of such communication and the attempt to control the less favorable images result in a systematic effort to control audience perceptions. The aspect of control is sometimes inocuous. Given that candidates represent groups of people, publics ascribe traits to these leaders that they perceive themselves to hold as followers. Other unflattering images are not likely to take root unless the bond is broken and voters perceive themselves in isolation from their leader. In the process of spinning an image, most people do not perceive their own attempts to control outcomes as unethical. By association, rarely do they perceive as manipulative the attempts by those who truly represent them. Control is most often recognized and repudiated by those who represent interests other than a person's own.

Association with a leader can at times blind an audience to the candidate's negative characteristics. For example, in the 1990 elections, many people were upset that Congress had failed to pass a budget reduction plan. Fliers and bumper stickers proclaiming, "This fall fire them all—re-elect nobody," appeared everywhere. The sentiment was high to oust the scoundrels who had caused the mess. However, when people went to the polls, they somehow felt that it was another district's representative that had caused the problem. Other people should throw their congressional representative out of office, they reasoned. Their own representative was a good person who, if involved at all, only became entangled because of the mistakes made in other districts. The public relations work fostered by most incumbent campaigns was effective in keeping their voters united and projecting an image of the candidate that was reflective of the public's attitude. These positive images were capable of overriding the mass dissatisfaction over the budget issue. Presenting positive images of their client is not only the responsibility of every effective public relations agent but, as this case illustrates, is essential for molding and holding constituents together.

The public generally fails to recognize the use of propagandistic techniques in political campaigns as inherently evil, and so do the people who practice the art. Few consultants that I have known view what they do as manipulative or exploitive. However, most of them would readily admit that their opponents sometimes use such techniques. Knowing the potential for manipulation and being cognizant of the techniques through which the public can be misled permits the democratic system to counter campaigns' natural proclivity to utilize techniques of propaganda.

PROPAGANDISTIC TENDENCIES AND PUBLIC CONTROL

Public relations work shares many of the characteristics of propaganda. Ellul (1973) defined propaganda as the work of "any organization that sets out to propagate a principle or belief" (p. 63). More recently, the term has been used to describe the persuasive techniques used to change opinions and spread political doctrines.

The use of propaganda is of great concern to many people. It carries negative connotations. The general impression is that propaganda is evil because it attempts to manipulate audiences and restrict people's choices by limiting their understanding of the choices available to them. Propagandists pretend to provide the audience with sufficient information on which to base a conclusion while in actuality supplying only the information that benefits their purpose. These characteristics are certainly applicable to political campaigns and are issues for concern in current electoral politics.

Significant indictments of propaganda result not from its use of persuasive techniques but from concerns about deceit and control. Jowett and O'Donnell (1986) in their book *Propaganda and Persuasion* identified five characteristics of modern propaganda, four of which must exist simultaneously in order to reap the negative consequences that distinguish it from persuasion. They are (1) a concealed purpose, (2) a concealed identity, (3) the control of information flow, (4) the management of public opinion, and (5) the manipulation of behavior.

Because the stakes are so high in political campaigns and the fear of propaganda techniques is so great, certain legal restrictions have been placed on campaigns to thwart these manipulative tendencies. In all political advertisements the source of the message must be clear. The use of "paid political advertisement by" is standard fare at the end of each radio and television spot and appears on all printed matter the campaign sends out. In this way, the audience can identify the source and the nature of the message. Further, in order to qualify for the best rates, candidates' voices must be heard on radio advertisements. Usually they are heard making the disclaimer at the end of the advertisement.

Laws have also been adopted to prevent one campaign from locking out other campaigns' access to the media. Equal time provisions, which are constantly changing with deregulation and various legal interpretations, have as their purpose the prevention of one candidate or party controlling the information that flows to the public. The guarantee of equal treatment is important if the audience is to be guaranteed access to opposing points of view.

Two areas are not regulated by statute. The first is political advertising. The courts and Congress have been reluctant to limit the nature of political messages in deference to the First Amendment rights of free speech. Whereas commercial products undergo the scrutiny of various commissions, there is no truth-in-advertising law applicable to political advertisements. Advertising firms are at liberty to use reenactments, create images via electronic devices, or even mislead the public, secure in the knowledge that the premises of free speech will protect them.

In the 1990 Alabama gubernatorial election, for example, Governor Guy Hunt's campaign actually manufactured a headline about Hunt's opponent to use in an advertisement. No such headline had ever been printed. The use of the headline was intended to build credibility for Hunt's argument. It implied that an objective party (the newspaper) had drawn the same conclusions about Paul Hubbert as had the Hunt campaign. Given that the evidence was falsified, the Hubbert campaign had a right to complain. However, Hunt had done nothing illegal.

Similarly, the 1990 Bill Cabaniss senatorial campaign in Alabama used a scene of what appeared to be a toxic waste dump which had in actuality been created for purposes of the advertisement. The visualization was intended to serve as proof of the impact of waste dumping in Alabama.

Given that the scene was fabricated, the evidence was misleading. As might be expected, the opposition candidate protested its use.

One of the major problems with current political advertisements is that the public has a hard time distinguishing between factual accounts and reenactments. Actors play the roles of concerned citizens speaking out for or against a particular campaign. Visual reenactments or staged settings project images that the audience may view as real. The result is that people either become jaded and mistrustful of all advertising or remain susceptible to its abuse.

The press, which readily proclaims itself as a watchdog when politicians serve selfish purposes, appears to be concerned with the misleading nature of political events but is plagued by many of the same problems itself. Reenactments of crime scenes, daring rescues, and news events have also blurred the distinction between fantasy and reality. It is difficult for political figures to accept standards applied to their business that the press does not apply to its own.

No doubt the standards by which we judge advertisements should be raised. The efforts of some newspapers which run ad-watch columns is helping campaigns to reassess the validity of their claims. More and more often a generic source like the *Congressional Record* is not cited without a specific date and page citation. The failure of campaigns to provide substantiation for the claims presented in their ads may result in bruising editorials from the newspapers. As a result, campaigns are beginning to become more accountable for the content of their ads. This movement toward better free-market policing of standards is a great benefit to the system. However, there is much work to be done on this front. Local reporters attempting to write columns on the validity of certain ads found that one of the limiting factors was a competent research staff. Considering the number of ads run by candidates of both parties in major as well as down-ballot races, the task of serving as electoral umpire is forbidding. Local newspapers simply do not have the resources to serve as a watchdog over the entire political spectrum. The best that can be hoped for is a kind of trickle-down standard that reviews the top of the ticket but only examines the major abuses in down-ballot races.

Despite the abuses that may occur, the current system is preferable to one in which some small federal or state commission would regulate advertisements. A commission's determination of what is fit for political dissemination would certainly restrict free speech and perhaps even the right to dissent. Moreover, given that the courts' declaration that prior restraint of messages cannot be condoned, censorship restrictions on advertisements can only occur once the message has been broadcast. Lyndon Johnson's controversial 1964 "Daisy" spot, which indirectly attacks Goldwater on his nuclear weapons policy, is considered to have been the most effective television advertisement in history, yet it aired only one time. Even the Willie Horton advertisement, which was produced independently of the Bush campaign, was run only in a small geographic section of the United States. The amplification of both these ads came through the news media which reran the ads as legitimate news events. Without prior restraint, censorship restrictions on advertisements would likely have the effect of escalating the emotional content of the ads to a level that would be considered newsworthy.

The other sticking point over regulation is determining who is competent to rule over standards of truth in advertising. A commission itself could easily fall prey to political pressures. The best approach for the control of abuse is a more informed electorate, a stronger watchdog role for the press, and higher campaign standards among the ranks of the candidates.

Even with such standards in place, however, the airways will still be filled with claims and countercharges. Contestants in political elections must recognize that the function of each public relations team is to make its candidate look good. If the opportunity arises, it will also aid in establishing an audience's standard of judgment by noting the less desirable qualities of the opposition. Campaigns are well served by a team that knows the effect of certain persuasive techniques, understands response strategies, and is capable of challenging opponent assumptions. Not only does such an exercise of debate provide additional information to the voter, it also weakens the impact of misleading statements or images. Were it not for these challenges, the public would only get smoke and mirrors, spun out to present a pleasing facade. Further, the use of open debates gives voters a more accurate picture of the candidates and campaigns.

Another area that is unregulated by law is the manipulation of public opinion via public opinion polls (Wheeler, 1976). When polling techniques first became newsworthy, few reporters had any idea of how to read a poll, and most did not realize that polls can contain flaws that may affect the interpretation of results. George Gallup set out to teach reporters of major newspapers by hosting a series of seminars. Today, political reporters at major newspapers are typically well versed in interpreting these reports. On the local level, the scene is dramatically different, however. Judging by what many newspapers print, reporters have little understanding of the reliability of findings between a poll that questions 300 people and one that questions 1,200. Nor do reporters seem to understand that polling results can be manipulated. Campaigns that are aware of polling dates can actually influence outcomes, as in the following example.

During the 1990 Alabama Democratic primary, students supporting one campaign were asked if they knew when the Capstone poll would be going to the field. The Capstone is a polling group comprised of students at the University of Alabama's Tuscaloosa campus. If the campaign could learn the approximate dates when the polling would take place, a series of advertisements could be introduced just prior to the polling date in order to boost its candidate's numbers. The individuals advocating this manipulation saw nothing wrong with this since they had not tampered with polling techniques. They also subscribed to the Gallup argument that polls are merely "snapshots in time"; therefore, why not show one snapshot that is more favorable than another since the measurement of "reality" remains the same.

Internal polls commissioned by campaigns use public relations markers in order to judge the effectiveness of their messages. These polls are perfectly legitimate, and their use is strategic. The manipulation of so-called objective polls conducted by supposedly disinterested third parties is subject to ethical concerns. The public tends to interpret these findings as a measure of the climate of opinion. Although no conclusive evidence indicates that it actually sways a person's vote, the potential is clearly there.

Polls are also used to make headlines (Stovall & Solomon, 1984). Newspapers sell more in close races than in races in which there are clear winners and losers. Some scholars have even asserted that the media often helps to manufacture a close race by commissioning their own horse-race polls and extending coverage to the underdog in an attempt to even the odds. Regardless of the motivations, there are some obvious problems with polling techniques judged by the facts that polls hitting the field simultaneously often come up with vastly different "snapshots" of the population. Either the mechanism is useless or it was used poorly. (The latter is more likely the case.)

What we observe in U.S. politics is not just one group's attempts to control political outcomes. Almost every interested group with something at stake makes overt attempts to bolster its claims. As long as we have a system that keeps political speech free of government control, the possibility for abuse will remain a constant area of concern. Understanding how systems operate and the techniques of persuasion through which decisions are influenced offer the single best control.

FOUNDATIONS OF PUBLIC COMMUNICATION CAMPAIGNS

One important principle of human behavior is that people prefer to be united with others. This is a basic pattern of socialization that permeates our lives. Nonetheless more and more people have difficulty fulfilling this social role.

We live in an age in which technology isolates us by limiting more and more the amount of time available for personal interaction. In a generation accustomed to E-Mail and fax transactions, people may communicate more frequently but have fewer face-to-face interactions. Indeed, some people interact more with machines during an average workday than with people.

Many scholars feel that this isolation is fostered by devices like television (Meyrowitz, 1985). Today people learn everything they feel that they need to know by staying tuned to the daily news reports. There is no longer as pressing a need to interact with others to find out what is happening in the world. Even in times of national disaster, our grief is expressed publicly via television but viewed in the privacy of our living rooms.

The popular term for this electronic isolation in the late 1980s was "cocooning." People seemed to enjoy isolating themselves in their homes and locking out the outside world except for the company of their immediate family, their television, and their VCR.

However, despite the isolation that our technocratic society has invoked, people need the company of others. We seek out frequent opportunities to unite ourselves with others, whether through churches, social groups, or political campaigns. Television experiences also provide a means of linking people together if only because of the shared world they encounter through its images.

Significantly, once we unite with others, our behaviors change. A whole new set of operative values takes over. Numerous studies have confirmed the effects of peer pressure on the individual (see, e.g., Courtwright, 1978; Janis, 1972). Our behaviors become more uniform. Our dissent is quieted and expressed only through channels approved by the group. We develop what Elisabeth Noelle-Neumann (1984) has described as a spiral of silence rather than expressing views that we perceive would be rejected by the group.

Today we have opportunities for joining groups in detached formats similar to those we use in our "cocoons." People can join conservation societies or political action committees or belong to numerous philanthropic groups just by contributing money. In return, newsletters keep the membership informed.

These groups are capable of political impact. During the elections of 1990, the Sierra Club endorsed candidates for the first time. It is significant to note that the club's membership is united primarily through the donor/newsletter arrangement. Although there are some meetings and expeditions sponsored by the organization, hundreds more belong to the group than attend its functions. Nonetheless, the group played a significant role in helping its members determine which candidates had upheld the premises of conservation that the group's charter swears to protect.

The power of groups to influence behaviors has been well documented through research on social proof. Social proof is essentially determined by observing and interacting with other people. Its power as a persuasive device lies in the fact that people are more likely to believe claims when someone whom they know or with whom they identify believes the claims to be true (see Bandura, Grusec, & Menlove, 1967). Political campaigns make widespread use of testimonials and letter writing based on this principle.

Ultimately, groups are more powerful than single individuals. Campaigns are clearly more effective when groups become organized on their behalf. For these reasons, understanding the techniques that encourage group membership and participation are useful to public relations staffs. Two persuasive principles in particular are worth noting.

One technique used frequently in the cultivation of group members is the "foot in the door" technique (see, e.g., Freedman & Fraser, 1966). It works by getting an individual to agree to a small request that is later used as a stepping stone for compliance with a bigger request. The compliance rate for these larger requests is significantly higher than if no initial commitment had been secured. The reason is that people view themselves as following through on an earlier commitment even though they probably did not recognize the implications of that commitment at the time when it was made.

For example, during the last federal election, a grass-roots petition circulated in an attempt to send a united message to elected officials. The pledge affirmed that people were tired of politicians saying anything just so they could stay in office. It further called for people to vote incumbents out. At face value, the petition seemed innocent enough, yet it had specific implications. First, signing a petition took very little effort (the foot-in-the-door feature was accomplished). Second, the petition asked for people's commitment to a particular value and a specific behavior. No mention was made of any competing values or the names of particular candidates would be driven from office. People who signed became united around a common cause. The impact of the petition was to be demonstrated later. The next step was to make sure that those who signed knew who the names of the incumbent candidates in their district. The desired result was an attempt to rid the system of the incumbents, and also of the ruling Democratic majority.

There was a great deal of discussion around Democratic party headquarters in one district as a result of the petition. Fortunately, the petition drive began late in the campaign and was advanced by only a small number of people. Party officials, however, watched its development very closely. If enough people had actually signed the petition, behavioral studies indicate that incumbents would have been voted out solely on the basis of their incumbency status. To counteract the effect of this petition, party officials were prepared to "blow the whistle" on the technique by holding a press conference to tell the public that this was a Republican ploy. Whether or not the original intention had been non-partisan, it had partisan implications. The fear was that it would be bolstered by the Republican candidates, who would benefit most from its application.

This particular drive was not successful. Historically, however, petition drives have been effective in laying the foundation for future claims by a particular campaign. During the precampaign period, commitments are secured on some principled idea. The campaign then starts up as a response to the public outcry for the principle. The effect is to unite individuals into a single group with a unified purpose.

A companion technique is the use of the reciprocity principle. This principle works on the theory that people have a need to repay in kind what others do for them. In fact, there is evidence to suggest that people will refrain from asking for favors that they feel they will be unable to repay (Greenberg & Shapiro, 1971; Riley & Eckenrode, 1986).

Such techniques are frequently used in political campaigns. Campaigns may use give-away gimmicks both to gain access to a voter and to interject the reciprocity principle. In a recent election, we tested the theory to determine its effectiveness. One campaign staked out key entrances at a local ballpark to give brochures to the crowd as they entered the stadium. The other campaign was similar except for the fact that they not only gave out brochures, they gave out mints as well. In the first case, people attempted to avoid the workers if they could. Some took brochures only to throw them down moments later, often within the sight of the campaign workers. In the second case, people readily approached the workers, sometimes waiting to get their free gift. Some walked away when they realized the gift had a brochure attached to it, but most willingly accepted the brochure as an obligation for accepting the candy. The most interesting phenomenon was that in the first case, almost no one stopped the procession into the ballgame to look through the literature. In the second case, however, numerous people actually stood to one side and glanced over the materials. Some even engaged a campaign member in conversation.

Some people may view these acts as insignificant, but they actually have a specific effect. In the first case, the people entering the ballpark were doing the campaign workers a favor by accepting their materials. In the second, the trade was mutually beneficial. Establishing the perception of a give-and-take relationship between politicians and their constituencies can be very beneficial to later claims that the candidate cares and listens to the public.

In almost every case, campaign experience supports the research findings. The acceptance of small gifts (anything ranging from yard sticks to pencils) provides an entrance for future dialogue and resultant commitments. Those who were unwilling to consider a future commitment to a candidate generally refused to accept the gift in the first place.

In an age in which mediated messages have taken the stage from the logrolling techniques of past political eras, politicians have failed to recognize the principles of persuasion at work in people's daily lives. Mutually beneficial relationships are the cornerstone of democratic processes. A candidate who can demonstrate an understanding of audience needs and wants, and who can follow through with an appropriate action is often perceived as superior to others who do not.

Through the political grapevine I heard an excellent example of the use of these principles. The story, supposedly based on fact, tells of two candidates who were engaged in a tight race. In focus group studies conducted to find out what was on the voters' minds, several incidents occurred in which people spoke of the terrible mosquito problem that was occurring that year. The public relations person talked to more people to discover whether these were isolated cases or whether a lot of people sensed the presence of a problem. The sentiment turned out to be widespread. The campaign then contacted a firm to buy samples of insecticide. The free samples were given out in a door-to-door campaign that argued that when their candidate was elected to office there would be better mosquito control measures in place in order to make the citizens' time outside more enjoyable. The issue was not significant in itself. Rather, the significance lay in the fact that one candidate cared enough to listen to the problems that affected people's lives and then took steps to respond to those concerns. As a result, the public was more willing to listen to other ideas that the candidate offered. They were willing, in essence, to consider a future commitment.

Campaigns for major elective audiences typically have broad issues that unite a following. Within the major parties, for example, the Republicans may attract business interests, and the Democrats, those interested in social responsibility. Local campaigns, by contrast, must forge coalitions. Often they unite people by reminding them of their common experiences. They help bond people to one another and unite the group with the campaign. In order to further understand the nature of effective public relations, we must consider the language codes of unified groups. Then we should investigate the principles that mold them and that hold publics together.

THE NATURE AND CHARACTERISTICS OF
POLITICAL ENCODING

Publics are unified groups of people that work together with one accord. In a classical rhetorical sense, a functional diagram of the relationship between candidates and their public shows a one-to-one relationship of give and take. Humans are trained to function in dyads (groups of two). Research tells us that even when three people are locked in conversation together, only two function at a time (Wilmont, 1979). This dyadic function is the basic component of human interaction.

Three factors emerge from viewing publics through this dyadic prism. First, messages intended for a particular public may not be interpreted by observing third parties as clearly as by observing those to whom the message was directed. The third parties do not have the communication burden of listening as closely to messages directed to someone else as with messages directed to themselves. Second, directed messages are effective because they make assumptions about the common backgrounds and characteristics of the audiences which help them interpret meanings. Certain key words and phrases serve as cues to.the recall of shared experiences. These experiences serve as the unspoken premises in arguments. Third, the relationship fostered in a dyadic relationship is mutually beneficial. As in conversation, the participants exchange messages and respond to each other's needs. The relationship is fostered by this attentiveness and, conversely, will inevitably suffer if there is no response.

This understanding of the communication dyad is important to those who would offer suggestions about effective public relations. A public is not a mass grouping of people but rather a collection of individuals united in purpose. Some might contend that a "public" takes on the personality of a single, composite individual. In this sense, the dyadic relationship permits a unique communication flow to occur. Communication on this level is more intimate and personal. The receivers hear a message that is specifically meant for them. The message may be received by hundreds of like-minded individuals, but each individual responds out of the personal responsibility or identification he or she feels toward the communicator.

The relationship between speakers and their publics has been discussed at length by precursers to Freudian and propagandistic theorists. Not the least among these early analysts is the work of G. LeBon. In his seminal book *The Crowd*, LeBon ([1896] 1982) contended that publics take on unique characteristics that mere assemblages of people do not. From his perspective, in their unified state they are more susceptible to emotional appeals, more desirous of attention from the speaker, and more easily lead. LeBon's work was so insightful that not only did Sigmund Freud use it as a basis of much of his early work, but so did Hitler's minister of propaganda, Joseph Goebbels. Our understanding of crowds and crowd psychology has changed markedly since the work of LeBon, but many of the principles are still applied to the practice of public relations.

Many inexperienced public relations agents mistakenly fail to recognize these principles of persuasion. Effective messages are targeted to particular groups. In order to appeal to the broadest number of people, the uninitiated water down their message so that it has neither strength of purpose nor specific unifying themes.

Moreover, a failure to recognize the principles of persuasion at work in public relations campaigns provides the opposition with an unfair advantage. The works of many of the early teachers of rhetoric were based on the assumption that if the techniques of persuasion were understood by both sides, there would be a diminished chance that manipulative techniques would stand unchallenged (Aristotle, 1984). Message construction begins with a thorough analysis of the audience, which is the origin of public messages. Messages reside in an audience until a spokesperson articulates them.

Acting independently, Jack Gargan placed advertisements in newspapers around the country during the 1990 federal elections explaining why he was fed up with Congress and appealing to voters to reject the incumbents. This was not a new idea; people had been exchanging the same message for some time. However, no one acted on the notion until Gargan emerged as the movement's leader, appearing on shows like "Phil Donahue" and other informational programs. Although the emergence of the movement was not well timed, Gargan was able to attract a sizable, though relatively ineffective following. The success he achieved was not due to his persuasive abilities to introduce a new or profound idea but rather to his skill in building on a sentiment that was already present (for the effectiveness of this approach, see Edelman, 1988, pp. 37–38; Newsom, Scott, & Turk, 1989, pp. 154–165).

The necessity of understanding audience leanings cannot be underestimated. The early stages of message construction must be spent in thoughtful consideration of the messages and themes that will mold people into a public. Campaigns begin to isolate "hot spots" of voters' sentiments: the issues on their minds; the problems that affect their daily lives; and their hopes, dreams, and fears for the future (see Edelman, 1988, p. 8).

We should also note that it is not necessary to find a single message uniting a singular mass audience. Candidates may have more than one public. Effective campaigns build coalitions. As long as the messages do not conflict, a single candidate may represent blacks, the elderly, the poor, and any other interest group. In local elections, coalitions built on a number of neighborhood issues may be more effective than those based on a single umbrella issue like taxes. A coalition may support garbage disposal projects, slope development, and beautification projects at the same time.

Candidates must not make the mistake, however, of trying to be all things to all people. Many analysts believe that the problem with the Democratic party in recent years is that it has come to represent so many divergent groups and interests that it lacks cohesiveness. By contrast, Republicans are more homogeneous.

The larger the group that a campaign attempts to hold together, the more problems the candidate will encounter. The result is that campaigns that become overextended will spend more time attempting to resolve internal struggles than in getting their message across to undecided voters. Effective message targeting entails not only determining a message but also unifying the various publics into a cohesive whole.

Once the message has been determined, contenders then begin the ritual "dance" of defining their territory and sizing up the opposition by noting its vulnerabilities and weaknesses. The battle for early positioning is an attempt to clear the field of all nonessential players: that is, those who lack a significant following. At times, two or more potential contenders emerge to vie over the same constituent base. The effect of having competing contenders is to split the coalition, thus giving ground to another group's candidate. Early resolution of these disputes can strengthen a group's ability to affect election outcomes.

Resolution can be affected by several means. Occasionally these disputes are settled between the candidates themselves. One candidate may step aside for a particular office in return for his competitor's support for a different office. Perhaps the tradeoff is made for an appointed post after the election. While this sounds rational and is, perhaps, the best solution, politicians' egos rarely allow them to agree to this.

Another means of settling these disputes is financial. The pool of monied people backing coalitions on the state and regional level is small, and donations from its members constitute an unofficial vote for the candidate. Without money, campaigns cannot be successful. This is an area in which having an organized campaign can reap handsome dividends. People will often give money and support to the first qualified person who asks them. The candidate with the broadest network of supporters working on behalf of the campaign to secure these commitments is way ahead in the campaign. The number of times a client of mine has been rejected because another candidate asked first is staggering. The principle is simple; the order in which candidates approach people is also an ordering of the latter group's status. Many individuals prefer to give to someone who values them highly enough to seek them out first rather than the candidate who asks them apparently as a political afterthought.

The court of last resort is the voter. Many times multiple contenders for the same constituent vote force themselves out of a job. For example, the scenario in Alabama's Fifth Congressional District has been predictable. The district spreads across the northern portion of the state.

Typically, several viable candidates emerge from the Huntsville metropolitan area and split what could be a huge voting block. The result is that the less populous and more cohesive Shoals area has been more influential in selecting the representative. During the 1990 election, this scenario changed. Huntsville voters were able to build a coalition in favor of District Attorney Bud Cramer. Holding onto the Huntsville block meant that Cramer was able to take the Democratic nomination on the first ballot.

The divide-and-conquer philosophy is not just something parties read about; it is something they practice. For example, if a certain Republican candidate is worried about tough opposition in the primary, key party officials and contributors may be asked to back only one person. This is generally the candidate whom the party believes to be the strongest contender and who has the potential to unite the party against the Democratic opponent in the fall elections. This action, the party hopes, will discourage opposition in the primary that would otherwise deplete financial resources. The strength of candidates may be determined by an individual's coalition-building power. Campaigns waged in public arenas must use messages that serve to draw distinctions between competing groups. At the same time, a candidate's power base is measured by the public unity and support the campaign demonstrates. Although some candidates may appear to possess enough clout in terms of money and support to wage a campaign, it is not automatically guaranteed that the supporters will coalesce into a public. The intermediate stages of any effective public relations campaign is marked by the joining of potential supporters within the populace into a unified public and the development of the candidate as the representative of that public's agenda.

The initial burden of staking out ideological turf falls squarely on the candidates' shoulders. During the initial stages, the candidates must attempt to discover common ground with the public, link together opinion leaders, and establish a sufficient support base. Public leaders, as well as some candidates themselves, make the mistake of assuming that people will naturally seek out the best representative for their interests. This may be true, but only to the extent that voters understand what the choices are. The candidates' next job, then, is to make sure the voters know what defines them, how the candidates represent those various interests, and why a particular candidate is a viable choice. Failure to accomplish this task results in a formula for voter confusion and a candidate's defeat.

A candidate's singleness of purpose in the formative stages of the selection process is necessary to lay the foundation for what is ahead. The candidate must be willing to stake out an aggressive claim and to take any action necessary to secure selection. Voters are typically unwilling to go through the laborious task of investigating the various qualifications of all those who express interest in holding office. They are more likely to investigate the qualifications of the few who rise to the top.

THE TIES THAT BIND: CANDIDATES, THEMES, AND ACTIONS

Building powerful associations is accomplished by strength of leadership, ideas, or initiative. These areas account for public attraction to some political campaigns and the antipathy with which other campaigns are viewed.

Powerful leaders attract followers. Some people seem to have innate leadership skills. From elementary-school on, they command the playground and determine the rules by which others must live. Characteristics such as charisma, perceptual abilities of accurately reading other people and their motives, and physical attractiveness are, by and large, elements over which others have no control. Looking around at the political leaders, it takes but a moment to realize that not all leaders have these characteristics. Aside from their God-given traits, however, many of our leaders have acquired traits of leadership. Public relations people contend, in contrast to the old adage, that powerful leaders are made, not born to leadership (see, e.g., Hess, 1987). At the same time, no one set of traits can distinguish a leader from others (see Davis, 1972, p. 3). Candidates must remain true to their own character traits yet acquire skills that will assist them in executing leadership responsibilities.

Paradoxically, the first rule of leadership development is for candidates to keep their mouths shut until they understand the lay of the land. Too many would-be leaders enter a political career with their mouth "in gear." They talk but fail to listen. They project themselves as the only ones with real solutions to complex problems. History has shown that powerful leaders listen before they act. When they finally take a position, their words and actions carry greater weight and importance. As M. Edelman (1988) noted, "Political leaders must follow their followers. . . . History and theory suggest that followers create leaders rather than the converse" (pp. 37–38). In order to accomplish that purpose, leaders must comprehend the desires of their public.

Intelligent candidates begin the process of learning about their public either with a benchmark poll or through gossip at the local political watering hole. Few local elections or down-ballot races can afford the luxury of polling and would learn little more than a candidate's name recognition percentages if they did. Much of the work done on local elections is intuitive. However, it must be remembered that the task of identifying and building constituencies is not restricted to the candidate. Many people participate in this phase of the campaign. One important principle is that a community's opinion leaders like to be asked for their input. Soliciting the involvement of key community leaders is important in the battle to attract supporters (for the classic study of this phenomenon, see Lazarsfeld, Berelson, & Gaudet, 1944).

These opinion leaders talk frequently with other community members and can provide insight into key questions. If an incumbent is involved, why might the public want to change? Who are the other potential players and what groups will they attract or repel? How will the addition of a particular candidate change the balance of power within the current structure and who would stand to gain or lose?

Each of these lines of analysis is designed to determine the nature of the public that would be targeted in a particular race. They also help assess the potential strength of a particular candidacy. However, the key factor in staking out a claim to a legitimizing public is the candidate. The candidate holds these groups together and is the focus in the deliberations.

Candidates must, therefore, secure two kinds of loyalties. The first is personal commitment from people who know them. This typically emerges from among circles of friends or from friends of friends. This tight circle is necessary to give the candidate guidance in the process that follows.

Of course, for candidates to succeed they must expand beyond the circle of people who know them by becoming symbols for the ideas that unite constituents. Loyalty to the ideas that mold a campaign are stronger than personal commitments to someone whom voters may never know. Voters who were asked why they supported Ronald Reagan, for example, typically said it was because he stood for a strong America, a get-tough attitude, and a belief in the free-market system. Reagan did not rely merely on the support of friends; he came to represent ideals that appealed to the American people at large.

A second rule of political leadership is that successful candidates learn to credit others for their success. In exchange for public acknowledgment of their efforts, insiders continue to work on the candidate's behalf. Staying on good terms with the constituency's opinion leaders is crucial to maintaining internal harmony and conveying an image of strength.

In the 1988 presidential campaign, a significant error was made by Albert Gore's team. The University of Alabama in Huntsville extended invitations to all candidates to speak in hopes of using the university setting as a forum for public ideas. Gore accepted. As a courtesy, the university contacted a local representative for the Gore campaign to coordinate schedules and such issues as transportation. The problem was that one of Gore's more prominent backers had not been informed that Gore was coming. Not only was this leader overtly hostile (even claiming at one point that the university was surely mistaken in its understanding that Gore would speak), he felt betrayed by the campaign. He believed that he should have known about the decision before Gore publicly accepted the invitation. Such a courtesy would have demonstrated the person's privileged status and rewarded his loyalty to the campaign. Unfortunately, the Gore campaign only alienated someone who had been an influential backer.

A third rule that candidates learn is how to build the perception of leadership. The most noted aspects of perception building are authority and image.

Candidates project authority, in part, by knowing how government works and being well versed in the specific problems their constituents face. Candidates lose credibility when they make major mistakes in their understanding of important issues of the day. Research teams can assist candidates in learning these details. In a recent Georgia race, high school and college debaters were hired to conduct opposition and issue research. This was good money for the students and relatively inexpensive for the campaign. At the same time, the candidate amassed a tremendous amount of detailed information about the opponent's publicly stated positions and the variables relating to the problems.

Candidates must possess personal qualities of leadership in order to be viewed as authorities. This is critical since studies confirm that people respond as authority figures tell them to (see Milgram, 1974). Sometimes they are even bounded in allegiance to authority whether or not the authority is legitimate. In a public opinion report regarding the Lieutenant William's Calley's order to shoot the residents of the Vietnam village of My Lai, 1968, 51 percent of those surveyed said they would have followed orders in the same way (see Kelman & Lawrence, 1972). Similarly, people respond when leaders whom they assume have special authority make requests of them. Dollars pour into Christian television ministries when someone whom viewers regard as God's spokesperson tells them to send money. Many remember the problem that arose in 1978 when Jimmy Carter asked people to stop using credit cards. Thousands responded. The bottom line is that people are waiting for leaders to offer solutions to their problems. They are willing to follow people who seem to know what they are doing. For better or worse, candidates who project that kind of authority succeed better than those who do not.

Perceptions of authority are created in any number of ways. Sometimes they are created by a person's title (see Cialdini, 1988, pp. 210–214). University professors, for example, are considered wise in their areas of research specialty and are granted the title of doctor to establish that authority. Military officers use titles, as do CEOs and executive managers. Candidates who use the title of an office they have won, such as Judge Hamilton, gain authority that is attributed to their office. Similarly, powerful people bestow titles on others. Like the queen who knights members of her court, other individuals in positions of power are recognized in part by their capacity to dispense titles.

Campaigns have numerous people with titles. Candidates learn to disburse them generously throughout the campaign. They are easy to invent, and people like the recognition. More subtly, however, in the process of "crowning" people with titles, the candidate gains more authority.

The trappings of authority are also pervasive images. Powerful candidates travel with an entourage. They are in constant access to seemingly important people by phone. Their schedules are laid out for them. Aides stand by to take down phone numbers and jot down suggestions. Any number of pseudo-events lead even the most casual observer to conclude that the candidate is someone of great importance.

Studies demonstrate that perceptions of authority affect what people think they see. For example, people who are perceived to be in authority are judged to be taller than those around them (see, e.g., Wilson, 1968). In a kind of weird analytical reversal, public relations specialists attempt to project authority images by controlling for these variables. In debates, platforms are often built so that the candidates appear to be of equal height (Germond & Witcover, 1989, pp. 428–429). These professionals reason that if people perceive those in authority to be taller, then the visual contrast of a person they had previously perceived as powerful to a taller opponent might alter their perceptions. This is even evidenced in the concern for the height of the people who travel with the candidate. In some cases there is a desire to assure that no one dominates the candidate visually, whereas in other instances a large supporter (Rosie Greer, for example) ads to the candidate's appeal. Spectators reason that the candidate must be a strong leader if he can keep such a big man on his team. Even though there is no substantiation for the interpretation of these claims, public relations crews would obviously rather not leave anything to chance.

The perceived talent, leadership abilities, power, and authority of the candidate certainly affect public adherence to candidates. However, candidates themselves are not always the glue that holds the campaign together. Candidates may emerge because of their ability to articulate the important themes and doctrines of a public.

Candidates who represent narrowly defined constituencies may not become symbols for a larger public. They may serve instead as tokens that people use to identify a specific belief system or political ideology. A token is, after all, a small part of a larger whole. We are all familiar with the broken heart, each half held by one of a pair of lovers. When put together, the symbol represents their commitment to one another. Similarly, Christians in the days of Roman persecution would draw a mark in the sand that, when completed by a second person, would look like a fish (or IXOUS). In this manner, they could identify themselves and know with whom they could share confidences.

U.S. politics has a need for such tokens. Although these candidates rarely win, they succeed in presenting agendas that might be suppressed in the normal system of political trade-offs. Jesse Jackson, for example, emerged initially as a representative of the black population. Before he became successful in expanding his constituency base to a more broadly defined group, his agenda was narrowly focused. He represented a point of view and a constituency that had previously been underrepresented by the more mainstream candidates. Similarly, Pat Robertson was a token of the religious conservatives in 1988. While achieving great success with that specific constituency, he was unable to define himself as a representative for more broadly based beliefs. In both cases, the candidate and the constituency belonged together in a unique fashion.

In both these scenarios, candidates came to represent more than the selfish interests of a politician who wanted to get ahead. Murray Edelman (1988) discussed the phenomenon that takes place in campaigns as the candidate is elevated to a status different than that of the members of the organization and comes to represent an ideal set of group values and characteristics. This perspective is instructive.

Elevation to the level of leadership carries with it unique problems and opportunities. Publics hold their leaders more accountable than others. They expect more from leaders because they represent group values. The obvious caveat to this worship of group norms is that the candidate lives in a fishbowl under the watchful eye of a crowd that will inevitably find fault with the performance. No human can live up to these standards of excellence.

The position has its advantages as well. As leaders, candidates' pronouncements carry more weight. Once Jesse Jackson had demonstrated his ability to attract a voting block, the issues that he represented were no longer the concerns only of an isolated group. The potential to have a brokered Democratic convention in 1988 meant that the winner would have to accommodate Jackson and his constituents.

Leaders also have media access which gives them the avenues through which to proselytize their views. Part of the success of any campaign rests in its ability to get a message out to a receptive audience. That process is very expensive. It can be prohibitive to message dissemination, particularly when the financial burden is carried by the campaign. Access to free public media for a constituency's leaders is a recognition of the strength of the public in whose name the campaign is waged.

Publics, as we have discussed, may be united either by candidates or by themes. They may also be united by action. Those leaders who wage more than token campaigns expand their constituent base by accommodating groups that are not already represented by mainstream candidates. Victors of electoral politics must be capable of forging coalitions based on real change within the governmental or social system. Campaigns are identified by their leaders and unified by their themes, but they are sustained by their ability to take action. Many people view campaigns as windows of opportunity through which to get goals accomplished. Thomas Jefferson believed that campaigns served a revolutionary function. The system included an ability to throw people out or put better representatives into office as a matter of course. The government conceived by our Founding Fathers included a method of ousting leaders without overthrowing the system.

This system of government also requires a spirit of accommodation. At the critical junctures that elections provide, officials are called into account for actions they have taken and plans they intend to implement in the future. Through the competitive political system, ideas and proposals for the future are weighed against one another.

In some ways, viewing campaigns permits voters to assess the ability of a candidate to get things done. The campaign functions like a minigovernment. Candidates may claim to be concerned about the welfare of black constituents yet fail to go into the neighborhoods where they live or the businesses where they work. A candidate's commitment to the principles he or she espouses is judged by the public through the actions of the campaign.

Events drive campaigns. The core of workers who offer their time and services use campaign events as benchmarks to measure the success of their efforts. Rallies measure the level of enthusiasm and commitment that the general public has for a campaign. The success of phone banks and Get Out the Vote drives are measures of a candidate's ability to organize and follow through on commitments secured.

These measures of effectiveness are critical for aiding in public assessments of a candidate's abilities. Even though we do not expect candidates to be able to perform all the tasks related to a campaign themselves, they are accountable for seeing that things get done. For example, people are drawn by major campaign events. Whether to get a free meal or to satisfy their curiosity, observers watch political events and make judgments about the candidates. Nothing is more disastrous to a campaign than to have a hot dog feast ready for 2,000 people and have only 500 show up. Numerous campaign events fall apart because of lack of planning. Sometimes preparations are not made well, directions are inadequate, locations are changed without notifying the participants, or alternative cites are not announced in advance for outdoor activities that may be canceled due to inclement weather. Such failures indicate poor timing and planning. Events that are well executed produce positive images for the campaign, while those that are poorly planned may have serious negative effects.

APPLICATIONS OF UNITY

Once campaigns are successful in uniting a public, the next step is to provide them with the trappings of unity. In every successful political campaign, symbols are used to foster group identification.

Insiders are marked by access to the candidate's private phone number, schedule, or computer access code, or by inclusion in strategy meetings. A second tier of supporters merit tokens of inclusion such as keys to the headquarters, purchase authority, or a title. Loyalists are identified by symbols such as campaign buttons, T-shirts, or bumper stickers. A larger population may be united by a slogan or theme.

These tokens indicate that group members belong together, and may represent the concept that is said to unite them. Often their similarity is marked visually. The hats, badges, and T-shirts mark their alliance with each other. Rank within the campaign may also be demonstrated visually. Campaign hacks are often identified as the suited persons attending the picnic. Each symbol is a visual cue to indicate membership and status in the group.

There is a difference between merely dispensing traditional trinkets like buttons and T-shirts and having them work as symbols. Sometimes candidates do not understand this. They stock the headquarters with objects for which no one claims ownership. Even if people take the T-shirts, they may use them only as night shirts or dust rags. These keepsakes take on meaning only if membership in the group takes on meaning.

People who become part of unified publics are often drawn by common interests. Sometimes those interests concern agreement on approaches to issues such as tax plans, medical care programs, or education reform. Other people may be drawn together out of fear (Mewborn & Rogers, 1979). The elderly may fear losing Social Security, the poor may fear losing entitlement programs, and the middle class may fear a decline in the standard of living.

Uniting with one another empowers the members of these groups. Working in isolation, they have little influence on political structures. Working together, however, in a united front with a strong spokesperson, they may present enough force to be reckoned with.

Like-minded groups are not always empowered by uniting their voices. Groups may agree on issues that bring them together but be divided on their solutions. In the 1984 presidential election, much speculation was made about the effects of the gender gap. There was reason to believe that because women supported Ronald Reagan less strongly than their male counterparts, the presence of a qualified female on the Democratic ticket would give that party an edge. The problem was that while many women supported the presence of a woman on the ticket, they were unwilling to vote for the Democrats merely *because* they offered that option. The theme of equality that united this group contended that a woman should be judged no differently than her male counterpart. Given this foundation, it was hard for them to argue that women should vote for the Walter Mondale–Geraldine Ferraro ticket just because Ferraro was a woman. To be consistent with their own analyses, Ferraro should be judged no differently than any other political figure. Given that perception, many people then decided that she was not as seasoned as George Bush to serve in the number two post. Her presence on the ticket did not provide any significant strength to an already belabored Mondale candidacy. The consequence was that the action to place a woman on the ticket fostered good-will toward the Democrats on the part of women's groups but did not unite a public to produce the desired outcome that the action had been designed to elicit. For all the stickers, buttons, and trapping that praised women's victory in the Ferraro candidacy, the symbols did little to compel a committed public to elect a woman to such a powerful position.

Unity efforts can be created by the candidate and the campaign. For example, Alabama state senator Bill Smith sought to find a perceptual wedge to use to get people to consider his record. Smith had three unresolved issues. First, Smith was not a grandstander. He did not take free media licks at every opportunity. A lot of people simply did not know the many things he had done for the people of his district. Second, people knew he was well-financed, but word on the street was that they had seen little evidence of the trappings of his campaign. Third, his campaign had also developed a problem over the years of having a number of older professionals in his camp but very few high school and college workers. This younger contingent is important to a campaign not only because of their energy and enthusiasm but also because of their innovative ideas.

During the general election, the campaign sought out high school and college groups that were in need of funds to handle certain campaign tasks. For example, an honorary fraternity was used to stuff envelopes for a mass mailing. Other groups were used on a massive Get Out the Vote drive on Halloween evening. This act of recruitment signaled the voters that Smith's money stayed in the district to help district residents. It also helped build a younger constituent base.

Mass mailings helped to get the Smith record out. In addition, during three hours on Halloween evening, over 2,000 households were targeted in a door-to-door campaign. Recipients not only got campaign literature that spelled out Smith's voting record, they were also given yardsticks with the slogan "One candidate measures up: Bill Smith State Senate District 7." The Smith campaign gave each household something it could use. At the same time, it asked that in return that the households look over the literature. The campaign was convinced that once people had viewed Smith's record, they would find him the better choice. This effort was also highly successful. The students even reported receiving a lot of Halloween candy although they made it clear that they were not asking for it.

CONCLUSIONS

Public relations work is not just a matter of performing a series of "feel-good" tasks. Its aims are communication and persuasion of the voter. Good public relations agents intentionally set out to thwart the negative effects of information or images that might be counterproductive to a candidacy and, more important, to build positive images. The role of public relations in the campaign is to direct the public discourse of important issues, to set the agenda in that discussion, and to present the candidate as the best possible choice for the public.

Chapter 11

Fund-Raising: Turning Images and Arguments into Capital

Long before any formal campaign is initiated, the competition for campaign monies begins. For many would-be politicians, this is the most difficult aspect of the entire process. People who are drawn to public service are often not adept at asking others for money.

The scenario during the early months of a campaign is repetitive and predictable. The candidate assembles a finance committee and identifies a finance chairperson. Then the candidate, the committee, and whatever staff has been assembled familiarize themselves with campaign-financing laws and begin mining for prospects. A fund-raising strategy is then devised. The strategy typically details the methods that will be used to solicit funds along three fronts: major contributors requiring personal contact, social contributors mined through functions and direct mail, and political action committees (PACs).

In the wealthier campaigns, fund-raising specialists are hired to teach campaign workers proper fund-raising techniques. Smaller campaigns rely on a carefully selected finance committee. That group of people must have sufficient power and influence as well as strong interpersonal skills that permit them to harvest contributors.

Almost from the beginning of the fund-raising effort, the realization sets in that asking for and receiving the money are two different tasks. Contributors find it easy to offer pledges, but find parting with the cash more difficult.

An even tougher task is to get the pledge payments by the time the bills are due. As simplistic as this analysis may at first appear, the ramifications are numerous. First, candidates in state and regional elections cannot realistically spend pledged monies. Most television and print sources require payment up front. This is particularly true for challengers. After years of experience, businesses have learned that it is easy for a candidate to drop out—or be forced out—of a race before the debts are paid.

Second, it takes dollars to get the campaign into operation. Basic supplies, phone service, and printing costs are necessary up-front expenditures. Fund-raising firms and other consultants also may either require a flat fee or front-load the majority of their fee with monthly payments thereafter. Therefore, in order to get the public campaign started, there must be money in the bank.

Third, getting a realistic appraisal of the budget is critical for campaign planning. One campaign manager who seems to be forever working for underdogs routinely budgets from election day backwards. This is done in order to assure that media time and funds for the Get Out the Vote (GOTV) effort are available for the closing days of the campaign. Obviously, the amount of money raised directly affects the type of campaign a candidate can wage. Modern media-saturation campaigns are very expensive, as are a host of standard budgetary items such as preparing campaign literature, kickoff rallies, advertising specialty items (bumper stickers, buttons, balloons, and palm cards), polling, mass mailings, headquarter operating expenses, travel, research, special events, and staff salaries.

Fourth, money is a key determinant for early positioning. Candidates are often treated by the media as serious contenders if they have accumulated sufficient money to wage a fierce campaign. Early accumulations of cash reserves also imply that the "smart money" has been bet on the success of the recipient candidate. A substantial cash reserve will also have the effect of scaring out of the race some people who realize that they cannot compete with a candidate who is much better financed than they are.

Fifth, money—and the wise appropriation of money—are vital to the development of a successful image (see Alexander, 1980, pp. 8–32). The way in which a candidate spends money in a campaign is often taken as indicative of the way he or she will utilize money once in office. Therefore, a candidate whose campaign is able to expand as election day nears will be seen as a winner who can keep up the momentum. The candidate who barely pays the bills, is forced to ask people to work for little or no salary, and has to concentrate during the most critical campaign periods on raising money rather than recruiting voters will be perceived as desperate.

Finally, money is viewed as an indicator of viability (see Thomsett, 1988). While being an underdog can be an advantage, there are limits to a challenger's ability to beat the odds. Funding must be available for voter contact activities. The voter will usually not select a candidate with low visibility. The candidate must be seen as a viable choice rather than a throw-away vote. Further, few people are willing to contribute financially to support a losing proposition. If the candidate cannot ignite public support, funds will dry up in a hurry.

Consultants have the ominous task of reminding the candidate of the implications surrounding each decision in the election process. Without such counsel, many critical decisions for the campaign will be made de facto. For example, political action committees may offer funds if a candidate will support a particular position. The consequences of accepting such contributions are obvious: The candidate cannot legitimately accept money from competing PACs, is publicly aligning with a particular issue that will influence position statements throughout the campaign, and runs the risk of estranging relationships with individual contributors who oppose the PAC for personal reasons.

All these issues contribute to a candidate's precampaign positioning (see Ries & Trout, 1981). In yet another paradox of politics, living with the strings attached to contributed money can be difficult—it gives the candidate less room to maneuver later in the campaign. It commits the campaign to the dictates of contributors but also signals the opponent as to the direction the campaign will take as issues emerge. That is one reason why some candidates delay accepting money from any individual or group that may signal a position until the campaign is in full swing.

For most candidates, the process of gathering contributors involves a daily list of potential clients to telephone, with follow-up correspondence confirming the commitment and arranging for the transaction to take place. The candidate may also be required to make personal visits to potential donors, as the phone itself is often considered too distant and impersonal a means of communication. The techniques by which a candidate solicits funds will be clearer once the motives of the contributors have been clarified.

MOTIVES

Although numerous fund-raising specialists develop extensive plans for achieving financial objectives, rarely do they train candidates on how to approach the target audience. Fewer candidates in local elections know how to close a deal with a contributor. One much needed area of counsel and advice is in the analysis of communication strategies for accomplishing this task. A review of the dominant motive patterns is a productive first step.

Although there are many motives for people to give money to a particular campaign, there are at least four recurring and prominent factors. Perhaps the most obvious one is to demonstrate power and influence. Campaigns provide an excellent opportunity for rewarding egos. Generally, the perception exists that the early phases of the campaign are limited to political elites. The reason is simple: Few people can afford to pay the ante to get into the game. In states that have no limits on the size of personal contributions, the primary targets are individuals who can give $10,000 or more. In federal elections, the law limits personal contributions to $1,000 per person per election cycle. The intent of the law is to limit the influence of the wealthy in the political process and to make the system more egalitarian. However, even at a "modest" $1,000, only a limited number of people have a large enough cash flow to risk that much money on an election. However, for people who are motivated by power and influence, early campaign events provide the opportunity to publicly demonstrate their elite status.

A second motivating factor for contributors is ideological in nature. Jean-Jacques Rousseau's theory of competing elites contended that in every society there are elites who compete ideologically for power. They play tug-of-war with the masses, attempting to sway the course of events in their favor. This perspective permits us to understand why some groups of people select candidates to support because of the candidate's ideological stance. A quite reasonable extension of this theory in democratic governments is the use of candidates as agents of influence.

In this perspective, candidates are viewed as pawns in a larger game for influence over the public mind. Clearly, one gauge for the ideological preferences of the masses is the analysis of election outcomes. Funds may be donated to campaigns, then, either to maintain the current value system or to help overthrow it.

A third motivating factor for contributing to a campaign is social fulfillment. The clients for whom the candidate offers the finest cuisine are among the community's social elite. These people are frequently asked to host fund-raising dinners or cocktail parties for the campaign. Given the expense of invitations, mailings, food, and drink, such parties are rarely hosted for less than $100 a couple and frequently cost much more. The goal is to treat these people to a nice evening out while simultaneously accumulating money for the campaign kitty.

The primary motivation for these people is to see and be seen. This is a social event with political overtones. Unlike the other classes of contributors, this group does not perceive their presence as a sine qua non of allegiance to the candidate. Frequently the candidate is viewed as the excuse for rather than the life of the party.

A fourth motivator is revenge. Rarely do books on political strategy discuss the "dark" emotions. It is as if not talking about them makes them seem less real or less intrinsic to the political process. But this is a powerful motivator. I am constantly amazed at the number of people who tell me privately that they are attending a particular fund-raiser not so much because they support the candidate but because they detest the opponent—or the other political party—or the opponent's circle of friends. The list is endless, and it accounts for why current polling techniques attempt to manage a candidate's "negatives" while simultaneously exploiting those of the opposition.

Another prominent motive pattern stems from a donor's feelings of civic duty and citizen participation in the electoral process. Donors view their contributions as proof of their commitment to the process of democratic government.

Developing an awareness of the various motive patterns of potential contributors helps determine fund-raising strategies for target audiences. Money is essential to running a campaign, yet strategists must concern themselves equally with the political costs of accepting contributions. This is particularly sensitive during the precampaign period when the candidate does most of the fund-raising in person.

DIRECT MAIL STRATEGIES

Over the past few years, campaigns have realized the difficulty of gathering crowds at fund-raisers and rallies. The realization that a larger audience can be targeted in one television spot than in a whole afternoon's rally has convinced many pundits that campaign time and money can be more appropriately spent elsewhere. That is not to say that rallies and dinners no longer have their place, but these events are certainly becoming more limited.

The purpose of fund-raising events is typically twofold: to raise money and to establish direct personal contact with the candidate's constituency. These same objectives can also be met through direct mail fund-raising. National campaigns have successfully utilized direct mail as a fund-raising method for the past two decades. Local and regional races can also profit from its use, particularly since the limited scope of the race permits more personalized approaches than the national campaigns can achieve. Direct mail raises money and also permits the campaign to test themes; receive direct, unfiltered feedback; explore the strength of certain issue positions; and provide the public with detailed information that is not readily available through other channels of communication. The efficacy of direct mail, then, lies not only in its financial potential but also in its ability to persuade voters.

Direct mail has numerous advantages for those who learn to use it well. First, given current technology, direct mail can be targeted to those people who vote. Unlike television and radio, through which a number of people who are not registered to vote receive campaign messages, direct mail is more specifically targeted. Therefore, every dollar spent is effectively utilized.

Second, the message of the direct mail piece can be specially targeted to voter concerns. Voter lists describe constituent concerns based on issues, age, ethnic origin, and a host of other demographic variables. An environmental message can be targeted to those who have specific passions in that area. Those who are concerned about zoning ordinances and their impact on the community can be similarly targeted. In terms of discussing issues that are on the voters' minds, perhaps no other medium permits the intense analysis that direct mail does. Unlike thirty-second radio or television spots, the candidate can more fully explain his or her position on an issue.

Third, this is the only communication medium that has the ability to be cost-effective. The early phases of a direct mail campaign can be quite expensive. This is the phase in which the campaign is searching for the right target audience for its message. However, once a good "house list" has been constructed, the return rates are quite acceptable. Timothy Roper, direct mail specialist for George Bush's presidential campaign in 1988, claimed that in one fund-raising drive the campaign spent over $900,000 but recovered $3.9 million *before* federal matching funds were added. That kind of success warrants the continued use of this technology.

Fourth, direct mail permits voters to get as involved in the campaign as they wish. Most people have other pressing agendas that do not permit them to spend hours assisting a candidate. However, many of those same people are quite willing to participate by contributing financially to the effort. Direct mail permits those who are reluctant to perform other campaign functions to become involved in the political process by opening up their checkbook. Moreover, direct mail also is an important tool for locating those who wish to participate in more active ways. Many times we have found people who are willing to distribute campaign literature, host a neighborhood coffee, display a yard sign, work on the phone campaign, work in the office, or perform various other functions merely by asking them to indicate areas in which they would be willing to assist on a mail-back portion of our letter. People are willing to help if there is a pressing need. They just need to know what must be done and how they can make a meaningful contribution to the effort.

Finally, direct mail is an effective form of grass-roots campaigning. For many people, personalized mail is as significant as shaking the candidate's hand. It establishes a line of communication that cannot be replicated outside of personal contact.

The personal contact established through direct mail cannot be underestimated. People prefer a personal approach when being asked for their vote and support. Political folklore abounds with stories of people who did not vote for a particular candidate because they were never asked. Democratic Congressman Tip O'Neill is credited with having said that he discovered quite by accident that a long-time neighbor did not vote for him. When he asked her why, she replied, "You never asked." Voters do like to be asked for their vote. Perhaps they assume that if candidates are not concerned enough to ask for their vote and their financial support, they do not deserve to win. Given that candidates cannot possibly reach all their constituents to make their requests in person, direct mail services as one solution to the task.

Considerations

Candidates are often alarmed at the initial high cost of direct mail efforts. Stamps and paper supplies are often difficult to afford in the early months of campaigning, to say nothing of the fees that direct mail consultants charge. The key to this, like any communication medium, is to understand its limitations and its capabilities.

Initially, the campaign must determine if a direct mail campaign is appropriate. Remember that there are two distinct types of direct mail campaigns: fund-raising and voter persuasion. Most consultants will advise the candidate to remember that every supporter is a potential donor. Therefore, voters should be given an opportunity to donate in each correspondence.

The first rule for launching a successful direct mail fund-raising campaign is to make sure that the campaign is in a financial position to see it through. The initial process of finding a list of people who respond to direct mail messages takes what consultants call prospecting money (equivalent to a grub stake in gold-mining parlance). By some conservative estimates, response rates to a first "cold call" mailing is approximately 1 percent. At those rates, it may very well cost more money to distribute the information than is received back in contributions. However, the real money will be made from the successive mail efforts. People who contribute become part of a house list. Response rates to a second solicitation from that list will be approximately 10 percent. At this level, the direct mail costs are more than covered by return response. The secret is to construct a good list. Obviously, the least cost-effective phase is during the list construction.

Incumbents have an advantage in that they can develop their house lists over a number of years. The more effective lists are those that candidates build while in office. Every time they perform a specific service or fulfill a legitimate request of a constituent, the constituent's name goes on the list. In essence, the campaign is identifying people who are pleased with the candidate's performance. The odds are that these are the people who will both vote for and contribute to the candidate during a reelection bid.

Challengers have a more difficult time constructing effective lists. Those who have been active participants in civic and social groups or who have been prominent in community affairs are more successful than those who lack close community relations. The more local the race, the more voters have a sense about a candidate's values and abilities to perform the task. The larger the campaign, the more campaigns have to rely on party lists and lists purchased from mailing houses. The essential point is that these initial efforts at list construction are expensive. Candidates often withdraw their support for direct mail efforts before they can pay off. If the campaign is not willing to complete the process, they should not attempt to utilize this medium.

The second consideration involves volunteer support and cost. The better-financed campaigns can pay direct mail firms to handle everything from the required postal permits and sorting procedures to the production of the materials and messages. Less financed campaigns must rely heavily on volunteer support. The latter is tricky. A good team must prepare and test the message, target the audience, find the appropriate mailing lists, address the mailing, sort it according to postal regulations, and get it mailed within a relatively short period of time. Moreover, once responses are received, tracking each response and identifying the list from which it came is crucial to an understanding of how the message is working with a targeted audience. Finding a team of volunteers this organized and systematic about their task is difficult. Most in-house direct mail projects are more hit-and-miss efforts than systematic attempts to gain responses.

The third consideration for utilizing direct mail is to effectively assess the campaign's chances of success before beginning. It is difficult to raise money if the candidate has little or no name recognition. People are reluctant to give money to people about whom they know very little. Name recognition is an important first step. In better-financed campaigns, media efforts aimed at name identification begin just before direct mail solicitation gets under way in order to bolster the latter's response rates. In campaigns in which this is not a realistic consideration and the candidate has low name recognition, direct mail is not likely to succeed.

Candidates who have no ideological turf find it difficult to raise money (Luntz, 1988, p. 161). Many fund-raising specialists avoid moderate (middle-of-the-road) candidates because issue extremes serve direct mail efforts well. Someone who is pro-choice or against gun control can raise a great deal of money from supporters of those positions alone. Issue extremes are effective for attracting money. Candidates who have no strong stance on ideological issues need other compelling factors to advance their mail campaigns.

Candidates also have trouble raising money if they lack a well-defined constituency. Those people who use a scatter gun approach to attract a general public will find the results of direct mail efforts unsatisfactory.

The advantage of direct mail, like any other communication medium, is its ability to target the audience to whom it is directed. By targeting messages for specific groups, the message strategy has a better opportunity for success. No one would consider giving a speech without considering the characteristics of the audience who will hear the address. No one should attempt direct mail with any less analysis. The secret of a good campaign is its ability to turn a larger number of people into a *public*. Good campaigns unite people and provide some commonality of purpose, while those that scatter their message will diffuse its effect.

Finally, direct mail efforts are disastrous when campaigns assume that the only thing necessary is a computer and a laser printer. The skill of the persuader is as necessary in direct mail appeals as in speeches or advertisements. People will not typically open up their wallets just because they are informed that a campaign needs money. Persuasion is necessary. Further, the letter must be well written. Many of my colleagues in English departments have claimed that this generation has become so dependent on the oral media of television and radio that they are losing their ability to write good prose. Campaigns may find verification for that claim when they review drafts of direct mail literature. Additionally, control over the layout and design is required. Direct mail may take many forms, it need not be confined to a letter on stock stationary. Working with a good printer and understanding the principles of design are necessary for an effective presentation of the materials.

Given these constraints, campaigns should recognize that direct mail can be very useful but that using it demands careful strategy.

The Mail Message

Once it has been determined that a direct mail campaign is warranted, the campaign must consider the message content. A successful direct mail campaign requires a message that blends the interests of the sender and the receiver. Some direct mail firms will suggest gimmicks that have worked in other campaigns. For example, if the candidate has a birthday during the campaign period, a letter from a spouse or friend asks for a contribution claiming that it would be a great birthday gift to help the candidate buy the next round of television ads (or whatever). Another stock mail-out asks for script approval. Copies of two radio scripts are sent with a request for feedback as to which one the campaign should run. Of course, candidates always enclose a contribution card as part of their ballot. Probably the most popular direct mail approach is to ask for contributions to fight an opponent's smear campaign. The letter appeals to voters to help set the record straight in a very public way (via a costly medium: usually television). The other most widely touted device is to send a survey form asking the voters to identify the important issues and agendas that their representative needs to address. As usual, voters are asked to contribute to campaigns or, at the very least, to contribute for the purpose of paying for and disseminating the polling results.

Although these gimmicks are successful, they only work as long as campaigns do not treat them as routine. The problem with these devices is that they are often exploitive. In many cases they lead people to believe that they are contributing to campaigns in some significant way other than their financial support. If that is not true, the campaign faces ethical questions.

Gimmicks like these may be effective for a while, but once people begin to recognize that their emotions have been manipulated, they cease to be persuaded by the appeals. This may explain why direct mail on the national level is beginning to lose its effectiveness (see Luntz, 1988, p. 227). It further contributes to the declining prestige of politicians and the apathy with which voters view political contests. Additionally, stock gimmicks are fundamentally lazy approaches to direct mail solicitation. Firms use them because they work, because they have stock letters ready, and because they do not have to get too involved with the campaign to make the direct mail segment successful. A lot of campaigns that do not keep up with political trends may not even recognize these as standard fare. They may actually believe that their effort is original. Candidates, too, become irritated when they find that they are buying the same gimmick that hundreds of other politicians have used. This is unnecessary since campaigns and candidates are loaded with opportunities for original direct mail ideas.

District court judge candidate Laura Jo Hamilton had a unique opportunity. Hamilton was reputed to be related to half the county. As her opponents in the primary quickly found out, she really did have a family with roots in almost every segment of the electorate. During the 1990 fall campaign, a cousin came up with an idea for a door-to-door campaign called "Cousins across the Country." On the Saturday before the election, family members would target key neighborhoods in a walking campaign followed by a family cookout. Those who could not participate were asked for contributions. The campaign created a unique "public" and provided an opportunity to bring that group together in an enjoyable celebration.

Many hardened politicos forget that one of the main attractions of campaigns is that they can be fun. Providing an event that had some personal appeal for the family was a compelling way to get them to help the campaign in a substantive way.

In another campaign that year, State Senator Bill Smith announced to his staff that his son was getting married. Everyone was excited until he announced that the ceremony was to be held just ten days before the election. The staff went crazy with worry that the senator would not be able to make what they considered to be critical campaign appearances. Those on the staff who knew the senator personally expected that he would stand by the young couple's decision. Smith explained to the staff how important the election was to him. Then he reminded everyone how important the wedding was to his son and soon-to-be daughter-in-law. They had a right to make their wedding the way they wanted to remember it fifty years from now. The event did not go unnoticed. The more the staff thought about it, the more it became apparent that this event revealed greater insights into the senator's character than any commercial they could envision. A simple, honest, and eloquent act of caring became part of the campaign. People were asked to help the Smith family celebrate by lining the roads with yard signs and contributing to the campaign in the couple's honor. The message was effective. People were able to participate in a campaign that reflected their values and simultaneously to join in a festive occasion.

The critical component of an effective message is that it is honest and expressive of the candidate's attitude toward public life. Candidates who engage in direct mail with the intent of conning people out of money are contemptible and serve as liabilities for more ethical candidates who want to remain in office for longer than just the upcoming term. Messages can be inventive and creative without being insincere or pejorative.

In a song from the musical *Gypsy*, the singer claims that "you've gotta have a gimmick if you want to get ahead." Perhaps the same can be said of good direct mail efforts. Something has to compel the reader to review the documents and motivate him or her to make some response. To be creative in developing a letter is not necessarily to be exploitive. The purpose of any gimmick is to gain the attention of people who are often so overloaded with information that it is hard to get their notice. Getting noticed is half the battle of getting the job done.

Packaging the message is also a critical component. Magazines that specialize in political information such as *Campaigns & Elections* or *Campaign Magazine* routinely print examples of some of the better material being used across the country. Similarly, much can be learned by reviewing the various nonpolitical direct mail pieces that arrive everyday. Carefully notice the ones you choose to open first. Ask yourself what makes some more compelling than others. Observe the use of color and graphics to enhance the image. Also notice the amount of time you spend reading the enclosure once you have decided to open it.

Given these perspectives, several key points should be clear. First, letters that are hand-addressed specifically to the receiver are the first to be opened. Letters addressed to "occupant" are seldom given priority. Second, the image of a general mailing matters. A recipient might be concerned if a local store that emphasizes low costs in its advertisements produces a slick brochure. Potential buyers might assume that the store valued the brochure more than it valued keeping costs down. Similarly, consumers would be disappointed if the luxury department store Neimann-Marcus marketed a catalog that did not compel them to browse for luxury items.

The same principles apply to politics. Alabama State Representative Tom Butler had a campaign that reached from Huntsville to the rural areas of the country. Even as an incumbent he had only limited campaign resources for the 1990 contest. Instead of spending money on fancy brochures, he used a xerox machine and a lot of volunteers who hand-addressed his mail-outs to target rural voters. Even his generic palm card and campaign newsletter were simple and cost-effective productions. His attempt was to demonstrate his frugality in a time of economic uncertainty, and the message played well. By contrast, Howell Heflin, Democratic senator from Alabama, had over $2.7 million dollars on hand after the June 1990 primary period ended (see *Campaign Magazine*, September 1990, p. 12). The fact that Heflin had a lot of money did not go unnoticed by the voters. His campaign was able to mount an impressive, and expensive, campaign. His billboards were elegantly designed, complete with a flattering photo of the senator. His brochures were attractively laid out, and printed in four colors on expensive paper stock. To distribute materials of less quality would make people wonder why he was trying to save money. After all, he had been given money to help him run his campaign; people expected some of it to be spent courting their votes.

Candidates who use direct mail as their only fund-raising component are likely to find themselves in jeopardy. Used as a supplement to other fund-raising efforts, however, this communication medium can prove a valuable asset.

PERSONAL FUND-RAISING BY THE CANDIDATE

Despite the presence of a finance committee to direct fund-raising efforts, the ultimate responsibility for soliciting the needed funds from major contributors falls squarely in their lap of the candidate. One test of suitability for office seems to be a candidate's ability to find a large enough constituent base to financially support the campaign. Further, in this way the candidate is assessed for an ability to woo the voter. In a way, the procedure of collecting/donating money resembles ritualized courting procedure. Although the candidate would like the check early, and in one lump sum, that rarely occurs.

The story is told of a man who was getting ready to donate a large sum of money to an election campaign. His friend stopped him from writing a check, noting that if he gave the money in one lump sum early in the campaign, his influence would be limited, If, however, he gave only a portion of the money now, he could give the remainder later when campaigns inevitably come back asking for more. The interesting moral of the story concerns the subject of influence. Who has the most influence, the person who donates early or the person who donates and then gives yet again when the campaign needs the money most? This explains, in part, the strategies that a candidate must master in order to successfully build a war chest. Moreover, it demonstrates three political principles that apply to dealing with major contributors: they demand to be courted, they expect to be viewed as worthy of the candidate's time and attention, and they want to be periodically asked for advice concerning the use of their funds. Although in fact, they rarely are, major contributors generally regard themselves as members of the candidate's inner circle throughout the campaign.

The candidates have to understand that they alone are accountable for raising the money since donors participating at the higher levels require the candidate's personal attention. Steve Jost, a fund-raising specialist noted for his early work for the Democratic Congressional Campaign Committee (DCCC), raised one point that candidates sometimes fail to understand—people do not contribute to fund-raisers; they contribute to candidates. In part, this is because a substantial contribution is thought to guarantee at least some degree of access to the candidate. A candidate who is unwilling to call or talk to them personally now, when asking for a favor, would not be likely to provide access later once he or she is in office. This principle does not change when a reputable fund-raiser is hired; the candidate still bears the responsibility for "reeling in" the big cash contributors. Clearly, larger contributors are often motivated by power and influence. To deny them access to the candidate is to say "Your money is not needed here."

For most people who are just beginning a life of politics, the daily routine of asking for money is draining. Even many seasoned incumbents will acknowledge that this aspect of the campaign is the most personally taxing. It demands a great deal of the candidate's time. Those employed or holding office during the campaign period must juggle responsibilities. This greatly increases the demands of performing well.

Pressures are also created by the constant struggle with moral and ethical issues. In part, the difficulty arises because the candidate must recognize that money is often contributed to buy influence. Kept in its proper perspective, nothing is wrong with that. If, however, political pressure keeps the candidate from making decisions based on merit rather than favoritism, the moral climate changes.

Perhaps equally constraining to the candidate is the feeling that contributions are personal favors that he or she may not be able to return in kind. Numerous studies indicate that people refrain from asking for favors unless they can repay them (see, e.g., Greenberg & Shapiro, 1971; Riley & Eckenrode, 1986).

Effective fund-raising consultants spend time helping the candidate reject some of these misgivings. Candidates do not usually have problems accepting a promise of a vote or a small donation that is offered voluntarily. The mental picture of such events is that the implied repayment is to be a good representative of the will of the constituents. However, our society puts so much value on material wealth that somehow when a donor gives $1,000, the bargain appears to change. Candidates have to remember that, in fact, however, the bargain does *not* change. A donor still gives money under the assumption that the candidate will represent constituents better than the opposition. The greater amount of the donation may mean that certain courtesies (such as personal access to the officeholder) will be extended to that donor and not to other voters, but there should be no greater trade-off implied. If one is implied, the candidate should not accept the donation.

Note that access to an officeholder is a courtesy; it is not an assurance of influence. No doubt each contributor has an agenda when donating large sums of money to a campaign, but for ethical candidates, accepting donations does not equal a capitulation of basic civic responsibilities. What the candidates can legitimately offer that donor is access to the candidate, once elected, for the sole purpose of expressing his or her views. Donors are granted the opportunity to attempt to influence policy through legitimate means of persuasion.

Cialdini (1988) claimed that one way to ensure a proper mental balance in the fair exchange of favors is to:

accept the offers of others but to accept those offers only for what they fundamentally are, not what they are represented to be. . . . To engage in this sort of arrangement with another is not to be exploited by that person through the rule for reciprocation. Quite the contrary; it is to participate fairly in the "honored network of obligation" that has served us so well, both individually and societally, from the dawn of humanity. However, if the initial favor turns out to be a device, a trick, an artifice designed specifically to stimulate our compliance with a larger returned favor, that is a different story. (p. 53)

Adopting this perspective enables the candidate to make the difficult choices concerning which contributions to accept and which to refuse.

Do candidates actually turn down funds? It happens more than people might imagine. In fact, candidates may actually return money to donors after the election if they demand favors that are out of line. Two motivations are involved in this. First, returning the donation relieves the candidate from any perceived obligation. Second, it is more honorable to return the money and reject the favor than to keep the money and have a very disgruntled patron.

Campaigners require the proper perspective to keep money from driving the candidate the way it must drive the campaign. With careful planning, shrewd use of resources, and effective utilization of limited funds, campaigns can be run for rather modest amounts of money. However, if the candidate is repeatedly told, "Unless we get more money you are going to lose," a begging mentality will set in. Not only is it unattractive for a candidate to look needy, it also makes potential donors less certain about the candidate's ability to pull off a close election. In campaign after campaign, managers confirm that once a candidate is viewed as a potential winner, the cash starts rolling in. The attitude of the candidate toward the fund-raising aspects of the campaign are partially responsible. The whole pitch for money changes from "I need money" to "You need to help this campaign because people like you will be well represented."

The campaign manager's role in the campaign is critical in this area. That person is ultimately in control of the campaign resources. An effective manager keeps the pressure up but prevents a panic mentality from developing in the campaign and affecting the candidate.

One way in which a campaign manager can keep the candidate on track is by aiding in the development of the candidate's daily call list. Most successful politicians understand the value of setting aside time for making direct telephone contact with key supporters. However, anyone who has ever worked in direct sales knows how difficult it is to be rejected time after time—sometimes even rudely. In larger, well-financed campaigns, field personnel are hired to make cold (initial) calls mining for financial support. The truly hot leads are then passed along to the candidate for follow-up. This greatly reduces the number of bashes the candidate must personally sustain.

In most campaigns, candidates have to rely on the campaign manager, members of the finance committee, and close friends to develop the call list. Careful development and scrutiny of the list gives the candidate a more systematic approach to fund-raising and increases the probability for success. Further, the judicious manager will work to see that a number of potentially successful calls are on each day's list. Otherwise, the candidate will become disheartened and find excuses not to solicit money in this manner.

Those surrounding the candidate must recognize the importance of the candidate's mental state. Ego and self-gratification play a large part in controlling the interpretation of events. When a campaign is lagging for lack of resources, the candidate must remain hopeful. Problems must be worked through, not ignored or avoided. Candidates with a positive self-image are in a better position to take positive action.

A consultant's most important role is to provide the candidate with honest reassurance. Although some panic may set in during a campaign, the experts should signal that steps are being taken to work problems out. One client told me that surviving critical days of a campaign is like living through an airline crash. Everything seems out of control. The consultants are reassuring only to the extent that you believe that they offer the best strategies for survival. Once events are underway, the "passengers" can only hold on and pray for everything to work out all right.

FUND-RAISING EVENTS

Fund-raising events are time-consuming organizational tasks. Nonetheless, they are the backbone of many political campaigns. One of their assets is the number of people involved in the planning, preparation, and execution of the event. These events are also important in that they gather in one place a number of supporters. They are critical in establishing proof of a solid campaign. These events are also vital components of fund-raising efforts because, when properly executed, they relieve stress on the candidate, provide money for the campaign, and permit the candidate to play a starring role. Given that much of a candidate's time during an election is spent convincing undecided voters and talking with those who are disgruntled, these events provide, at least temporarily, a warm and sustaining environment.

The traditional fund-raising dinner has gone by the wayside with the exception of prestigious events. Most local and regional candidates cannot garner enough interest to sustain an expensive dinner in which dining with the candidate is the only attraction.

Successful events require imagination to be appealing. They also require the consideration of a number of factors that help to guarantee their success. One of the initial tasks is determining whom to invite. Good attendance at these functions is critical. Fund-raising events are more successful when guests are members of some highly cohesive group. In Laura Jo Hamilton's 1990 campaign for district court judge, for example, the invitation lists were drawn from organizations of which she was an active member. Those included such cohesive groups as the Junior League, her church, and the local Democratic women's groups. Because she has been a board member or active participation in some fifteen highly visible community groups, Hamilton's name alone attracted a number of well-wishers, many of whom contributed to a campaign for the first time.

Similar cohesiveness may be derived from the participant's connection to the host of the fund-raiser. People will often attend because the event is being hosted by a friend despite the fact that they may not know the candidate personally or have a particular interest in the race.

By building fund-raising events around cohesive groups, a campaign gains a number of advantages. First, it allows the participants to remind each other of the upcoming event. Some people with good intentions of attending functions may forget or let other events take priority. Having close associates who are also planning to attend makes it less likely that other events will take precedence. Second, it begins to provide social proof for the acceptability of the candidate. After all, when friends are supporting a candidate, they will feel more comfortable announcing similar support (for elaboration on this aspect of social proof, see Noelle-Neumann, 1984). Third, highly cohesive groups are not offended when one of their members calls another to remind him or her of an upcoming event. Interestingly, some of our focus group interviews have indicated that participants are often irritated by follow-up phone calls when they do not personally recognize the caller. They frequently made comments such as, "If I had wanted to go I would have. But I don't want to be harassed." Others went so far as to tell us that our follow-up might cause them to change their minds. Allowing people to participate was viewed as acceptable. Anything else was viewed as harassment.

Once the invitation list has been constructed, the theme or nature of the event can be determined. There are no hard-and-fast rules for what will work. Events should typically be festive, appealing, and cost-effective. Beyond that, imagination is a campaign's only limitation. It is important to note that the way in which invitations to events are developed can increase the response rate. In interviews with numerous consultants, several guidelines emerged. First, hand-addressed invitations are better received than typed ones. They seem to foster the perception that the invitation is personal and that the person invited is worth a little extra effort. Second, a contribution amount should be specified. This is particularly true for events that are more social in nature. Unless an amount is specified, people will feel unsure of themselves. Many first-time contributors may not know what is considered acceptable. The result is that people will choose not to attend rather than feel insecure about their behavior at an important social gathering. Third, a reply card should be enclosed. This card usually contains a check-off space for attendance or regrets as well as a list of other campaign services that could be contributed such as distributing campaign materials or displaying a yard sign. This provides a ready list of people who want more substantive roles within the campaign or who desire specific campaign service.

Assuming that most people oblige the request to RSVP, the campaign will get a better sense of what is going on in the community by using a reply card. One reason is that the card necessitates a yes–no response: It forces the respondent into making a commitment of some sort. Those who choose not to support the candidate in any way, either financially or materially, can be evaluated for further persuasion. They may, for example, require a personal visit or letter from the candidate. However, it also assures that they will not be petitioned by the campaign to attend other events. Without the reply card, a phoned-in regret provides little information. It may be that the person had other commitments that evening, or perhaps they could not afford to come at this particular time. Whatever the reason, with a telephone regret, the campaign almost inevitably assumes that the person will attend another event. Consequently, that person is added to yet another fund-raising event list.

The reply card also provides an advantage for the fund-raising team. If people return the reply card with regrets, they are more likely to submit some token amount to demonstrate support for the candidate than if they were to phone in their regrets. This helps in bolstering the "take" for an event.

One final note: Consultants continually stress the importance of donor tracking. Each pledged requires a timely follow-up to secure the offer. A letter serves as both a reminder of the promise made and a means of following up on the commitment to see that it arrives. Further, donor tracking permits the campaign to show the proper appreciation for contributions received.

People expect to be acknowledged for the efforts on behalf of a campaign. One person recounted the story of his fund-raising efforts on behalf of a gubernatorial candidate a few years back. After collecting a sizable sum, not only did the candidate fail to thank him for his efforts, his efforts were further devalued when another person was publicly recognized and credited for the efforts. Such actions at the very least reduce the possibility that this donor would participate in a fund-raising effort for the candidate again.

Campaigns must also be aware that receiving money from a donor does not ensure that person's vote. One of the more difficult tasks is to convert those who attend fund-raising events into voters. People who attend these parties and dinners do not necessarily view their actions as a commitment to vote for the candidate. In part, their attitude is that they paid their money to see the show. Once the admission price has been paid, they are under little or no further obligation to act. Additionally, it is not uncommon for some people to attend the fund-raisers of competing candidates. The Southern expression is that a person thus "butters both sides of the bread," so that no matter who wins, the contributor wins as well. The candidates, on the other hand, have an entirely different agenda, as they require both money and the votes to get elected.

Several strategies can be implemented by the hosts to aid in the "conversion" process. First, the hosts should make their guests aware that by attending they have made a substantial contribution to the election of the candidate as well as a public statement of support. Since people usually want to follow through on commitments they have made, every attempt should be made to reinforce the attendees' commitment. Sometimes campaigns publish newsletters containing pictures of those in attendance. At other events, people are given special campaign pins to wear as a sign of their support for the candidate.

Momentum can also be advanced during the event. The candidate should be projected as the de facto winner of the race that is yet to be run. As such, the candidate is referred to by titles such as "the candidate," the "next Governor," or the current office title, such as "the Congressman." This builds respect for the position and provides the aesthetic distance required by officeholders. After all, people expect a candidate to be like them to some extent, but they also want someone who is a little different. In some ways, being an effective statesman is like being a good preacher: People expect more of you. They want you to be a model worthy of emulation. The use of titles helps foster that image.

Even the use of a candidate's first name can be strategic. If the hosts and campaign staff refer to the candidate by title, then those on a first-name basis with the candidate will feel more privileged (thus, appealing to the insider mentality). The juxtaposition is important: The staff and hosts portray the candidate as somewhat regal, and the candidate counters this with a "plain-folks" approach in which first names are acceptable. Adlai Stevenson is credited with having said, "I am now seasoned enough to have learned that the hardest thing about any political campaign is how to win without proving that you are unworthy of winning." To be common is important, but to be set apart is equally important.

A winning mentality can also be established by reinforcing participant choice. Getting people actually to say that they will vote for the candidate, tell others of that decision, or demonstrate support through some other visible means all build a campaign's momentum. At the events targeted at a less affluent audience, bumper stickers and buttons may serve this purpose. In as many events as possible, some public manifestation of the night's event should be evident.

Campaigns should recognize the buttons and bumper stickers as favors, not as an advertising function. The public is accustomed to, and even expects, these standard campaign advertisements. The fact is that they are not effective in low-visibility campaigns. In all but the most visible public office races, few people actually wear their buttons on a regular basis or attach the stickers to their cars. Candidates give them out primarily because they give the illusion that the campaign is underway and because it fulfills public expectations about what campaigns do.

Attendance at a fund-raising event and the acceptance of campaign materials do not demonstrate sufficient support for the campaign. More is required for a successful effort. Primarily, candidates need votes. They also need other kinds of support that can take numerous forms. Money is always needed, but participants should also be made aware that in-kind donations can be accepted and are equally tax-deductible when properly reported. A surprising number of people have office supplies available which they can easily donate. Computer ribbons, stamp pads, office furniture, flags, pencils, and other equipment are always needed.

At every event the campaign should have volunteer cards available. Collecting names, phone numbers, and time available to work at major events can save a great deal of time. In addition to volunteering time, providing lists of in-kind donations or the names of other prospects who might be willing to contribute to the campaign can be included. If yard signs are going to be available during the campaign period, getting permission to put up the signs immediately provides volunteers with a ready-made call list rather than making them from scratch. It also serves as a courtesy to have the first public displays of the campaign shown by those who have contributed financially. Through the effective use of volunteer cards, a week's worth of assistance can be generated from each event.

FUND-RAISING CLUBS

Since people have a natural desire to be associated with a winner, once an election is drawing to a close, contributions generally begin to flow in. Monies promised but not delivered suddenly appear along with a note apologizing for forgetting to send them sooner. Contributors who were earlier afraid of offending someone now decide that the political environment is safe enough to make an open contribution. Manager after manager will confirm that money never comes when you need it; it comes when you no longer need it—when the victory is already in sight.

Once in office, the candidate generally recognizes the power of a large war chest. The obvious reason is to fend off potential challengers. Large cash reserves give an opposing candidate pause before setting out with insufficient comparable financial backing to unseat a well-financed incumbent. Having a substantive cash reserve, then, works much like an insurance policy: It protects the candidate by narrowing the field of serious challengers to the well-financed, the well-intentioned, or the politically naive.

Incumbents have many strategic advantages over challengers, not the least of which is the ability to sustain an ongoing program for enhancing their campaign war chest. Although the technique is used most often in presidential and top-of-the-ballot races (see Luntz, 1988, pp. 172–173), fund-raising clubs are becoming more widely used as an incumbent strategy.

The idea is relatively simple. The candidate's principal campaign committee (or other body, as permitted by law) organizes what is tantamount to a club formed to provide continued support for and supply information to the officeholder. For a yearly fee, which may be paid annually, quarterly, or monthly, members are permitted the opportunity to dine with the candidate and exchange ideas on an informal basis in a closed-door meeting. The down side to the scheme arises when the membership is comprised of only PAC members or the financially elite. Ideally such clubs can also provide a powerful grass-roots access point to campaign workers and supporters with limited financial resources. One club was designed to maintain contact with the people who had worked so hard to put the candidate in office. Simultaneously, it was capable of building a campaign fund for future elections.

These clubs are actually tailored to a specific audience. The club mentioned above, for example, was especially tailored to the working-class participant. This was important since this group had comprised the candidate's primary supporters during the campaign. Like most volunteers whose work during a campaign is a sacrifice of personal time and energy, these stalwarts had returned to their routine activities after the election. The donor club offered them the same personal contact and input they had enjoyed during the campaign for a minimal sacrifice in terms of time and money. Moreover, it still allowed them to demonstrate their allegiance to the candidate.

This strategy is particularly effective for candidates who win on the platform of opening up government to the average citizen. Such clubs demonstrate that it is not just the "fat cats" whose money counts. It provides visible support for the contention that the officeholder still values the contributions of those who supported the campaign.

These clubs also serve indirectly as a measuring stick of job performance. Good membership numbers and high attendance at these functions signify continued support for the candidacy whereas a significant drop-off in numbers and interest may very well indicate a change in the electoral climate. In both cases, the information is of great value.

Another decided advantage of fund-raising clubs is that they take the pressure off the candidate during the election season. Numerous clients have commented about feeling torn between their continual need to raise money for future elections and performance of their civic tasks. Ethical questions abound. Are speaking fees appropriate? If so, are there groups that should be exempted from paying the fee? Additionally, many politicians feel that since they are only offered public appearance fees because of the office they hold, they would be ill-advised to use that money for partisan campaign purposes. These are not easy questions to answer. What is legally correct and what is ethically correct often differ. The effective use of fund-raising clubs helps eliminate many of those concerns. The candidate can thus afford to waive speaking and other fees, knowing that the campaign is being sustained in other ways. Those who want to contribute can do so directly to the club.

Donor clubs have to be strategically orchestrated. There are a host of problems that naturally arise almost from the inception. Donor clubs function as political action committees that support one particular candidate. Usually that support is directed toward a particular office as well. Thus, for example, a club may be formed to support a candidate who is currently serving in the Senate. The problem arises when that candidate decides to seek another elected office. Those who were avid supporters in one race may be opposed to the same candidate in another elected position. Given their political nature, organizations can be ripped apart by such internal controversy.

Additionally, organizers must be careful to abide by legal restrictions governing the use of such committees. If, for example, by law the group functions as a PAC, it must spend its money independently of the campaign. Direct evidence that the campaign controls the spending could become a front-page headline during an election. In recent elections, the truthfulness of the claim that such PACs are truly independent of the campaign has been brought into question. Given that members are usually dedicated supporters, they are bound to have inside information on the issues, themes, and presses points of contention that the campaign considers vital. The upshot is that such groups may inadvertently engage in unethical behavior.

Perhaps the greatest perceptual weakness of these organizations is that people may come to believe that they are having to pay to see a publicly elected official. Care must be taken to assure participants that this is not a "pay-per-view" approach to politics. Such a scenario could create a campaign's worst nightmare for the next election should the opponent claim the candidate is controlled by monied interests.

Used wisely and well, fund-raising clubs allow sustained voter participation at levels that most people can afford. They provide monitoring of the issues and the candidate's job performance. They may also help ensure that candidates do the job they were elected to perform.

CONCLUSIONS

The fair exchange of services for financial support is a cornerstone of U.S. politics. Ideologically, people want to ensure that their government leaders reflect the values and standards of the community. Voters truly wish to support good candidates for office.

Unfortunately, majority rule can easily take a back seat to financial rule. Campaigns are expensive propositions. Effective consultants can help ensure the democratization of the political landscape. By following not only the letter but also the spirit of campaign spending laws, campaigns can get people involved in grass-roots efforts to influence their government. Such efforts are time-consuming but effective.

In the glamour races for Congress and the presidency, few people in mainstreet America have a chance to get involved. Unless you live in one of the early presidential primary or caucus states, you may never meet a candidate face to face. In such races, the widow's mite is valued only if it comes unsolicited.

Local and regional campaigns are different. Although there is a decided trend to bring the new politics into local elections, people who know you and live next to you serve as a constant reminder that "we the people" know you and are watching.

Bibliography

Aaker, D. A., & Stayman, D. H. (1988). Are all the effects of ad-induced feelings mediated by the ad? *Journal of Communication Research, 15,* 368–373.

Adams, G. R. (1977). Physical attractiveness research: Toward a developmental social psychology. *Human Development, 20,* 217–239.

Agranoff, R. (1976). *The management of election campaigns.* Boston: Holbrook.

Ailes, R., & Kraushar, J. (1988). *You are the message: Getting what you want by being who you are.* New York: Doubleday.

Albert, J. A. (1986). The remedies available to candidates who are defamed by television or radio commercials of opponents. *Vermont Law Review, 11,* 33–73.

Alexander, H. E. (1980). *Financing politics: Money and elections* (3rd ed.). Washington, DC: Congressional Quarterly Press.

Alger, D. E. (1990). The media in elections: Evidence on the role and impact. In D. A. Graber (Ed.), *Media power in politics* (2nd ed., pp. 147–160). Washington, DC: Congressional Quarterly Press.

Allen, C. (1990). GOTV: C & E's grassroots blueprint for success on election day. *Campaign & Elections, 11,* 38–44.

Allen, J., Long, K. M., O'Mara, J., & Judd, B. (1987). Candidate image, voter values, and gender as determinants of voter preference in the 1984 presidential campaign. In L. B. Nadler, M. K. Nadler, & W. R. Todd-Mancillas (Eds.), *Advances in gender and communication research* (pp. 291–305). New York: University Press of America.

Allgeier, A. R., Byrne, D., Brooks, B., & Revenes, D. (1979). The waffle phenomenon: Negative evaluation of those who shift attitudinally. *Journal of Applied Social Psychology, 9,* 170–182.

Almond, G., & Verba, S. (1963). *The civic culture.* Princeton, NJ: Princeton University Press.

Alston, C., & Hook, J. (1988). An election: Money can be dangerous. *Congressional Quarterly Weekly Report, 46,* 3366–3367.

Anderson, K. (1975). Working women and political participation (1952–1972). *American Journal of Political Science, 19,* 439–454.

Anderson, K., & Clevenger, T. (1963). A summary of experimental research in ethos. *Communication Monographs, 30,* 59–78.

Aristotle. (1984). *The rhetoric and the poetics of Aristotle* (W. R. Roberts, Trans.). New York: Modern Library.

Arnold, W. E., & McCroskey, J. C. (1967). The credibility of reluctant testimony. *Central States Speech Journal, 18,* 97–103.

Arterton, F. C. (1990). Campaign organizations confront the media-political environment. In D. A. Graber (Ed.), *Media power in politics* (2nd ed., pp. 161–169). Washington, DC: Congressional Quarterly Press.

Asch, S. E. (1965). Effect of group pressure upon the modification and distortion of judgments. In J. H. Campbell & H. Hepler (Eds.), *Dimensions in communication* (pp. 170–182). Belmont, CA: Wadsworth Publishing.

Atkin, C. (1969). The impact of political poll results on candidate and issue preferences. *Journalism Quarterly, 46,* 515–521.

Atkin, C. K. (1981). Mass media effects on voting: Recent advances and future priorities. *Political Communication Review, 6,* 13–26.

Baer, D. L., Bositis, D. A., & Miller, R. E. (1982). A field experimental study of a precinct committeeman's canvassing efforts in a primary election: Cognitive effects. In M. Burgoon (Ed.), *Communication yearbook 5* (pp. 651–666). New Brunswick, NJ: Transaction Publishers.

Bailey, F. G. (1983). *The tactical uses of passion: An essay on power, reason, and reality.* Ithaca, NY: Cornell University Press.

Bandura, A. (1973). *Aggression: A social learning analysis.* Englewood Cliffs, NJ: Prentice Hall.

Bandura, A., Grusec, J. E., & Menlove, F. L. (1967). Vicarious extinction of avoidance behavior. *Journal of Personality and Social Psychology, 5,* 16–23.

Bart, J., & Pfau, M. (March 1989). *Turning the tables as campaign strategy: A study of the 1986 Dakota senatorial race.* Paper presented at the annual meeting of the Central States Speech Association, Kansas City, MO.

Bassett, R., Staton-Spicer, A., & Whitehead, J. (1979). Effects of source attire on judgments of credibility. *Central States Speech Journal, 36,* 282–285.

Baukus, R. A., & Payne, J. G. (April 1984). *Trend analysis of the 1984 GOP senatorial commercials: The Diamond Bates perspective.* Paper presented at the meeting of the American Culture Association, Atlanta, GA.

Beaman, A. L., Steblay, N. M., Preston, M., & Klentz, B. (1988). Compliance as a function of elapsed time between first and second requests. *Journal of Social Psychology, 128,* 233–242.

Belch, G. E. (1982). The effects of television commercial repetition on cognitive response and message retention. *Journal of Consumer Research, 9,* 56–65.

Benneson, R. (1982). *Women and politics.* Washington, DC: Congressional Quarterly Press.

Bennett, W. L. (1977). The ritualistic and pragmatic bases of political campaign discourse. *Quarterly Journal of Speech, 63,* 219–238.

———. (1988). *The politics of illusion* (2nd ed.). New York: Longman.

Berelson, B. (1948). Communication and public opinion. In W. Schramm (Ed.), *Communication in modern society.* Chicago: University of Illinois Press.

Berelson, B., Lazarsfeld, P., & McPhee, W. (1954). *Voting*. Chicago: University of Chicago Press.

Berger, C. R., & Calabrese, R. J. (1975). Some explorations on initial interaction and beyond: Toward a developmental theory of interpersonal communication. *Human Communication Research, 1*, 99–112.

Berlo, D., Lemmert, J., & Mertz, R. (1969). Dimensions for evaluating the acceptability of message sources. *Public Opinion Quarterly, 33*, 563–576.

Berscheid, E. (1966). Opinion change and communicator–communicatee simiarlity and dissimilarity. *Journal of Personality and Social Psychology, 4*, 670–680.

Berscheid, E., & Walster, E. (1974). Physical attractiveness. In L. Berkowitz (Ed.), *Advances in experimental social psychology* (Vol. 7, pp. 157–215). New York: Academic Press.

Bickman, L. (1974). The social power of a uniform. *Journal of Applied Social Psychology, 4*, 47–61.

Blumenthal, S. (1988). *Our long national daydream: A political pageant of the Reagan era*. NY: Harper and Row.

Bogart, L. (1981). *Press and public: Who reads what, when, where, and why in American newspapers*. NJ: Erlbaum.

Boorstin, D. (1962). *The image*. New York: Atheneum.

Bormann, E. G. (1961). Ethics of ghostwritten speeches. *Quarterly Journal of Speech, 47*, 262–267.

Bositis, D. A., & Miller, R. E. (1982). The successful communication of cognitive information: A study of a precinct committeeman. In M. Burgoon (Ed.), *Communication yearbook 5* (pp. 651–666). Beverly Hills, CA: Sage.

Boster, F. J., & Mongeau, P. (1984). Fear-arousing persuasive messages. In R. N. Bostrom (Ed.), *Communication yearbook 8* (pp. 330–375). Beverly Hills, CA: Sage.

Bostrom, R. E., & Tucker, R. K. (1969). Evidence, personality, and attitude change. *Communication Monographs, 36*, 22–27.

Bostrom, R. N. (1983). *Persuasion*. Englewood Cliffs, NJ: Prentice-Hall.

Bovee, C. L., & Arens, W. F. (1982). *Contemporary advertising*. Homewood, IL: Irwin.

Bowen, W. (1981). How to regain our competitive edge. *Fortune, 102*, 84.

Brockner, J., & Rubin, J. Z. (1985). *Entrapment in escalating conflicts: A social psychological analysis*. New York: Springer-Verlag.

Brummett, B. (1980). Towards a theory of silence as a political strategy. *Quarterly Journal of Speech, 66*, 288–303.

Burke, K. (1969). *A rhetoric of motives*. Berkeley: University of California Press.

Burnell, P., & Reave, A. (1984). Persuasion as a political concept. *British Journal of Political Science, 14*, 393–410.

Bushman, B. J. (1984). Perceived symbols of authority and their influence on compliance. *Journal of Applied Social Psychology, 14*, 501–508.

Byrne, D. (1971). *The attraction paradigm*. New York: Academic Press.

Cacioppo, J. T., & Petty, R. E. (1979).Effects of message repetition and position on cognitive response, recall, and persuasion. *Journal of Personality and Social Psychology, 37*, 97–109.

Campbell, A., Converse, P. E., Miller, W. E., & Stokes, D. E. (1960). *The American voter*. New York: Wiley.

Carbone, T. (1975). Stylistic variables as related to source credibility. *Speech Monographs, 42*, 99–106.

Carlson, J. M., & Boring, M. L. (1981). Androgyny and politics: The effects of winning and losing on candidate image. *International Political Science Review, 16*, 481–490.

Carmines, E. G., & Gopoian, J. D. (1981). Issue coalitions, issueless campaigns: The paradox of rationality in American presidential elections. *Journal of Politics, 43*, 1170–1189.

Carroll, S. J. (1989). Gender politics and the socializing impact of the women's movement. In R. S. Sigel (Ed.), *Political learning in adulthood* (pp. 306–399). Chicago: University of Chicago Press.

Ceci, S. J., & Kain, E. L. (1982). Jumping on the bandwagon with the underdog: The impact of attitude polls on polling behavior. *Public Opinion Quarterly, 46*, 228–242.

Chaiken, S. (1987). Attitudes and attitude change. *Annual Review of Psychology, 38*, 575–630.

Chasteen, D. (November 1988). *Harriet Woods vs. Kit Bond: Television commercials as argumentation*. Paper presented at the annual meeting of the Speech Communiation Association, New Orleans, LA.

Choi, H. C., & Becker, S. L. (1987). Media use, issue/image discriminations, and voting. *Communication Research, 14*, 267–291.

Chubb, J. E., & Peterson, P. (Eds.). (1985). *The new direction of American politics*. Washington, DC: Brookings Institution.

Cialdini, R. B. (1988). *Influence: Science and practice*. Glenview, IL: Scott, Foresman.

Cobb, R. W., & Elder, C. D. (1972). Individual orientations in the study of political symbolism. *Social Science Quarterly, 53*, 79–90.

Cohen, S. (1978). Environmental load and the allocation of attention. In A. Baum, J. E. Singer, & S. Vallins (Eds.), *Advances in environmental psychology* (Vol. 1, pp. 43–57). New York: Halstead Press.

Collins, R. L., Taylor, S. E., Wood, J. V., & Thompson, S. C. (1988). The vividness effect: Elusive or illusory? *Journal of Experimental Social Psychology, 24*, 1–18.

Combs, J., & Nimmo, D. (1985). *Politics through movies: Quest, community, and the American dream*. Berkeley, CA: University of California Press.

Cook, C. (1990). Attention grabbing ads wake-up the apathetic voter. *Campaign Magazine, 4*, 8.

Courtwright, J. (1978). A laboratory investigation of groupthink. *Communication Monographs, 45*, 229–246.

Cover, A., & Brumberg, B. S. (1982). Baby books and ballots: The impact of congressional mail on constituent opinion. *American Political Science Review, 76*, 347–359.

Cragan, J. F., & Shields, D. C. (1981). *Applied communication research: A dramatistic approach*. Prospect Heights, IL: Waveland Press.

Cundy, D. T. (1986). Political commercials and candidate image: The effects can be substantial. In L. L. Kaid, D. Nimmo, & K. R. Sanders (Eds.), *New perspectives on political advertising* (pp. 210–234). Carbondale: Southern Illinois University Press.

Cunningham, C. (1990). Smoke and mirrors. *Campaign Magazine, 4*, 16–17.

Danziger, J. N., Dutton, W. H., Kling, R., & Kraemer, K. L. (1982). *Computers and politics: High technology in American local government.* New York: Columbia University Press.

Davis, D. F. (1981). Issue information and connotation in candidate imagery: Evidence from a laboratory. *International Political Science Review, 2*, 461–480.

Davis, K. (1972). *Human behavior at work.* New York: McGraw Hill.

Deighton, J., Romer, D., & McQueen, J. (1989). Using drama to persuade. *Journal of Communication Research, 16*, 335–343.

Denton, R. E., Jr., & Hahn, D. F. (1986). *Presidential communication.* New York: Praeger.

Denton, R. E., Jr., & Woodward, G. C. (1988). *Persuasion and influence in American life.* Prospect Heights, IL: Waveland Press.

Diamond, E., & Bates, S. (1984). *The spot: The rise of political advertising* (rev. ed.). Cambridge, MA: MIT Press.

Dye, Thomas R. (1988). *Politics in states and communities* (6th ed.). Englewood Cliffs, NJ: Prentice-Hall.

Edelman, M. (1964). *The symbolic use of politics.* Urbana: University of Illinois Press.

———. (1988). *Constructing the political spectacle.* Chicago: University of Chicago Press.

Einhorn, L. J. (1988). The ghosts talk: Personal interviews with three former speechwriters. *Communication Quarterly, 36*, 41–47.

Elder, C. D., & Cobb, R. W. (1983). *The political use of symbols.* New York: Longman.

Elebash, C., & Rosene, J. (1982). Issues in political advertising in a Deep South gubernatorial campaign. *Journalism Quarterly, 59*, 420–423.

Ellul, J. (1965). *Propaganda: The formation of men's attitudes.* New York: Vintage Books.

Erikson, R. S., Luttbeg, N. R., & Tedin, K. L. (1980). *American public opinion: Its origins, content, and impact* (2nd ed.). New York: Wiley.

Ewen, S. (1988). *All consuming images: The politics of style in contemporary culture.* New York: Basic Books.

Faison, E.W.J. (1961). Affectiveness of one-sided and two-sided mass communication and advertising. *Public Opinion Quarterly, 25*, 468–469.

Flora, C. B., & Lynn, N. B. (1974). Women and political socialization: Considerations of the impact of motherhood. In N. L. Jacquette (Ed.), *Women in politics* (pp. 37–53). New York: Wiley.

Freedman, J. L., & Fraser, S. C. (1966). Compliance without pressure: The foot-in-the-door technique. *Journal of Personality and Social Psychology, 4*, 195–203.

Garramone, G. M. (1984). Voter responses to negative political ads. *Journalism Quarterly, 61*, 250–259.

———. (1985). Effects of negative political advertising: The roles of sponsors and rebuttals. *Journal of Broadcasting & Electronic Media, 29*, 147–159.

Garramone, G. M., & Smith, S. J. (1984). Reactions to political advertising: Clarifying sponsor effects. *Journalism Quarterly, 61*, 771–775.

Germond, J. W., & Witcover, J. (1989). *Whose broad stripes and bright stars?* New York: Warner Books.

Goodman, N. (1978). *Ways of worldmaking.* Indianapolis: Hackett Publishing.

Gordon, G. N. (1971). *Persuasion: The theory and practice of manipulative communication.* New York: Hastings House.

Graber, D. (1976). *Verbal behavior and politics.* Chicago: University of Illinois Press.

Graber, D. A. (1990). *Media power in politics* (2nd ed.). Washington, DC: Congressional Quarterly Press.

Greenberg, M. S., & Shapiro, S. P. (1971). Indebtedness: An adverse effect of asking for and receiving help. *Sociometry, 34*, 290–301.

Greenfield, J. (1980). *Playing to win: An insider's guide to politics.* New York: Simon & Schuster.

Gronbeck, B. (1989). Mythic portraiture in the 1988 Iowa presidential caucus bio-ads. *American Behavioralist Scientists, 32*, 351–364.

Grush, J. E. (1980). Impact of candidate expenditures, regionality, and prior outcomes on the 1976 Democratic presidential primaries. *Journal of Personality and Social Psychology, 38*, 337–347.

Grush, J. E., McKeough, K. L., & Ahlering, R. F. (1978). Extrapolating laboratory exposure experiments to actual political elections. *Journal of Personality and Social Psychology, 36*, 257–270.

Hahn, D. F., & Gonchar, R. M. (1972). Political myth: The image and the issue. *Communication Quarterly, 20*, 57–65.

Haiman, F. S. (1949). The effects of ethos in public speaking. *Speech Monographs, 16*, 190–202.

Harms, L. S. (1961). Listener judgments of status even in speech. *Quarterly Journal of Speech, 47*, 164–169.

Hart, R. (1987). *The sound of leadership.* Chicago: University of Chicago Press.

Hellweg, S. A., King, S. W., & Williams, S. E. (1988). Comparative candidate evaluation as a function of election level and candidate incumbency. *Communication Reports, 1*, 76–83.

Hershey, M. R. (1984). *Running for office: The political education of campaigners.* Chatham, NJ: Chatham House.

Hess, S. (1987). "Why great men are not chosen Presidents": Lord Bryce revisited. In A. J. Reichley (Ed.), *Elections American style* (pp. 75–94). Washington, DC: Brookings Institution.

Hesse, M. (1981). Strategies of the political communication process. *Public Relations Review, 7*, 32–47.

Hiebert, R. E., & Reuss, C. (1988). *Impact of mass media* (2nd ed.). New York: Longman.

Hofstetter, C. R., & Buss, T. F. (1980). Politics and last-minute political television. *Western Political Quarterly, 33*, 24–37.

Hovland, C. I., Lumsdaine, A. A., & Sheffield, F. D. (Eds.) (1949). *Experiments on mass communication.* Princeton, NJ: Princeton University Press.

Hovland, C. I., & Weiss, W. (1951). The influence of source credibility on communication effectiveness. *Public Opinion Quarterly, 15*, 635–650.

Howell, S. E., & Oiler, W. S. (1981). Campaign activities and local election outcomes. *Social Science Quarterly, 62,* 151–160.

Husson, W., Stephen, T., Harrison, T. M., & Fehr, B. J. (1988). An interpersonal
communication perspective on images of political candidates. *Human Communication Research, 14,* 397–421.

Iglitzen, L. (1974). The making of the apolitical women: Femininity and sex
stereotyping in girls. In N. L. Jacquette (Ed.), *Women in politics* (pp. 25–
36). New York: Wiley.

Infante, D. A. (1976). Persuasion as a function of the receiver's prior success of
failure as a message source. *Communication Quarterly, 24,* 21–26.

———. (1978). Similarity between advocate and receiver: The roles of instru-
mentality. *Central States Speech Journal, 29,* 187–193.

———. (1988). *Arguing constructively.* Prospect Heights, IL: Waveland Press.

Infante, D. A., & Gordon, W. I. (1981). Similarities and differences in the communicator styles of superiors and subordinates: Relations to subordinate
satisfaction. *Communication Quarterly, 30,* 67–71.

Iyengar, S., & Kinder, D. R. (1987). *News that matters.* Chicago: University of
Chicago Press.

Jacobson, G. (1981). Incumbents' advantages in the 1978 U.S. congressional
elections. *Legislative Studies Quarterly, 6,* 183–200.

Jacobson, G. C. (1975). The impact of broadcast campaigning on electoral outcomes. *Journal of Politics, 37,* 769–793.

Jacobson, G. C., & Kernell, S. (1981). *Strategy and choice in congressional elections.*
New Haven: Yale University Press.

Jamieson, K. H. (1984). *Packaging the presidency.* New York: Oxford University
Press.

———. (1988). *Eloquence in an electronic age.* New York: Oxford University Press.

Janis, I. (1972). *Victims of groupthink.* Boston: Houghton Mifflin.

Jewler, A. J. (1981). *Creative strategy in advertising.* Belmont, CA: Wadsworth
Publishing.

Johnson, B. T., & Eagley, A. H. (1989). Effects of involvement on persuasion:
A meta-analysis. *Psychological Bulletin, 106,* 290–314.

Jones, C. (1983). *How to speak t.v.* Marathon, FL: Video Consultants.

Joslyn, R. (1984). *Mass media and elections.* Reading, MA: Addison-Wesley.

———. (1986). Political advertising and the meaning of elections. In L. Kaid, D.
Nimmo, & K. Sanders (Eds.), *New perspectives on political advertising*
(pp. 139–183). Carbondale: Southern Illinois University Press.

Jowett, G. S., & O'Donnell, V. (1986). *Propaganda and persuasion.* Newbury Park,
CA: Sage.

Kaid, L. L. (1976). Measures of political advertising. *Journal of Advertising Research, 16,* 49–53.

———. (1982). Paid television advertising and candidate name identification.
Campaigns and Elections, 3, 34–36.

Kaid, L. L., & Boydston, J. (1987). An experimental study of the effectiveness
of negative political advertisements. *Communication Quarterly, 35,* 193–201.

Kaid, L. L., Nimmo, D., & Sanders, K. R. (Eds.). (1986). *New perspectives on
political advertising.* Carbondale: Southern Illinois University Press.

Katz, E., & Lazarsfeld, P. F. (1955). *Personal influence.* Glencoe, IL: Free Press.

Kelman, H. C., & Lawrence, L. (1972). Assignment of responsibility in the case of Lt. Calley: Preliminary research on a national survey. *Journal of Social Issues, 28,* 177–212.

Kenski, H. C. (1988). The gender factor in a changing electorate. In C. M. Mueller (Ed.), *The politics of gender gap: The social construction of political influence* (Sage Yearbooks in Women's Policy Studies, Vol. 12, pp. 38–60). Beverly Hills, CA: Sage.

Kepplinger, H. M. (1982). Visual biases in television campaign coverage. *Communication Research, 9,* 432–446.

Kern, M. (1989). *30-second politics.* New York: Praeger.

Kinder, D. R., & Sears, D. O. (1985). Public opinion and political behavior. In G. Lindzey & R. Aronson (Eds.), *Handbook of social psychology* (3rd ed., Vol. 2, pp. 315–458). New York: Random House.

Kirkwood, W. G. (1983). Storytelling and self-confrontation: Parables as communication strategies. *Quarterly Journal of Speech, 69,* 58–74.

Klapper, J. T. (1960). *The effects of mass communications.* New York: Free Press.

Kraus, S. (1962). *The great debates: Kennedy versus Nixon.* Bloomington: University of Indiana Press.

————. (1988). *Televised presidential debates.* Hillsdale, NJ: Erlbaum.

Lang, K., & Lang, G. E. (1968). *Politics and television.* Chicago, IL: Quadrangle Books.

Larson, C., & Sanders, R. (1975). Faith, mystery and data: An analysis of "scientific" studies of persuasion. *Quarterly Journal of Speech, 61,* 178–193.

Larson, C. U. (1982). Media metaphors: Two models for rhetorically criticizing the political television spot advertisement. *Central States Speech Journal, 33,* 533–546.

————. (1983). *Persuasion: Reception and responsibility* (3rd ed.). Belmont, CA: Wadsworth Publishing.

Lazarsfeld, P., Berelson, B., & Gaudet, H. (1944). *The people's choice.* New York: Duell, Sloan & Pearce. (Rev. ed., 1968). New York: Columbia University Press.

LeBon, G. ([1896] 1982). *The crowd.* Atlanta, GA: Cherokee Publishing.

Leuthold, D. (1968). *Electioneering in a democracy: Campaigns for Congress.* New York: Wiley.

Linsky, M. (Ed.). (1983). *Television and presidential elections.* Lexington, MA: Lexington Books.

Littlejohn, S. W., & Jabusch, D. M. (1987). *Persuasive transactions.* Glenview, IL: Scott, Foresman.

Lowell, A. L. (1913). *Public opinion and popular government.* New York: Longmans, Green, & Co.

Lumsdaine, A. A., & Janis, I. L. (1953). Resistance to "counter propaganda" produced by one-sided and two-sided "propaganda" presentations. *Public Opinion Quarterly, 17,* 311–318.

Luntz, F. I. (1988). *Candidates, consultants, and campaigns.* New York: Basil Blackwell.

McCabe, E. (12 December 1988). The campaign you never saw. *New York Magazine, 21,* 32–48.

McCain, T. A., & Koch, N. S. (1985). Gender differences in political communication: A look at the 1980 presidential election. In K. R. Sanders, L. L. Kaid, & D. Nimmo (Eds.), *Political communication yearbook, 1984*. Carbondale: Southern Illinois University Press.

McCroskey, J. (1967). The effects of evidence in persuasive communication. *Western Speech, 21*, 189–199.

McCroskey, J. C., Richmond, V. P., & Daly, J. A. (1975). The development of a measure of perceived homophily in interpersonal communication. *Human Communication Research, 1*, 323–332.

McCroskey, J. C., Young, T. J., & Scott, M. D. (1972). The effects of message sidedness and evidence on inoculation against counterpersuasion in small group communication. *Speech Monographs, 34* (Special Reports), 205–212.

McDonald, L. (1969). Myths, politics and political science. *Western Political Quarterly, 22*, 141–150.

McGee, M. C., & Nelson, J. S. (1985). Narrative reason in public argument. *Journal of Communication, 35*, 139–155.

McGinniss, J. (1969). *The selling of a president, 1968*. New York: Trident Press.

McGuire, W. J. (1969). The nature of attitudes and attitude change. In G. Lindzey & E. Aronson (Eds.), *The handbook of social psychology* (2nd ed., Vol. 3, pp. 136–314). Reading, MA: Addison-Wesley.

Malone, G. (1988). *Political advocacy and cultural communication* (Vol. 11). New York: University Press of America.

Manheim, J. B. (1975). *The politics within*. Englewood Cliffs, NJ: Prentice-Hall.

Martel, M. (1983). *Political campaign debates*. New York: Longman.

Matthews, C. (1988). *Hardball: How politics is played—Told by one who knows the game*. New York: Summit Books.

Mauser, G. A. (1983). *Political marketing: An approach to campaign strategy*. New York: Praeger.

Mayo, E. (1962). *The great debates*. Santa Barbara, CA: Center for the Study of Democratic Institutions.

Meadow, R. G. (1981). Political dimensions of nonproduct advertising. *Journal of Communication, 31*, 69–82.

Medhurst, M. J., & Dreibelbis, G. C. (1986). Building the speechwriter–principal relationship: Minority leader Robert Michel confronts his ghost. *Central States Speech Journal, 37*, 239–247.

Melder, K. (1989). Creating candidate imagery: The man on horseback. In L. J. Sabato (Ed.), *Campaigns and elections: A reader in modern American politics* (pp. 5–11). Glenview, IL: Scott, Foresman.

Merritt, S. (1984). Negative political advertising: Some empirical findings. *Journal of Advertising, 13*, 27–38.

Newborn, C. R., & Rogers, R. W. (1979). Effects of threatening and reassuring components of fear appeals on physiological and verbal measures of emotion and attitudes. *Journal of Experimental Social Psychology, 15*, 242–253.

Meyers, W. (1984). *The image makers: Power and persuasion on Madison Avenue*. New York: New York Times Book Company.

Meyers-Levy, J. (1989). The influence of a branch name's association set, size, and word frequency on brand memory. *Journal of Consumer Research, 16*, 197–207.

Meyrowitz, J. (1985). *No sense of place: The impact of electronic media on social behavior.* New York: Oxford University Press.

Mickelson, S. (1989). *From whistle stop to sound bite.* New York: Praeger.

Milgram, S. (1970). The experience of living in cities. *Science, 13,* 1461–1468.

———. (1974). *Obedience to authority.* New York: Harper & Row.

Miller, G. R. (1963). Studies on the use of fear appeals: A summary and analysis. *Central States Speech Journal, 14,* 117–125.

Miller, G. R., Boster, F., Roloff, M., & Siebold, D. (1977). Compliance-gaining message strategies: A typology and some findings concerning effects of situational differences. *Communication Monographs, 44,* 37–51.

Minnick, W. C. (1968). *The art of persuasion* (2nd ed.). New York: Houghton Mifflin.

Morello, J. T. (1988). Argument and visual structuring in the 1984 Mondale–Reagan debates: The medium's influence on the perception of clash. *Western Journal of Speech Communication, 52,* 277–290.

Morgan, G. (1986). *Images of organization.* Newbury Park, CA: Sage.

Mueller, C. (1973). *The politics of communication.* New York: Oxford University Press.

Newsom, D., Scott, A., & Turk, J. V. (1989). *This is PR: The realities of public relations* (4th ed.). Belmont, CA: Wadsworth Publishing.

Nimmo, D. (1970). *The political persuaders: The techniques of modern election campaigns.* Englewood Cliffs, NJ: Prentice-Hall.

Nimmo, D., & Combs, J. E. (1980). *Subliminal politics.* Englewood Cliffs, NJ: Spectrum Books.

———. (1990). *Mediated political realities.* New York: Longman.

Nimmo, D., & Savage, R. L. (1976). *Candidates and their images: Concepts, methods, and findings.* Pacific Palisades, CA: Goodyear Publishing.

Nimmo, D., & Ungs, T. D. (1967). *American political patterns.* Boston: Little, Brown.

Nimmo, D., & Sanders, K. R. (Eds.). (1981). *Handbook of political communication.* Beverly Hills, CA: Sage.

Noelle-Neumann, E. (1973). Return to the concept of the powerful mass media. *Studies of Broadcasting, 9,* 67–112.

———. (1974a). The spiral of silence. *Journal of Communication, 24,* 43–51.

———. (1974b). Turbulences in the climate of opinion: Methodological applications of the spiral of silence theory. *Public Opinion Quarterly, 41,* 113–158.

———. (1979). Public opinion and the classical tradition. *Public Opinion Quarterly, 43,* 143–156.

———. (1980). Mass media and social change in developed societies. In G. C. Wilhoit & H. DeBock (Eds.), *Mass communication review yearbook 1* (pp. 657–678). Beverly Hills, CA: Sage.

———. (1981). Mass media and social change in developed societies. In E. Katz & T. Szecsko (Eds.), *Mass media and social change* (pp. 137–165). Beverly Hills, CA: Sage.

———. (1983). The conflict between effects research and journalists. *Journal of Communication, 33,* 17–25.

———. (1984). *The spiral of silence.* Chicago: University of Chicago Press.

Olson, K. M. (1989). *The emergence of the refutative media attack: A comparative analysis of Agnew and Hart's attacks on the news media.* Paper presented at the annual meeting of the Speech Communication Association, New Orleans, LA.

Patterson, T. E., & McClure, R. D. (1973). *Political advertising: Voter reaction to televised political commercials.* Princeton, NJ: Citizen's Research Foundation.

Petty, R. E., & Cacioppo, J. T. (1979). Issue involvement can increase or decrease persuasion by enhancing message-relevant cognitive responses. *Journal of Personality and Social Psychology, 37,* 1915–1926.

————. (1981). *Attitudes and persuasion: Classic and contemporary approaches.* Dubuque, IA: Wm. C. Brown.

————. (1984). The effects of involvement in responses to argument quantity and quality: Central and peripheral routes to persuasion. *Journal of Personality and Social Psychology, 46,* 69–81.

————. (1986). The elaboration likelihood model of persuasion. In L. Berkowitz (Ed.), *Advances in experimental social psychology* (Vol. 19, pp. 123–205). New York: Academic Press.

Petty, R. E., Cacioppo, J. T., & Goldman, R. (1981). Personal involvement as a determinant of argument-based persuasion. *Journal of Personality and Social Psychology, 41,* 847–855.

Pfau, M., & Burgoon, M. (1988). Inoculation in political campaign communication. *Human Communication Research, 15,* 91–111.

————. (1989). The efficacy of issue and character attack message strategies in political campaign communication. *Communication Reports, 2,* 53–61.

Pfau, M., & Kenski, H. C. (1990). *Attack politics: Strategy and defense.* New York: Praeger.

Poole, K. T., & Zeigler, L. H. (1985). *Women, public opinion, and politics: The changing political attitudes of American women.* New York: Longman.

Quintilian. (1977). *The institutio of oratorio of Quintilian.* (H. E. Butler, trans.). Cambridge: Harvard University Press.

Rappaport, R. B. (1981). The sex gap in political persuading: Where the "structuring principle" works. *American Journal of Political Science, 25,* 32–48.

Rasberry, R. W. (1981). *The "technique" of political lying.* Washington, DC: University Press of America.

Reichley, A. J. (Ed.). (1987). *Elections American style.* Washington, DC: Brookings Institution.

Ries, A., & Trout, J. (1981). *Positioning: The battle for your mind* (rev. ed.). New York: Warner Books.

Riley, D., & Eckenrode, J. (1986). Social ties: Subgroup differences in costs and benefits. *Journal of Personality and Social Psychology, 51,* 770–778.

Robinson, J. P. (1974). The press as king maker: What surveys from the last five campaigns show. *Journalism Quarterly, 51,* 587–594.

Roshwalb, I., & Resnicoff, L. (1974). The impact of endorsements and published polls on the 1970 New York senatorial election. *Public Opinion Quarterly, 35,* 410–414.

Rudd, R. (1986). Issues as image in political campaign commercials. *Western Journal of Speech Communication, 50,* 102–118.

Runkle, D. R. (1989). *Campaign for president: The managers look at '88*. Dover, MA: Auburn House Publishing.

Rybacki, K. C., and Rybacki, D. J. (1991). *Advocacy & opposition: An introduction to argumentation*. Englewood Cliffs, NJ: Prentice-Hall.

Sabato, L. J. (1981). *The rise of political consultants: New ways of winning elections*. New York: Basic Books.

Salmore, S. A., & Salmore, B. G. (1985). *Candidates, parties, and campaigns: Electoral politics in America*. Washington, DC: Congressional Quarterly Press.

Sandage, C. H., Fryburger, V., & Rotzoll, K. (1988). *Advertising: Theory and practice*. New York: Longman.

Schwartz, T. (1973). *The responsive chord*. Garden City, NY: Doubleday.

Schweitzer, D. (1981). How to buy media (in political campaigns): Getting the most for your money. *Campaigns and Elections, 2*, 34–39.

Shabad, G., & Anderson, K. (1979). Candidate evaluations by men and women. *Public Opinion Quarterly, 43*, 18–35.

Sharp, J., Jr., & McClung, T. (1966). Effects of organizations on the speaker's ethos. *Communication Monographs, 33*, 182–183.

Smith, C. R. (1976). Contemporary political speechwriting. *Southern Speech Communication Journal, 42*, 52–67.

Smith, L. D., & Golden, J. L. (1988). Electronic storytelling in electoral politics: An anecdotal analysis of television advertising in the Helms–Hunt Senate race. *Southern Speech Communication Journal, 53*, 244–258.

Spillman, B. (1979). The impact of value and self-esteem messages on persuasion. *Central States Speech Journal 30*, 67–74.

Stewart, C. W., Smith, C. A., & Denton, R. E., Jr. (1989). *Persuasion and social movements* (2nd ed.). Prospect Heights, IL: Waveland Press.

Stewart, L. P., Cooper, P. J., & Friedly, S. (1986). *Communication between the sexes: Sex differences and sex-role stereotypes*. Scottsdale, AZ: Gorsuch Scarisbrick.

Stovall, J. G., & Solomon, J. H. (1984). The poll as news event in the 1980 presidential campaign. *Public Opinion Quarterly, 48*, 615–623.

Sullivan, P. A. (November 1985). *Campaign 1984: Shoot-out at gender gap*. Paper presented at the meeting of the Speech Communication Association, Denver, CO.

Surmanek, J. (1987). *Media planning*. Lincolnwood, IL: NTC Business Books.

Swanson, D. L., & Nimmo, D. (Eds.). (1990). *New directions in political communication*. Newbury Park, CA: Sage.

Tedeschi, J. T., Schlenker, B. R., & Bonoma, T. V. (1971). Cognitive dissonance: Private ratiocination or public spectacle? *American Psychologist, 26*, 685–695.

Teger, A. I. (1980). *Too much invested to quit*. Elmsford, NY: Permagon.

Thomasett, M. (1988). *The little black book of budgets and forecasts*. New York: Basil Blackwell.

Trent, J. S., & Friedenberg, R. V. (1983). *Political campaign communication: Principles and practices*. New York: Praeger.

Ullman, W. R., & Bodaken, E. M. (1975). Inducing resistance to persuasive attack: A test of two strategies of communication. *Western Speech Communication, 39*, 240–248.

Verba, S., & Nie, N. H. (1972). *Participation in America*. New York: Harper & Row.

Wakshlag, J. J., & Edison, N. G. (1979). Attraction, credibility, perceived similarity, and the image of public figure. *Communication Quarterly, 27*, 27–34.

Welch, S. (1977). Women as political animals. *American Journal of Political Science, 21*, 711–730.

Wheeler, M. (1976). *Lies, damn lies and statistics*. New York: Liverright Publishing.

Whitney, C. D., & Goldman, S. B. (1985). Media use and time of vote decision. *Communication Research, 12*, 511–529.

Wilmont, W. W. (1979). *Dyadic communication* (2nd ed.). Reading, MA: Addison-Wesley.

Wilson, P. R. (1968). The perceptual distortion of height as a function of ascribed academic status. *Journal of Social Psychology, 74*, 97–102.

Wise, D. (1973). *The politics of lying: Government deception, secrecy, and power*. New York: Random House.

Woodward, G. C., & Denton, R. E., Jr. (1988). *Persuasion and influence in American life*. Prospect Heights, IL: Waveland Press.

Wright, P. L. (1973). The cognitive processes mediating acceptance of advertising. *Journal of Marketing Research, 10*, 53–62.

Zillman, D. (1979). *Hostility and aggression*. Hillsdale, NJ: Erlbaum.

Index

gress and, 129; credibility of, 91; crisis in leadership, 11; direct mail and, 207; fund-raising clubs and, 220–22; isolation and, 22; responding to challenger claims, 172; sentiment against, 27–28; state senate race and, 19–35; unseating, 7–8; winning percentages, 129

information: from attacks, 116; backing rumors with, 157; credible sources, 151; flow of, 179; method of processing, 112; motivation to sort through, 113; newspaper readers biased toward, 110; one sided, 85; organization of, 84; planted, 157; story form and, 141–45; two-sided, 86; visually reinforced, 131. *See also* messages

"inoculation strategy," 86

integrity, 111

insider, 142

intelligence, 111

interpersonal skills, 92

interviews, 103, 125, 132, 134

issues: candidates as symbols of, 192; candidate's image and, 139; controversial, 86; defining opposition with, 23–24; effective, 97–98; feedback loop and, 62; fund raising and, 208; "hot spots," 25–27, 188; human connections and, 87; knowledge about, 94–95, 191–92; localizing, 94, 95–96, 160; media and, 160–61; novice politicians and, 100; personality important, 113–14; polling data and, 13, 26, 94, 160, 162; positive associations with, 27, 135; pseudo-, 97, 161–62, 163; research on, 94–98, 193; rhetorical comments and, 98–101; saliency, 140; selection objectives, 23; sense of unity for various, 141; special-interest, 80; substantiated, 97–98; swing, 140; voter familiarity with, 78, 87; as weapons, 159–66; well-constructed theme, 11

Jackson, Jesse, 115, 133, 195

Jacobson, G. C., 10

Jamieson, Kathleen Hall, 101, 117, 124

Janis, Irving, 67, 73

Jefferson, Thomas, 196

Johnson, Lyndon, 180

Jordan, Barbara, 99

Jost, Steve, 59–63, 213

Kennedy, Jacqueline, 168–69

Kennedy, John F., 73, 132

Lazaras, Ed, 142

leadership, 45–46, 111; in action, 28; bold, 11; credentials, 27; crisis in, 11; perception of, 193; powerful, 191; skills, 11–12, 191; theme, 10–11

LeBon, Gustave, 187

legal community, fund-raising and, 47

legal issues, family and, 43

legislative successes, 11

letter writing, 184

letters of endorsement. *see* testimonials

Lincoln, Abraham, 131

local elections, 100; coalitions and, 186; image and, 126; learning about voters and, 191–92; media coverage, 92, 135; radio adverstising and, 105–7; rumor mill and, 153; television strategy, 103–5

MacDonald, Albert, 133

macho mentality, Southern politics and, 20

magazines, political information, 211

mail fraud, 72

mailings. *See* direct mail

Matthews, Christopher, 42

McLean, Joe, 63, 71

media, 16, 83; access, 179; as audience, 136–37; camera crew and, 136; consistent messages and, 88; covering smear campaigns, 71, 72; distortion and, 135; equal time provisions and, 179; image control via, 114–19; issues and, 160–61; leaders' access to, 195; lead position in sto-

ABOUT THE AUTHOR

RITA KIRK WHILLOCK is Assistant Professor of Communication at Southern Methodist University in Dallas. She was previously an assistant professor of communication at the University of Alabama in Huntsville. She has served as a political analyst for WAFF-TV and WAAY-TV in Huntsville. She is currently a media consultant for Alabama and Texas political races.